PHILOSOPHICAL ESSAYS & LECTURES, VOL. 3

THE TRIAL OF SOCRATES

by

GREG JOHNSON

Counter-Currents Publishing Ltd.
San Francisco
2023

Copyright © 2023 by Greg Johnson
All rights reserved

Cover image:
Paulus Pontius, *Socrates Sophronisci Filivs: Atheniesis*, 1638

Cover design by
Kevin I. Slaughter

Published in the United States by
COUNTER-CURRENTS PUBLISHING LTD.
P.O. Box 22638
San Francisco, CA 94122
USA
http://www.counter-currents.com/

Hardcover ISBN: 978-1-64264-018-2
Paperback ISBN: 978-1-64264-019-9
E-book ISBN: 978-1-64264-020-5

Contents

Preface ❖ iii

1. Introduction ❖ 1

2. The Background to Aristophanes' *Clouds* ❖ 28

3. Aristophanes' *Clouds* ❖ 56

4. Plato's *Theages* ❖ 96

5. Plato's *Euthyphro* ❖ 121

6. Plato's *Apology of Socrates* ❖ 143

7. Plato's *Crito* ❖ 170

8. Plato's *Phaedo* ❖ 194

Index ❖ 219

About the Author ❖ 230

Preface

This volume began as a series of eight lectures entitled *The Trial of Socrates* presented to about a dozen students in The Invisible College, my adult education organization, in Atlanta. The class was held on Tuesday evenings, beginning September 1, 1998 and ending on October 20. This is the outline of the class:

Lecture 1: Introduction
Lecture 2: The Background of Aristophanes' *Clouds*, which discusses myth, pre-philosophical concepts of order, pre-Socratic natural philosophy, and the sophists
Lecture 3: Aristophanes' *Clouds*, which gives a very unflattering portrayal of Socrates
Lecture 4: More on the *Clouds*/Plato's *Theages*, which can be read as a rebuttal to the *Clouds*
Lecture 5: Plato's *Euthyphro*, which is set just before the trial of Socrates and deals with one of the accusations against him, namely impiety
Lecture 6: Plato's *Apology of Socrates*, which is Socrates' speech to the jury at his trial
Lecture 7: Plato's *Crito*, which is set in Socrates' prison cell as he awaits execution
Lecture 8: Selections from Plato's *Phaedo*, which tells of the last conversations and death of Socrates

All of the lectures were taped, but the lecture on selections from the *Phaedo* was loaned out and never returned. Fortunately, I saved my quite detailed notes, which allowed me to reconstruct it. I did not deal in detail with Socrates' accounts of the immortality of the soul and the afterlife, reserving those for the very next course I taught, which dealt entirely with the *Phaedo*. I also delivered a lecture on the *Phaedo* to the Theosophical Society in Atlanta. Those recordings survived, and I will eventually release them. Perhaps they would make a nice sequel called *The Death of Socrates*. In the meantime, if you are curious about my further thoughts on the *Phaedo*, see my lecture "The Myths of Plato," published in *From Plato to Postmodernism*.[1]

This book is based on a course of lectures for intelligent laymen drawn to philosophical questions. If I were to sit down and write a book on the same topic from scratch, it would be very different. It would surely be drier, more compressed, and more scholarly. As I edited the source materials, I had to fight the temptation to turn this into another academic book. Thus I have tried to make as few changes as possible to the general informal feel of the lectures.

Nevertheless, I think it is a good policy to cut every manuscript by at least ten percent before publication, and lecture transcripts afford many such opportunities. Thus I eliminated many needless repetitions, wordy constructions, and false starts. I introduced some qualifications, made some tweaks to increase clarity and precision, deleted weasel words, and quietly corrected a few factual errors. I removed questions from the students but tried to work my answers into the flow of the lecture. Unless there is a citation to a particular source, the words I attribute to other writers are paraphrases or quotes from memory, not verbatim quotes. To make these passages clear, I use single rather than double quotation marks. I also added section headings.

Although most of the chapters have been cut ruthlessly, I actually added to the lecture on the *Theages*. This was the first of three occasions when I taught the *Theages*, and subsequent discussions were more detailed and refined, so I fleshed out the *Theages* chapter based on my notes for and recollections of later lectures. I also substituted Nicholas D. Smith's translation for Thomas Pangle's when it was more readable.

The process of editing the *Phaedo* notes was almost the opposite of editing the transcripts: more like putting meat on bones than trimming fat.

Why have I decided to publish these lectures? For the same

---

[1] Greg Johnson, *From Plato to Postmodernism* (San Francisco: Counter-Currents, 2019).

reasons that I taught them in the first place: the love of philosophy and the love of sharing. Philosophy is the pursuit of wisdom. Wisdom is the most reliable way of securing a good life, and we are all pursuing the good life. Therefore, philosophy is of paramount importance to every serious human being.

If this is the case, then philosophy is too important to abandon to the embalming rooms of academia. Philosophy needs to address the general public. Thus we need accurate but simple and engaging introductions to the great philosophers and their questions. Plato and Aristophanes are two of the greatest writers to survive the fall of ancient Europe. They are both philosophically deep and literarily engaging. Thus the drama surrounding the trial and death of Socrates is one of the most compelling places to begin one's philosophical education.

But beyond that, I'm simply proud of these lectures and wish to share them with a much wider audience. They do more than just cover the essential facts and arguments. They go deeper. I also think there are some original ideas and turns of phrase here. I am particularly pleased with how much philosophy I managed to tease out of Aristophanes' *Clouds*. Indeed, I argue that Aristophanes was the first Socratic philosopher — meaning that all the essential ideas of Socratic philosophy are outlined in the *Clouds* — and thus the *Clouds* is the oldest extant work of Western philosophy.

I incurred many debts in the creation of this book.

The greatest influence on these lectures is Thomas Prufer of the Catholic University of America. I am still catching up to his class on Sophocles' *Oedipus the King*, Aristophanes' *Clouds*, and Plato's *Apology of Socrates* and *Phaedo*. We read Aristophanes' *Clouds* and Plato's *Apology* in the *Four Texts on Socrates* collection translated by Thomas G. West and Grace Starry West, which I used in this class as well.[2] Another abiding influence is Leo Strauss. Prufer assigned Strauss' *The Rebirth of Classical Political Rationalism*,[3] specifically the lectures on "The Problem of

---

[2] Plato and Aristophanes, *Four Texts on Socrates: Plato's* Euthyphro, Apology, *and* Crito *and Aristophanes'* Clouds, trans. Thomas G. West and Grace Starry West (Ithaca: Cornell University Press, 1984).

[3] Leo Strauss, *The Rebirth of Classical Political Rationalism: An Intro-

Socrates," as a supplementary text. Strauss also influenced the West and West edition. My understanding of Socrates' philosophical mission was also deeply marked by Donald W. Livingston's magisterial study *Hume's Philosophy of Common Life*.[4] Finally, another important influence was my friend Glenn Magee. Many of the ideas here were worked out in my conversations with him in the 1990s.

I wish to thank everyone connected to The Invisible College, especially the students in the room during these lectures. You brought out my best as a teacher.

I want to thank Michael Polignano for digitizing these recordings and teaching me how to edit them and improve their sound quality.

I am deeply grateful to V.S. for his enormous efforts as a transcriber.

I also wish to thank Collin Cleary, Buttercup Dew, John Morgan, and David Zsutty for their careful proofing, Alex Graham and James O'Meara for their help with the index, Kevin Slaughter for his work on the cover, and Collin Cleary, Mark Gullick, F. Roger Devlin, and Anonymous Heidegger Scholar for their kind words of praise.

This book is dedicated to the memory of Mary Ann Martini. I was really looking forward to sharing it with her.

---

duction to the Thought of Leo Strauss, ed. Thomas Pangle (Chicago: University of Chicago Press, 1989).

[4] Donald W. Livingston, *Hume's Philosophy of Common Life* (Chicago: University of Chicago Press, 1984).

INTRODUCTION

"... Socrates the sole turning point and vortex of so-called world history."

—Friedrich Nietzsche, *The Birth of Tragedy*[1]

"Socrates idea stem into modern thought and rationalization."

—Undergraduate plagiarist, 2000

Socrates is an epochal thinker, in a very literal sense, because epochs in the history of philosophy are named in relation to him. Before Socrates, philosophy is called pre-Socratic. After Socrates, it is called Socratic or post-Socratic. It is analogous to dividing history into years Before Christ and *Anno Domini*. Socrates is a watershed figure in the history of thought, just as is Jesus in history in general.

One can say that Socrates is a *pivotal* figure in history. The hinges of history turn on the life and teachings of Socrates, at least the history of philosophy. And, because philosophy has had such an influence on every other dimension of culture, Socrates would have to be considered one of the men who created the world we live in, including shaping our minds in ways that we might not be aware of, unless we actually study what he taught and what he did.

So, this is not just a book about somebody called Socrates. Because Socrates left such a deep impression on human life and human history, it's really a book about us. Therefore, understanding Socrates is a way to understand the deep tangled roots of our own civilization and our own selves.

---

[1] "... Sokrates den einen Wendepunkt und Wirbel der sogenannten Weltgeschichte ... ," Friedrich Nietzsche, *Die Geburt der Tragödie aus dem Geiste der Musik* (1872), ch. 15.

SOURCES ON SOCRATES

There are six sources of knowledge on Socrates.

The first source, historically speaking, is Aristophanes' comic play *Clouds*, which is a very nasty and very funny satire of Socrates and what we now call "pre-Socratic" philosophy. Aristophanes saw no difference between Socrates and the pre-Socratics, because at the time he wrote, there *was* no difference. Before Socrates became Socrates, he too had a pre-Socratic phase.

The second source is Xenophon's set of writings on Socrates. Xenophon was an Athenian general and nobleman who became a student of Socrates.

The third and primary source of knowledge on Socrates are the dialogues of Plato. We will read four dialogues: *Theages, Euthyphro, Apology of Socrates*, and *Crito*. We will also look at excerpts from the *Phaedo*.

Fourth, Aristotle provides important information about Socrates.

Fifth, there are Socratic dialogues written by people other than Plato and Xenophon. Socrates had many followers and imitators. Crito, who we will meet in the dialogue called the *Crito*, wrote Socratic dialogues, even though Plato portrays him as not particularly philosophical.

The sixth and final category can be labelled "other." These are testimonies about Socrates' life and teachings preserved by historians like Diogenes Laertius and philosophers like Cicero.

I will draw primarily upon Aristophanes and Plato, plus the testimonies of Aristotle and others. Space does not permit looking at Xenophon and other Socratic writings from antiquity.

Because of all these sources, the life of Socrates is fairly well-documented for a person who died in the fourth century BCE.

THE LIFE OF SOCRATES

Socrates was born in Athens in 469 BCE and he died at age 70 in 399 BCE. His father, Sophroniscus, was a sculptor. His mother, Phaenarete, was a midwife. Socrates had two wives. One was Xanthippe, who was a notoriously difficult woman with whom he had a son named Lamprocles. There are many stories about how shrewish Xanthippe was. People asked him, 'Socrates, why do you put up with this woman? She's so difficult!' And he said, in effect, 'Just like some people like spirited horses, I like a spirited wife. Besides, if I can get used to dealing with Xanthippe, I can deal with anybody.'[2] She was with him until the very end.

Near the end of his life, though, Socrates took a second wife named Myrto, who had two children with him named Sophroniscus and Menexenus, who were just babies when he died at 70. It's interesting that Xanthippe and the two young children are present at his death, which indicates that he had children from a second woman while he was still married to his first wife, and Diogenes Laertius argues that this was exactly what happened.[3] The Athenians, because of the great loss of population during the Peloponnesian War, passed a law allowing any citizen to take a second wife, not officially, but as a sort of concubine to increase the population. So apparently Socrates did his civic duty even in his extreme old age by taking on a second wife and having two more children.

Diogenes Laertius records many odd stories about Socrates. He was reputed to have helped Euripides write his plays, which is quite a remarkable claim.[4] He was said to have been a student of natural philosophers like Anaxagoras, Damon, and Archelaus. We'll deal with that in the next chapter. He was alleged to have never been interested in natural philosophy as well. He was rumored to have been a slave, which is probably entirely false. He was born the son of Athenian citizens, and he died an Athenian citizen.

He was alleged to have followed his father's craft of being a sculptor and was credited with some statues of the three graces at the Acropolis. A poet named Timon wrote an epigram on this: "From these diverged the sculptor, a praetor about laws, the enchanter of Greece, inventor of subtle arguments, the sneerer who mocked at fine speeches, half-Attic in his irony."[5]

---

[2] Diogenes Laertius, *Lives of the Eminent Philosophers*, trans. R. D. Hicks, 2 vols. (Cambridge, Mass.: Loeb Classical Library, 1959), II, 37.
[3] Diogenes Laertius, II, 26–27.
[4] Diogenes Laertius, II, 18.
[5] Diogenes Laertius, II, 19.

He was reputedly a formidable public speaker and capable of persuading and dissuading people on any point. He was supposed to be the first teacher of rhetoric, which we know is historically false. According to Diogenes Laertius, "he was the first philosopher who discoursed on the conduct of life and the first philosopher who was tried and put to death."[6]

He was supposedly a moneylender and an investor, although most sources say he lived in complete poverty and walked around barefoot wearing dirty clothes full of holes. He prided himself on simple living, which is one of the sources of his conflicts with his wife. She wanted him to earn money, and he wanted to hang around talking philosophy. He really did value freedom rather than money or security, and so he chose to live in voluntary poverty in order to have as much free time as possible in order to think.

He did not travel at all except when he was sent on military expeditions by Athens during the Peloponnesian War. He was an exercise fanatic. He was very scrupulous about keeping himself in shape until he died. He was sometimes seen dancing alone, and he was asked why he would dance alone, and he said, 'It's good exercise.'[7]

Frequently, because of the vehemence of his arguments in the gym or marketplace, people would physically assault him. He would also stand around the marketplace not buying things but talking philosophy. He enjoyed looking at the wares in the marketplace, thinking, 'How many things I can do without!'

He claimed, according to some sources, that virtue equals knowledge and vice equals ignorance, and we find those claims are borne out in Plato. He was renowned for courage in battle and for moderation and self-control, and we find this attested to quite dramatically in Plato's dialogue *Symposium*. Alcibiades described how he slipped into Socrates' bed at night and tried to seduce him, and Socrates remained completely unmoved by the whole experience, which is probably not an easy thing to do given that Socrates apparently had a wild crush on Alcibiades.

---

[6] Diogenes Laertius, II, 20.

[7] Diogenes Laertius, II, 32.

The earliest dated event in Socrates' life happened when he was 46 years old, in 423 BCE, when Aristophanes' play *Clouds* premiered. It came in dead last in the competition of comedies in the great festival of Dionysus in Athens. Of course, the other plays have long since disappeared, but this play has maintained itself as a classic ever since. Words of encouragement for aspiring writers, I suppose. The *Clouds* is Socrates' debut on the stage of history, and it's a very unflattering portrait.

A couple of years later, 421 BCE, is the date of one of Xenophon's works called the *Symposium,* or the drinking party, and here Socrates is shown to be somewhat similar to the Socrates of the *Clouds* but somewhat different too.

Socrates was sent off to fight a couple of battles during the Peloponnesian War, which lasted from 431 to 404 BCE and ended with Athens' defeat and the downfall of her empire. A few years after the war was over, Socrates was put on trial for a number of charges. Basically, he was charged with disbelieving in the gods of the city, i.e., impiety, which, to the minds of the ancient Greeks, was equivalent to taking an interest in nature. For the ancient Greeks, natural philosophy or the investigation of nature by science or reason was equivalent to atheism, and we'll see how that is the case. That's very much the portrait of Socrates you find in the *Clouds*.

Socrates was also accused of corrupting the youth by disbelieving in the gods and also by teaching them how to make the weaker argument the stronger, which has come to be known as "sophistry": the art of public speaking. Spin-doctoring might be our most exact contemporary analogue.

Socrates was tried, condemned, and executed in 399 BCE. It was a fairly painless and humane death. They had him drink some hemlock, which caused him to expire. The Athenians were good to their own citizens even when they were executing them. They were remarkably humane by the standards of the time.

Socrates could have avoided the trial to begin with but chose not to. And he could have escaped from prison after he was condemned, but he chose not to and ended up dying. One of the things we'll examine in this book is why he did this.

Xenophon says in his *Apology of Socrates to the Jury* that Socrates had decided it was time for him to die. That would explain his behavior. I think there is more to it than that, but it's a start. It's very peculiar that he chose to suffer execution unjustly.

Immediately after Socrates' execution, the Athenians had a fit of remorse. Socrates' friend, Aristippus, brought charges against the people who put Socrates on trial: Lycon, Anytus, and Meletus. Meletus was executed. Anytus and Lycon were banished.[8] Eventually the Athenians erected a bronze statue of Socrates at public expense. The "dying Socrates" became an ideal that young Athenians aspired to. He seemed heroic and gained an extraordinary mystique that has clung to him throughout history. He's a martyr for philosophy, and it sealed his fame in the history books. Such a hope might have been part of his decision to remain and suffer execution.

PHILOSOPHY BEFORE SOCRATES

Why do we divide philosophy into pre-Socratic and post-Socratic periods? Because something very fundamental happened with Socrates.

First of all, philosophy before Socrates was pretty much *amoral* philosophy. There was no such thing as moral philosophy before Socrates. Among the pre-Socratic schools are two approaches to philosophy that show up quite prominently in the *Clouds*.

There was natural philosophy, which was simply what we would call science today. It was *value-free* science. The natural philosophers looked out at the world of nature and didn't see any norms written in nature, any rights and wrongs. They simply saw what we see today: nature red in tooth and claw, the ugly struggle for survival, and that's about it. They looked upon morality as merely a matter of social convention.

Another movement at the time, the sophists, who were teachers of public speaking and how to get ahead in politics, also held basically the same framework. They thought that nature does not provide any moral norms, but it does provide certain desires, and the sophists were there to equip people with the necessary tools to satisfy their desires to the best of their ability.

---

[8] Diogenes Laertius, II, 43.

And in ancient Greece the best way of satisfying one's desires was to go into politics.

For the ancients, politics was much more central than it is today. Anybody who was from a good family and wanted to make his way in the world would go into politics. It was simply not considered gentlemanly to go into business. That was a slavish activity. You were supposed to do business on the side to keep your estate functioning, but anyone who was seen to be too concerned with this kind of activity was looked down upon as a mere money-grubber.

The true activity of a free and noble individual was politics, so the sophists equipped people for politics. But they equipped them for politics by teaching them that beliefs about the gods and morality were merely conventional, that the teaching of nature was to satisfy one's desires, and that they should divest themselves of moral scruples in going about that.

So, neither strand of pre-Socratic philosophy had anything to do with morals. Morals were considered to be merely conventional and therefore outside the realm of philosophy. Indeed, morals were seen as beneath the dignity of philosophy. As conventions, they were seen as somewhat contemptible, somewhat stupid. You'd have to be something of an unreflective buffoon to be concerned with morality.

THE SOCRATIC DIFFERENCE

Socrates, however, is entirely different. Socrates was primarily a moral philosopher, at least the Socrates we find in Plato and Xenophon. Let's look at a few passages from the *Apology of Socrates* and the *Crito*. In the *Apology*, Socrates talks about his activity in the city.

> . . . I go around and do nothing but persuade you, both younger and older, not to care for bodies and money before, nor as vehemently as, how your soul will be the best possible. I say: "Not from money does virtue come, but from virtue comes money and all the other good things for human beings both privately and publicly." (30b)[9]

---

[9] All quotes from Plato's *Euthyphro, Apology,* and *Crito* and Aris-

The care of the soul, meaning the cultivation of one's moral character, was the central concern for Socrates. He said that you don't get good character from getting money. You might have money coming to you if you cultivate good character, but there's no guarantee about that either. But the primary concern for Socrates is the care of the soul.

Also in the *Apology*, after he's been found guilty, Socrates says to the jury:

> Perhaps, then, someone might say, "By being silent and keeping quiet, Socrates, won't you be able to live in exile for us?" It is hardest of all to persuade some of you about this. For if I say that this is to disobey the god and because of this it is impossible to keep quiet, you will not be persuaded by me, on the ground that I am being ironic. And, on the other hand, if I say that this even happens to be a very great good for a human being—to make speeches every day about virtue and the other things about which you hear me conversing and examining both myself and others—and that the unexamined life is not worth living for a human being, you will be persuaded by me still less when I say these things. (37e–38b)

That's a complicated passage, but the gist of it is this: Socrates, before he was convicted, tried to justify the activity of going around Athens and conversing about virtue and encouraging people to leave off the things that impeded them from developing their souls and their characters. He claimed that he did this because the god Apollo at Delphi had said that Socrates was wiser than anybody else in the world. His reaction was, 'Well, pious man that I am, I realized that this couldn't be true, so I must test what the god said.'

So he went around finding people who had a reputation for

---

tophanes' *Clouds*, are from *Four Texts on Socrates:* trans. Thomas G. West and Grace Starry West (Ithaca: Cornell University Press, 1984). Plato quotes will be cited by Stephanus numbers, the universal form of Plato citation, Aristophanes quotes by page number.

wisdom, namely the sophists. He also talked to the poets, who were teachers of morals. If anybody taught morals in ancient Greece it was poets. Homer was the moral teacher for the ancient Greeks.

Socrates would go to people who recited Homer or people who taught public speaking, and he would ask them to display their wisdom, and they would come up wanting. They would fail, and so he'd go away thinking, 'Well, maybe I am wiser than these people. Why? Because they think they're wise, and they're not, whereas I don't think I am wise, and that's true. I'm not wise.'

And so he says, in essence, 'Maybe I have some kind of wisdom. Call it human wisdom, if you will, which is knowledge of one's own ignorance and limitations.'

Now, in this passage he's saying, 'You didn't believe that, you jurors. You didn't believe that on account of the reputation I have for being ironic.' And we'll explain what that means later.

So, paraphrasing again: 'I'm going to tell you the true reason why I go around philosophizing now. It has nothing to do with the gods. It has to do with the fact that the examined life—the philosophical life of self-reflection and self-cultivation—is the only life worth living for a human being. Meaning that it's *intrinsically good* to engage in philosophical reflection and self-criticism and self-examination.'

Philosophy is the care of the soul. The activity of philosophy is intrinsically good. It needs no other justification than the effect that it has on you. Socrates tried to fob the Athenians off with the claim that he was sent to philosophize by a god, but it didn't work. But Socrates says it's even harder to persuade them of the truth. The truth being that the unexamined life is not worth living for a human being, and the philosophical life is the only life worth living. That's even harder to convince people of.

These are dramatic claims, but it gives a sense of the centrality of moral philosophy and self-cultivation to Socrates.

SOCRATIC IRONY

Socrates tells the jurors, 'You didn't believe me because I have a reputation for being ironic.' So, we need to know what it means to be ironic in the Greek sense.

For the ancient Greeks, irony has to be understood in the context of a rigidly hierarchical society ruled by a warrior aristocracy. One of the hallmarks of aristocratic good manners is that when you deal with people who are your inferiors, you don't make them *feel* inferior. It's considered crass and low-class to make people feel inferior.

This attitude is very much present in Jane Austen's novels. Think of *Emma*. Emma is chastised by Mr. Knightley (which is the perfect name for a magnanimous man) because she makes people who are her inferiors *feel* inferior. 'Badly done, Emma!' he says, 'That's the wrong thing to do.' Traces of this attitude still remain in Southern genteel society.

A sign of good breeding is that you don't make your inferiors feel their inferiority. How do you do that? You have to be somewhat dishonest. You have to pretend to be less than you really are. It's a kind of self-concealment and condescension designed to not ruffle the feelings of people who would otherwise feel put upon by their social superiors.

The crowning virtue of the gentleman, the aristocrat, is called magnanimity, meaning "greatness of soul." But great-souled people, when dealing with inferiors have to condescend to them. In order to prevent inequality of status from being painful, they have to downplay the distinction. So, they have to pretend to be less than they really are.

Now, if you look in Aristotle's *Nicomachean Ethics*, if you look in Theophrastus' book *Characters*, which are the primary sources we have from the time of Socrates on the nature of irony, this is exactly what irony is.

The modern sense of irony as saying one thing but meaning something different does not really come into existence until the century after Socrates' death, and it's not really formulated or defined clearly until the first century CE by the Roman orator Quintilian.

The primary sense of irony is this aristocratic, condescending, magnanimous refusal to display oneself fully. It's a kind of dissimulation.

Socrates has a reputation for irony. What does that mean? It means Socrates feels superior to people. He knows he's superior. He's certain of it, but he doesn't want to hurt their feelings, so he pretends to be less than he really is. Unfortunately, however, people saw through him, and irony only works if people are unaware of it. No one likes to be condescended to, so if you know someone is being ironical with you, it angers you. And Socrates angered a lot of people by being ironical.

Irony is a way of lubricating social interactions between unequals so that differences of class or breeding or social status do not cause friction. But on the other hand, if you see through it, then it exacerbates those differences all the more.

Here's Socrates, who goes around barefoot, looking like what would nowadays be delicately described as a "homeless person." Socrates' behavior would probably get him labeled a schizophrenic. He walks around barefoot. He talks about philosophy. He says he has a little voice that talks to him and tells him what not to do. Once he stood up all night just thinking about something. He would go into trances and lose track of reality.

Thus when Socrates condescended to the well-dressed, well-bred gentleman of Athens, and they saw through him, they felt deeply insulted. Because all of their good manners were being turned against them, when they were being condescended to by somebody who appears to be by all conventional standards a total bum.

Socrates' reputation for irony made his story that he philosophized out of piety to the gods completely unbelievable. The Athenians think Socrates is up to more than he admits, because he's ironical. They thought, in effect, 'He's talking down to us when he talks about the gods.' That assumes, of course, that Socrates doesn't really believe in the gods, which is one of the charges against him.

What's the real reason Socrates philosophizes, then? Socrates reveals the truth when he says, in effect, 'If you're not persuaded by the gods, you'll be even less persuaded by the truth, namely that there is nothing more important than the care of one's own soul.' And that is hard for people to swallow. Most Athenians would not adopt Socrates' lifestyle to save their own souls, much less care for them.

SOCRATIC IGNORANCE

Socrates is also reputed to claim ignorance. A lot of people, of course, take comfort in the fact that Socrates doesn't claim that he knows, because, well, if Socrates can't know, then who am I to be expected to know anything about virtue? So one can sink back into one's comfy chair, click on the television, and that's that. That's really not the message one wants to take away from Socrates' disavowal of knowledge.

I want to read the passages where Socrates talks about what he knows and doesn't know. We will encounter this theme throughout the book. So we might as well get it in our sights beforehand, so that when we encounter it again it will be fresh in our minds.

In the *Apology* Socrates says, "I, men of Athens, have gotten this name, this reputation for being a philosopher due nothing but a certain wisdom" (20d). So, he doesn't deny being wise. He claims that he has a certain wisdom.

> Just what sort of wisdom is this? That which is perhaps human wisdom. For probably I really am wise in this. But those of whom I just spoke might perhaps be wise in some wisdom greater than human or else I cannot say what it is. For I, at least, do not have knowledge of it, but whoever asserts that I do lies and speaks in order to slander me. (20d–e)

So, Socrates does avow wisdom, but he calls it human wisdom as opposed to a more-than-human kind of wisdom, which he does deny having.

To use terms completely out of context, he avows *anthroposophy* and denies *theosophy*. He has human wisdom or anthroposophy but not divine wisdom, theosophy. Those terms are being totally misused here. You shouldn't associate them with Madame Blavatsky or Rudolf Steiner. I'm just using the terms loosely.

After Socrates heard that the oracle of Delphi said 'No one is wiser than Socrates,' his reaction was, "I'm conscious that I'm not at all wise, either much or little" (19d). I want to amend the translation there, because I think it's better translated, "I am not wise in anything great or small."

Socrates denies wisdom about the great and small. But is great and small an exhaustive division of things? Is everything either great or small, so that if you have no wisdom great or small you have no wisdom at all? Or is something being left out? What about the middle-sized? What about the average?

Socrates is referring here to his portrait in the *Clouds*. In the *Clouds*, Socrates is shown having an interest in the feet of fleas and the anuses of gnats. Tiny little things. He's also shown to be interested in the cosmos as a whole and the Earth as a whole. Great big things.

But when it comes to dealing with the middle-sized things — namely his friends and neighbors, his fellow human beings, the city, the human world — the Socrates of the *Clouds* is a total boob.

In the *Clouds*, Socrates is portrayed as wise about great and small things and a fool in the middle-sized realm where human beings live. So, when he denies wisdom of things great and small in the *Apology*, he is denying the truth of the portrayal of himself in the *Clouds* as being interested in gnats and fleas and in the planets and the cosmos as a whole. Beyond that, when Socrates avows a human wisdom, that's equivalent to avowing wisdom about middle-sized things, namely us, the human world and human affairs.

SOCRATES ON EROS

Another sense of the "middle" is very important for Socrates. Socrates claims to know something. Not only does he claim wisdom about human things, he claims knowledge. He doesn't disavow all forms of knowledge. And there's one particular thing that he claims to know that I think is most astonishing.

In Plato's *Symposium*, Socrates says 'the only thing I say I understand is the art of love.' So, he does say he knows the art of love. Now, the Greek is just "the erotic things," *ta erotika*. He knows the erotic things.

In the *Theages*, Socrates also says he knows the erotic things:

Rather I always say, surely, that I happen to know, so to

speak, nothing except a certain small subject of knowledge: What pertains to erotic things. As regards this subject of knowledge, to be sure, I rank myself as wondrously clever beyond anyone, whether human beings of the past or of the present. (128b)[10]

Socrates is not bragging about his sexual prowess. Instead, he's speaking about his knowledge of the human soul, what we would today call "psychology."

In the *Symposium*, *eros* or love is spoken of as a being that exists *in the middle*. The Greek term is *metaxy*, the middle realm, the middle space. And what's it the middle between? Between mortals and the gods. Love or *eros* is treated as an intermediate being between the human and the divine. Not between the microscopic and the macroscopic, but between the human realm and the divine realm.

When Socrates claims not to have wisdom of things great and small but doesn't deny knowing about the middle, that's also equivalent to the claim that he knows *eros*, because *eros* is a god for him. Not a full-fledged god. A *daimon* is the Greek term. For the Greeks, a *daimon* refers to a quasi-divine being like an angel. It's not mortal, but it's not a full-fledged god either, and it hangs around between the realms of the gods and the mortals and carries messages or causes trouble. When Socrates claims that he has wisdom of the middle and knowledge of *eros*, that's equivalent to the same thing.

What is knowledge of *eros*, though, for Socrates? Well, when you boil it down it means knowledge of the human soul. Because for Socrates *eros* is a kind of pulsating, plastic, vibrating force, the energy of the soul. It's libido in Freud's sense, the reservoir of psychic energy that sets the whole soul in motion. It doesn't just refer to sexual libido. It refers to any kind of psychic energy and can take on any form, from attachment to another human being or one's pets and one's familiar surroundings to

---

[10] Plato, *Theages*, trans. Thomas L. Pangle, in *The Roots of Political Philosophy: Ten Forgotten Socratic Dialogues*, ed. Thomas L. Pangle (Ithaca: Cornell University Press, 1987).

love of the fine or the beautiful, of the just, of ideals. *Eros* is a power that human beings have in the soul to form passionate attachments to things. Not just sexual things but also ideals like justice or the good.

Plato and Socrates believe that the soul can be healthy or sick, and a healthy soul has a certain well-organized quality to it. It's erotically well-balanced, whereas a sick soul is unbalanced, erotically speaking.

The hallmark of a healthy soul for Socrates is that it exists in this middle realm. It's not caught up entirely in mere human affairs, in minutiae and trivia and the newspapers, because it also looks upward to things that are universal and ideal, and it tries to illuminate the messy flux of human affairs by something that's not merely human, that's ideal or universal in significance. So, in the healthy soul there's a kind of tension between the ideal and the merely real.

An unhealthy soul collapses into trivial affairs and gets caught up in the merely human, all too human. Another form of illness of the soul is to become entirely indifferent to human things and solely identify oneself with what's abstract or ideal. This is the error of the ideologue as well as what you call the "gnostic" impulse in philosophy: the mysticism, asceticism, even hatred of matter associated, for instance, with the ancient Pythagoreans, who looked upon the body as a prison and regarded the material world as such as evil.

There's a little emblem from a seventeenth century Rosicrucian named Daniel Cramer. The title is *Mors Lucrum*, which is Latin for "death is a profit," "death is a gain." It is the image of a man in stocks praying to death for release, and death is poised with a little arrow to deliver him. This is the gnostic attitude that the body is simply a prison and death is our only route to freedom.

Socrates doesn't have that attitude, because it denies man's middle place. We can't entirely leave the bodily world behind, and we shouldn't be concerned with that. Rather, the ideal of psychic health is to maintain oneself in a constant tension between the ideal and the merely real. An erotically healthy soul tries to maintain itself in that tension without collapsing into one extreme or the other.

When Socrates says he has "human wisdom" or wisdom about "the middle things" this means knowledge of how the soul can be healthy or sick. Socrates' primary concern is the care of the soul.

THE *DAIMONION*

Socrates was also reputed to have a *"daimonion."* *Eros* is supposed to be a *daimon*. It's a quasi-divine being between the gods and humans. Socrates claims that he has a *daimonion*, which just means a "little daimon." Socrates refers to his *daimonion* in the *Theages*, the *Apology*, and the *Crito*. It's sometimes translated as "divine sign." If Socrates was about to make a bad decision, the *daimonion* would say, 'Wait, Socrates, don't do it.' That's all it said to him. It just stopped him from making bad decisions.

It's worth noting that, according to the texts of Xenophon and Plato, the decisions the *daimonion* intervenes in all concern human affairs. Socrates is about to get involved with something—with politics or with a certain student—and then the *daimonion* says, 'No, Socrates, don't do it.'

Now, if Socrates was dismissed as being condescending when he spoke of the gods, we can't dismiss the idea that he was also being condescending when he spoke of the *daimonion*. My working hypothesis is that Socrates refers to the *daimonion* merely to personify his knowledge of erotic things, meaning his knowledge of the soul and how it can become good or go bad. The *daimonion* always warns Socrates away from dealing with bad characters. So, Socrates' *daimonion* is equivalent to his knowledge of human things, of the middle realm of the soul.

SOCRATES AS MORAL PHILOSOPHER

In what sense is Socrates a moral philosopher?

First of all, Socrates is a moral philosopher because he's concerned about how to live and how to die.

One of the wonderful things about Plato and Xenophon is they don't just report what Socrates *said*, they also narrate some of the things he *did*. He was courageous in battle. He was good to his friends. We don't know much about his home life, but we do have one record of him explaining to his elder son why he should be better to his mother, Xanthippe. There are many acts of decency, courage, self-control, and so forth narrated about Socrates' life. He lived well, and, as we shall see from the end of the *Phaedo*, he died well too. This is what moral philosophy is all about.

ALL MEN ARE PURSUING THE GOOD

Socrates was famous for defending the claim that all human beings are pursuing the good. Human action, if it is rational, always shows a certain pattern. When we have a choice of different options, we always choose the option that appears to be the best option available.

To be precise, Socrates is not saying that we're choosing what's *really* the best thing but what just *seems* to be the best to us. We are often mistaken—maybe more often than not—about what the good is. But we choose what we see as the good, and if we see it differently then we'll choose differently. But embedded in all human action is the deep concern to choose the better option. We can be mistaken, but that's beside the point. An orientation towards the good is an intrinsic part of all human action.

If that's the case, Socrates argues, we have to be very serious about life, because first of all we're already pursuing the good life, so we need to know exactly what's required of us to do this. The main requirement is practical wisdom. Moral wisdom, if you will. The virtues.

In the dialogue *Euthydemus*, Socrates goes through a little exchange with a young man named Clinias, who is somewhat confused about life. Socrates asks him, 'What do you want in life? What are the good things in life?' And Clinias gives a list of the good things in life.

Then Socrates says, 'Well, what about good fortune? Don't you need good fortune to make all of these things real? Because even if you have good looks and a good family and money and so forth, if you don't have good luck none of these things are actually going to lead to having a good life.'

Socrates is identifying two things that are really different: wisdom and good fortune. Most people depend on luck to make all the components of a good life *actually coalesce* into a good life. But depending on luck to have a good life is really foolish, because you might not luck out. Fortune is fickle.

So, the smart thing to do is to make your own luck. What's the wise person's substitute for luck? It's wisdom. And what is wisdom? Wisdom for Plato and Socrates is *the capacity to make right use of all things*. It's the capacity to take all of the advantages that life has dealt you—and all the disadvantages, for that matter—and manage them in such a way that the net result is a good life. This is a deeply practical and deeply moral sense of wisdom.

How do the virtues—things like courage and temperance and justice—relate to being morally wise? For Plato and Socrates, and for Aristotle too, virtue is a kind of *moral perceptiveness* about the right thing to do at the right time and the right place and the right circumstances.

If you have the virtue of courage, that means you know when it's good to fight and when it's good to run away, and you have the capacity to see the right thing to do in the particular emerging situation, not in hindsight. Most of us figure out the right thing to do six months later. Hindsight is 20/20. But virtue is the ability to discern the right thing to do in the moment.

Another Socratic moral claim is that virtue is a kind of knowledge, so if one knows what the good is, one does it. And if someone doesn't do the virtuous thing, then it's a sign that he doesn't really know it.

This is a very strange claim, and it's quite controversial, because of course there is an obvious objection. This is something that Euripides says in *Hippolytus*: We know what's good, but often times we don't *do* what's good. Isn't that true of all of us?

This phenomenon is called by the Greeks "weakness of will," *akrasia*. It is sometimes translated as "incontinence," which unfortunately also has the connotation of bed-wetting. So, let's just say "weakness of will."

You *know* it's good, but you don't *do* it.

Socrates held that if there is moral knowledge, action just follows as a matter of course. If you know, you do. There's no hiatus between knowing what's right and doing it. So, any example of weakness of will is really an example of not really knowing.

Aristotle actually criticizes Socrates on this point, but Aristotle's solution to the problem also boils down to saying that weakness of the will is ultimately not knowing. So, it's a hard position to shake off.

SOCRATES & THEORETICAL PHILOSOPHY

Wisdom in the older sense, which you could call *theoretical* wisdom, *natural science*, or *metaphysics* is of secondary importance to Socrates.

To put this in context, let's look at a passage from Cicero that talks about the theoretical model of wisdom that was held by the pre-Socratic philosophers.

> ... though we see that philosophy is a fact of great antiquity, yet its name is, we admit, of recent origin. For who can deny that wisdom itself, at any rate, is not only ancient in fact but in name as well? And by its discovery of things sacred and human, as well as of the beginnings and causes of every phenomenon [i.e., natural science], it gained its glorious name with the ancients. And so the famous seven (who were called *sophoi* by the Greeks) were both held and named wise men by our countrymen, whilst many generations previously, Lycurgus (in whose day according to tradition Homer also lived before the foundation of this city) and back in the heroic age Ulysses and Nestor were, as history relates, wise men and accounted wise. And surely tradition would not have told of Atlas upholding the heavens, or Prometheus nailed to the Caucasus, or Cepheus placed among the stars with his wife and son-in-law and daughter, unless their marvelous discovery of things heavenly had caused their name to be transferred to the fairy tales of myth.

He's saying that these mythic names originate from early natural philosophers, who learned the nature of things and whose names were transferred into the realm of myth.

> And with these began the succession of all those who devoted themselves to the contemplation of nature and were both held to be and named wise men, and this title of theirs penetrated to the time of Pythagoras, who, according to Heraclides of Pontus, the pupil of Plato and a learned man of the first rank, came, the story goes, to Phlius and with a wealth of learning discussed certain subjects with Leon, the ruler of the Phliasians. And Leon after wondering at his talent and eloquence asked him to name the art in which he put the most reliance, but Pythagoras said that for his part he had no acquaintance with any art, but was a philosopher. Leon was astonished at the novelty of the term and asked who philosophers were and in what they differed from the rest of the world. Pythagoras, the story continues, replied that the life of man seemed to him to resemble the festival which was celebrated with the most magnificent games before a concourse collected from the whole of Greece.

He's referring the Olympic Games, the Corinthian Games, and so forth.

> For at this festival some men whose bodies had been trained sought to win the glorious distinction of a crown. Others were attracted by the prospect of making gain by buying or selling. Whilst there was on the other hand a certain class, and that quite the best type of freeborn men, who looked neither for applause nor gain, but came for the sake of the spectacle and closely watched what was done and how it was done. So also we, as though we had come from some city to a kind of crowded festival, leaving in like fashion another life and nature of being, entered upon this life, and some were slaves of ambition, some of money, and there were a special few, who, counting all else as nothing, closely scanned the nature of things. These men gave themselves the name lovers of wisdom (for that is the meaning of the word philosopher). And just as at the games the men of truest breeding looked on without any

self-seeking, so in life the contemplation and discovery of nature far surpassed all other pursuits.

The word "theory" comes from the Greek word "*theorein,*" which means to be a spectator, to look upon. The word "speculation" is a Latinization of the same term, to be a spectator, to look on. Early pre-Socratic philosophy was primarily theoretical or speculative, gazing at nature, trying to know the nature of things as they are. It was entirely unconnected with practical activity, and, in fact, it regarded itself as noble precisely to the extent that it was divorced from any sort of practical activity.

This was very much a part of the Greek aristocratic ethos, which prized leisure above work. The best people didn't have to work. Some, of course, fell into self-indulgence. But the best devoted themselves to self-improvement, including the creation of beautiful and useless things. Most of what we call "high culture" is the result of aristocratic patronage going all the way back to the ancients.

The philosophers emulated this model of nobility, then intensified it. In fact, they beat the aristocrats at their own game, for the aristocrats, although they were liberated from material necessity, were still caught up with material luxury, whereas the philosophers were completely divorced from material and practical concerns, devoting themselves entirely to the most sublimely useless thing of all, which is knowing how the cosmos works. Not for any technological benefits, not for any "cash value" — which is what drives science today — but simply for the sake of knowing as an end in itself.

This is the original aim of philosophy. It's amoral because it's concerned with nature and doesn't see any moral law in nature. It's impractical because it measures its nobility by the extent to which it liberates itself from any concern with practical activity.

Nor was Pythagoras by any means simply the discoverer of the name but he extended the actual content of philosophy as well. After his arrival in Italy, subsequently to this conversation in Phlius, he enriched the private and public life of the district known as Magna Graecia with the most excellent institutions and arts—of his doctrines we can perhaps speak another time. But from the ancient days down to the time of Socrates, who had listened to Archelaus, the pupil of Anaxagoras, who were both natural philosophers too, philosophy dealt with numbers and movements, the problem whence all things came or whither they returned, and zealously inquired into the size of the stars, the spaces that divided them, their courses, and all celestial phenomena. Socrates, on the other hand, was the first to call philosophy down from the heavens and set her in the cities of men and bring her also into their homes and compel her to ask questions about life, morality, and things good and evil. And his many-sided method of discussion and the varied nature of its subjects and the greatness of his genius, which have been immortalized in Plato's literary masterpieces, have produced many warring philosophic sects of which I have chosen particularly to follow that one which I think agreeable to the practice of Socrates, in trying to conceal my own private opinion, to relieve others from deception, and in every discussion to look for the most probable solution . . .[11]

Cicero is a very important source. He gives us the tableau of pre-Socratic and post-Socratic philosophy. Socrates is the pivotal figure who called philosophy down from the heavens and put it to work on the problems of men and morals.

SPECULATIVE VS. HUMANISTIC PHILOSOPHY

The distinction between pre-Socratic and Socratic philosophizing is not merely historical. They are live options today. There are quite a few pre-Socratics running around right now There are many who think that reason cannot guide morals and character. There are many who think that the scientific investigation of nature can only lead to the collapse of moral conduct, and, well, so be it.

---

[11] Cicero, *Tusculan Disputations*, trans. J. E. King (Cambridge, Mass.: Loeb Classical Library, 1971), book V, iii–iv, pp. 431–35.

A central characteristic of pre-Socratic philosophy is its attempt to step outside the human world and the human perspective on things and see the world from a non-human point of view, somewhere far above or far below the human. The ordinary perspective of human actors is left behind, whereas with Socrates you find a resolution never to forget that we are human beings, that we are *human* spectators in the world, and never to forget that whatever we see in nature we see from the human point of view. We're never going to be able to step outside of the human condition and see the world as it would look if we didn't exist, which is the model of pre-Socratics ancient and modern. This struggle exists to this day.

For instance, if you look around any modern city, you can see a nice jumble of what you might call pre-Socratic and Socratic forms of architecture. I would call brutalist and Bauhaus architecture pre-Socratic in the sense that it steps out from the human point of view, the human perspective, and human scale. It's large, dwarfing, somewhat alienating, and not particularly homey. Before the age of the skyscraper, most architecture was built much more to the human scale. This is as true of palaces and public buildings as it is of townhouses and cottages. They're much more inviting and engaging. What's the difference?

With modern architecture the perspective of the human actor and agent has simply disappeared, and you have just people with mathematical models multiplying floors, maximizing value, getting the most bang for their buck. And that whole set of incentives is completely divorced from the human agent's perspective on things, which is why it's so hard to feel at home in Bauhaus or post-Bauhaus architecture.

There are many other dimensions of this as well, but the difference is between what you can call a *theory-centered* philosophy that tries to look at the world from a non-human point of view and what you could call a *humanistic* philosophy that always begins with the human condition as a starting point and never forgets that, no matter how much we learn about the cosmos, it's not going to make any sense unless we can fit ourselves into that picture.

SUFFERING VS. DOING WRONG

Another important thesis of Socrates' moral philosophy is that it is always better to suffer wrong than to do wrong. That's an extraordinary claim, and it all goes back to his primary concern with the health of the soul. Socrates ultimately argues that good character, virtue, is intrinsically good. Virtue is its own reward, in some sense. Many good things come from being virtuous. However, given the choice between those good things and your virtue, you'd always choose virtue. So, virtue is choiceworthy whether or not any additional rewards accrue to it. If that's the case, then when you're given the choice between doing injustice and suffering it, you have to think about your soul.

The reason Socrates chooses to suffer injustice is simple. If you suffer injustice, it doesn't harm your soul. To be a victim doesn't destroy your character. It could destroy you physically, but it can't destroy your moral nature. It can't make you into a monster. However, to do evil corrupts one's soul. Therefore, to do evil is to harm oneself morally speaking, whereas to suffer evil might be terribly inconvenient—it might even be fatal—but it can't make you a monster. If the primary concern is the health of one's soul, then given the choice between doing injustice and suffering it you should choose to suffer it rather than do it.

Of course, Socrates would rather avoid the choice to begin with. But sometimes life presents us with sticky situations where you have to choose one or the other. When Socrates' friend Crito offers to break him out of jail, Socrates is in one of those situations. Socrates argues that it would be unjust for him to escape, because he would be doing injustice and therefore harming himself.

Socrates also makes the strange claim that, in a sense, virtue makes one invulnerable, because virtue primarily resides in the soul. Think about Job. He loses his camel, he loses his wife, he's covered with running sores, and so forth. But if Job were a virtuous man—if his soul were in harmony rather than corrupt—in a sense he would be invulnerable to the last measure of degradation. He would certainly be unhappy, but it wouldn't make him into a monster. He wouldn't become an evil man for suffering all these things. In that sense, virtue makes one invulnerable to the worst sorts of harm, because nobody can force you to be a monster. They can kill you. They can take your camel and wives and servants and cover you with running sores, but they can't turn you into a bad person.

Consider this passage from the *Apology*:

> Perhaps then someone might say, ". . . are you not ashamed, Socrates, of having followed the sort of pursuits from which you now run the risk of dying? Aren't you ashamed to be in this situation?" I would respond to him with a just speech: "What you say is ignoble, fellow, if you suppose that a man who is of even a little benefit should take into account the danger of living or dying but not rather this alone: whenever he acts whether his actions are just or unjust and the deeds of a good man or a bad." (28b–c)

One's consideration is always 'Am I doing the right thing?' and not 'Is this going to accrue to my long-term benefit?' It's noble to do the right thing, come what may. So, again, we have to be concerned whether our actions are just or unjust, the deeds of a good man or a bad man.

A little further on he says, "This is the way it is, men of Athens, in truth. Wherever someone stations himself upholding that it is best, or wherever he is stationed by a ruler, there he must stay and run the risk." He's talking about a soldier's duty. ". . . as it seems to me, and not take into account death or anything else compared to what is shameful or noble" (28d).

And he says, "Just as I was stationed at Delium and Potidaea and Amphipolis" (28e), battles where he went and did his duty, he has his duty to philosophize, and he's going to do the right thing regardless of the consequences.

But he doesn't think the consequences are so bad in this case, because they can't fundamentally hurt him.

The very end of the *Apology* Socrates says: "There is nothing bad that can happen to a good man whether living or dead, and the gods are not without care for his troubles" (41d). Can a good man truly not suffer anything bad? You can lose your camel and your wife. These are bad things. But on the most *fundamental* level, on the level of what we prize the most, namely our own character, nothing can take that away from us. We have to consent to the corruption of our own souls. No one else can do it for us. So if you choose not to become a bad person, no one can force you to become one.

In the *Crito*, Socrates says, "But you wondrous man, Crito, the argument that we have gone through still seems to me at least like it did before. Consider again whether the following also stays so for us or not: not *living* but *living well* is to be regarded as the most important" (48b).

Life is not unconditionally good. Only a good life is unconditionally good, and a good life is a life of virtue, a life of moral and practical wisdom. Wisdom is the only unconditionally good thing for Plato. A life of wisdom is worth living, and a life without wisdom isn't worth living. This is what Socrates means when he says 'The unexamined life is not worth living.'

The life of a fool is not worth living. They're better off dead. This is an extreme claim. Socrates is not mealy-mouthed at all. But if you look at somebody who is a consistent fool, a prize fool, such people create so much misery for themselves and others that you can say in some ways that they'd be better off dead. The dead don't suffer, after all. The dead don't cause others to suffer either. Fools are better off being wise, but if that is not an option, maybe they're better off dead. That's a pretty brutal claim, but Socrates is not going to back down from it, even if you threaten to kill him.

Socrates goes on, "And don't we say that living well and nobly and justly are the same thing?" (48b). To live well is to be noble and just. So, if you're not noble, if you're not just, then your life isn't worth living. Life without virtue isn't worth living. Life without practical wisdom isn't worth living.

A little further on, Socrates says, "Therefore, from the things agreed upon, it must be considered whether it is just for me to try to go out of here although the Athenians are not permitting me to go or not just. And if it appears just let us try, but if it's not let's leave it aside" (48b–c). That's the only consideration, not whether or not he's going to live or die.

What do you say to someone like that? Ordinary people

would want to shake him: 'Snap out of it, Socrates! You're about to die! All this fine talk means nothing! You're about to die!'

Socrates goes on, "Since this is how the argument holds, nothing else is to be considered by us except what we were saying just now, whether we will do the just things by paying money and gratitude to those who will lead me out of here or whether in truth we will be doing injustice by doing these things" (48c–d). That's the only consideration.

So, Socrates is not only the first moral philosopher, but he's a rather strict moralist. But there's more to what's essentially Socratic than being a moral philosopher. Socrates' turn toward moral philosophy is part of a broader turn towards what you can call "humanistic philosophy" or humanism.

Humanism doesn't mean what we call "secular humanism" today. Humanism in the broad sense simply means a form of philosophy that always starts out from the *human condition* or the *human perspective* and never forgets about it and never tries to get outside of it.

In my view, Socrates' greatest philosophical achievement is to start out from a humanistic standpoint and a primary concern with moral philosophy — and then to resurrect metaphysical speculation, speculation about the whole, in a way that's consistent with the humanistic point of view. That's important, because we really do need to have a sense of where we fit into the big picture. But the pursuit of that kind of knowledge can also uproot us from the world we live in and alienate us from ourselves. So we might find ourselves a home in the cosmos, yet lose our place in this world. But that's too big a price to pay. We need to do justice to both human finitude and our desire to understand the big picture.

The Background to Aristophanes' *Clouds*

It's important to understand pre-Socratic philosophy before we read Socrates, because the two are defined in contrast to each other. Moreover, Socrates wasn't always the contrast term for the pre-Socratics, because for a long period in his life, Socrates himself was apparently a pre-Socratic. When we get to Aristophanes' *Clouds*, we're going to see a portrait of Socrates as a pre-Socratic philosopher.

Our understanding of Socratic philosophy is based primarily on Plato's dialogues and Xenophon's Socratic writings, although even in those texts there are clues that at one time Socrates was a pre-Socratic. But in the *Clouds*, we have a very clear portrait of Socrates as a pre-Socratic philosopher, so we need to get a sense of what pre-Socratic philosophy means.

Hence this little book *A Presocratics Reader*,[1] which collects the fragments, the *disjecta membra*, of philosophy before Socrates. It is said there are no full books of philosophy extant before Plato's dialogues. In the next chapter, I will argue that the *Clouds* is actually a work of philosophy. But most earlier philosophical writings survive only in fragments quoted by later writers. Other fragments were found by archaeologists. For instance, the passage from Antiphon we will look at very closely is from one of the Oxyrhynchus papyri discovered in Egypt in the late nineteenth century. These texts are fascinating, because you're going to find echoes of all these ideas showing up in the *Clouds*.

We won't be covering the greatest of the pre-Socratics, Heraclitus and Parmenides, because their ideas don't figure in the

---

[1] *A Presocratics Reader: Selected Fragments and Testimonia*, ed. Patricia Curd, trans. Richard D. McKirahan (Indianapolis: Hackett, 1995), henceforth cited in the text as Curd. I will also cite the standard numbers from *Die Fragmente der Vorsokratiker*, ed. Herman Diels and Walther Kranz, 10th ed. (Berlin: Weidmannsche Verlagsbuchhandlung, 1960), henceforth DK.

Clouds, although Parmenides had a powerful influence on both Socrates and Plato, whose dialogue *Parmenides* dramatizes an encounter between young Socrates and the aged Parmenides.

PRE-PHILOSOPHICAL CONCEPTIONS OF ORDER

As a background to the pre-Socratics, I'd like to talk about what came before the pre-Socratics, i.e., pre-pre-Socratic thinking. And that means pre-philosophical thinking, because in order to really understand what was revolutionary about early Greek philosophy you have to understand what came before it.

First, I want to talk about pre-philosophical conceptions of order, because every culture has some concept that names the order of things. The Chinese have the *tao*; the Indians have *dharma*; the Egyptians have *ma'at*; the Hebrews have *mishpat*; and the Greeks *nomos* and *dike*. They can all be translated as "the way."

"The way" is understood as the characteristic way of things, the way things have always been, the way things will always be, the patterns of behavior that they've exhibited from "time out of mind." These concepts encompass both natural processes (the sun, the stars, the seasons, and the behavior of animals) as well as human traditions, institutions, and practices.

Pre-philosophic thought makes no distinction between the way of natural things and the way of human things. But that's problematic. The way of animal natures is not as variable as the way of human things, which vary constantly from time to time and from place to place.

Imagine we're studying the mating habits of armadillos. It wouldn't really matter if we were studying armadillos north or south of the Rio Grande. It doesn't matter where the armadillo is. It's going to behave exactly the same way.

However, if we wanted to study the mating and dating habits of human beings, we would discover there are many different ways of doing that north and south of the Rio Grande. Why is that? Because there are different nations with different histories and different cultures. If we were to look at the way human beings date and mate in America today versus the way it happened before World War Two, we'd also see that there are amazing differences within the same culture in different times.

The enormous variability of human things, as opposed to natural things, seems to be important. But in pre-philosophic, traditional forms of thought, that distinction isn't made.

MYTH

Where does order come from? This brings us to the topic of myth. Myths are pre-philosophical and pre-scientific accounts of the origins and nature of order. This would include accounts of cosmic order and human order. It would be an account of particular traditions, customs, and institutions. Most importantly, it's going to be an account of the origin of right and wrong, the origins of moral law. There are several characteristics of myth that I want to talk about briefly.

Myths are always stories, narratives. One thing happens after another. There are stories about characters, and the characters are usually personifications of some force of nature, or they're gods, demi-gods, and mortals.

Once you personify a force of nature, you're projecting the idea that there's a mind behind it, which implies that we can enter a personal relationship with it. We can try to understand its motivations. And once you understand the motivations of these fearsome forces, we can try to change their behavior. If the gods want sheep, lots of them, slaughtered and burned, we can do that, if it wins their favor. If we give them enough sheep or human sacrifices or whatever, they'll stop the drought. Maybe we can even come to command the gods. This is the foundation of religion and magic.

Once you have personified the forces of nature, one must understand how they relate to one another. The way we relate human characters together is by telling stories about their interactions. The same is true of the gods. The narrative structure of myth comes about as a way of knitting together, or synthesizing, all these different forces of nature in an intelligible way. The most comprehensive myth would be an account of the whole of nature. You can find highly developed mythological accounts of virtually everything in a society that has existed long enough to refine its understanding of the world.

The Greeks had a myth to explain anything, and it's the replacement of myth with another kind of explanation, namely scientific explanation, that is one of the most monumental and revolutionary changes that marks the beginning of philosophy in Greece.

MORAL EDUCATION

Greek myths might have explanatory power, but they were not particularly morally edifying. For instance, you wouldn't want to model your family after Zeus' family. Zeus castrated his father Cronos and threw him into a pit. Cronos ate his own children. Zeus married his sister, Hera, and then cheated on her constantly. No one would want their children to imitate the Greek gods.

The Greeks looked instead to their great poets for examples of human excellence and vice. Indeed, the Greek poets seemed to have more authority than the gods themselves. Paul Veyne, a French scholar, has written a book called *Did the Greeks Believe Their Myths?*[2] It's a very good question, because their attitude towards their myths was quite different from, say, Jewish or Christian or Islamic attitudes towards the founding stories of those religions. It would not be permitted for a great Muslim novelist to come out with a new Koran with a different ending, for instance. Spice it up with a car chase, or something like that. It would be condemned as heresy.

But in ancient Greece the poets would rewrite their myths. Homer and Hesiod, the two most important poets of ancient Greece, would take up elements of the mythical worldview and transform it; they'd add to it; they'd embroider it. The great tragedians of Athens in the fourth and fifth centuries BCE would rewrite the myths and transform them.

When philosophy emerged, it immediately became a rival to poetry. Just as the poets had exalted themselves above the gods and installed themselves as the moral teachers of Greece, the philosophers exalted themselves over both the gods and the poets, and in their train followed new moral teachings as well.

---

[2] Paul Veyne, *Did the Greeks Believe their Myths?*, trans. Paula Wissing (Chicago: University of Chicago Press, 1988).

THALES

Thales, the first recorded Greek philosopher, was born in Miletus, which is now in Turkey, around 625 BCE. He was a remarkably odd fellow. He was born to a good family, yet he lived in poverty. He didn't get involved in politics, which all respectable upper-class Greeks did. Instead, he spent a lot of time outside the city walls not engaged in farming or war or any other useful thing. He just wandered around looking at nature. According to Plato's *Theaetetus* (174a):

> Once while Thales was gazing upwards while doing astronomy he fell into a well. A clever and delightful Thracian serving girl was said to have made fun of him since he was eager to know the things in heaven but failed to notice the things in front of him and right next to his feet. (DK 11A9; Curd, p. 9)

Thales was both a very impractical person, as far as worldly affairs are concerned, and very much interested in theoretical matters, interested in gazing upwards (the Greek verb is *theorein* from which we get the word theory). He was gazing upwards, looking at the course of the stars.

Thales wasn't looking at the stars as gods, as other ancient peoples did. He regarded them as natural phenomena. He was observing them very carefully trying to learn to predict and control natural phenomena:

> The story goes that when they found fault with him for his poverty, supposing that philosophy is useless, he learned from his astronomy that there would be a large crop of olives. It was still winter, he obtained a little money and he made deposits with all the olive presses both in Miletus and Chios. Since no one bid against him, he rented them cheaply. When the right time came, suddenly many tried to get the presses all at once, and he rented them out on whatever terms he wished and so made a great deal of money, and this way he proved that philosophers could easily be wealthy if they desire, but this is not what they

are interested in. (DK 11A10; Curd, pp. 9-10)

Thales was known for his poverty, but he had to demonstrate that he was poor not because of any defect but simply because he chose a different kind of life than that of respectable gentlemen. It was a theoretical life, a contemplative life. But his primary concerns were understanding natural phenomena, not human things. He was an astronomer. Thales is in some ways better understood as the first scientist than the first philosopher, because there's nothing particularly philosophical about what he's doing in the reports that have come down to us.

Thales' most famous claim is that everything is water. The water in the sink is water, and—appearances to the contrary notwithstanding—the sink too is water, and we're all water as well. Now, that sounds fanciful, but it's not a mythical claim, because it is an attempt to give an account of everything—the origins of everything, all the processes you observe in nature—based not myth but on a natural principle which he calls water.

Basically, the idea is that one can give a complete account of everything in terms of two things. First of all, you need an underlying substance, namely water, the stuff that everything is made out of. Second, you need a principle that accounts for the transformation of water into all the different forms that it takes. That's a very radical project, and it has nothing in common whatsoever with mythological accounts of the cosmos which are notoriously complex.

Laugh if you want, but "everything is water" represents an enormous step forward in the history of thought. Thales is really the first natural scientist. It's the first attempt to give a naturalistic, non-mythological account of the whole cosmos, and that's a remarkable achievement.

ANAXIMANDER

Thales was followed by his student Anaximander, another Milesian who was born around 600 BCE. Anaximander accounted for everything not in terms of water, but in terms of what he called the *apeiron* which means the "indefinite" or the "infinite." He chose the indefinite rather than water because to say that everything is water doesn't explain the characteristics of water. You just treat those as given. So it's not really a complete explanation of everything.

Anaximander argued that we can go deeper. We can come up with an even more comprehensive principle than Thales offered. So he said that everything *definite*, including water, arises out of the *indefinite*, the *infinite*. Beyond that, he offers an account of the process by which the indefinite takes on definite forms and flavors and becomes the world we see around us.

The earliest fragment of an actual text in the history of philosophy is from Anaximander, quoted in Simplicius' commentary on Aristotle's *Physics*: "... the things that are, perish into the things out of which they come to be, according to necessity, for they pay penalty and retribution to each other for their injustice in accordance with the ordering of time" (DK 12B1; Curd, p. 12).

The ordering of time refers to the processes of nature: change and transformation. Justice and injustice refer to a kind of law, if you will, natural law, that orders the transformations of things in time.

So for Anaximander, the cosmos consists of an indefinite stuff that gives rise to definite things, which then break up and return to the indefinite, recycled in accordance with a cosmic process he calls "necessity," which is governed by a kind of justice.

Necessity is a very important concept here. In mythical thought there's a notion of fate, but it is always connected with divine beings and their intentions. Necessity, however, is a force that moves the cosmos without ideas or intentions behind it. It is "dumb" luck, "blind" fate. It's a non-anthropomorphic, non-personified understanding of what moves the world.

Ask a person who has a mythical understanding of things 'Who moves the clouds?' and he'll say 'Zeus moves the clouds.' Whereas for Anaximander it is necessity that moves the clouds. This is a fundamental change. Nature is being de-personified. It's being de-anthropomorphized. Nature is no longer being understood on the model of the mind but simply as mindless things actuated and animated by mindless necessity.

Anaximander also tried to give an account of the origins of life that didn't make any reference to gods:

Anaximander says that the first animals were produced in moisture enclosed in thorny barks. When their age increased, they came out onto the drier part, their bark broke off, and they lived a different mode of life for a short time. (DK 12A30; Curd, p. 13)

He also declares that in the beginning humans were born from other kinds of animals, since other animals quickly manage on their own, and humans alone require lengthy nursing. For this reason, in the beginning they would not have been preserved if they had been like this. (DK 12A10; Curd, p. 13)

Anaximander believed that there arose from heated water and earth either fish or animals rather like fish, and these humans grew and were kept inside as embryos up to puberty then finally they burst, and men and women came forth already able to nourish themselves. (DK 12A30; Curd, pp. 13-14)

This is the oldest known purely naturalistic account of the origin of life. Moreover, it's the first evolutionary account, because it argues that human beings evolved in some way out of non-human and sub-human animals. All this is set in motion by forces of necessity. Design and intelligence are not at work here.

ANAXIMENES

Anaximenes of Miletus was a somewhat younger contemporary or student of Anaximander. Anaximenes is very important for understanding the *Clouds*, as is Diogenes of Apollonia who came many years later, because the whole idea of the clouds as presented in the *Clouds* seems to make reference to the doctrines taught by these people. Anaximenes and Diogenes of Apollonia both taught that the ultimate stuff out of which the cosmos arises is not water (like Thales) or the infinite (like Anaximander) but instead it's *air*. "Anaximenes determined that air is a god and that it comes to be and is without measure infinite and always in motion" (DK 13A10; Curd, p. 15).

Now, that may seem like back-sliding, because you can give the same objection to Anaximenes and this notion of air that you could give to Thales, which is that it explains everything except air. What explains air? Isn't there some underlying force from which airy qualities arise?

I think Anaximenes might have thought it's better to posit a principle that has some qualities to underlie things. Otherwise, how do you even know it's there? The trouble with the indefinite or the infinite is that it's precisely that which has no qualities of its own. It's indistinguishable from nothing. Anaximander's notion that being has no qualities makes being indistinguishable from nothing, because isn't nothing the absence of any qualities?

Anaximenes seems to want to have characteristics for his ultimate stuff, and the air is it. So, again, he comes up with the notion that there's one substance out of which all things arise, and there's a process by which this substance undergoes transformation, and so we have all the things that don't appear to be airy, like books, for instance, and ourselves. There's book air and human air. Then there's airy air, like the air around us, and then there's smoke and clouds, which seem to be intermediate between pure air and solid things.

"Anaximenes stated that clouds occur when the air is further thickened. When it is condensed still more rain is squeezed out. Hail occurs when the falling water freezes and snow when some wind is caught up in the moisture" (DK 13A17; Curd, p. 15). When you have even more condensed air, you get rocks and stones and animals and so forth. So it's one big spectrum of rarefaction and condensation.

It's an interesting idea because air is a very fluid thing, yet you can see air getting dense, like smoke or clouds and vapors. And if you look up into the clouds and watch long enough, you can see the clouds taking on shapes of things. So, it's not really silly to think that maybe everything is like a cloud formation, that the world of things around us is just composed of evanescent cloud formations, in which this airy stuff is gathered up and takes on a certain form for a particular period of time and then dissipates according to some cosmic process. Indeed, it is not mere poetry to say that you and I are merely clouds of atoms taking on a particular shape for a time.

Air is also a very good concept for understanding the principle of life. When we're alive we breathe. Air is going in, and air is going out. It's warm air. This is a particular point with Anaximenes. The air he's talking about is a kind of dense, warm mist. So, it would be almost like breath, which has a warmth to it. When we die, we no longer breathe, and we get cold. It sort of makes sense to think that if there's any one principle that underlies life and the transformations of all the things in the cosmos it would be something like warm, vital breath, and this is what he's talking about.

THE GODS

It's very interesting that Anaximenes says air is a god. Heraclitus is supposed to have said that there are gods in everything. What does that mean? Aristotle in his *Parts of Animals* relates the story. Heraclitus was supposedly warming himself by the stove, and some friends of his arrived and saw him doing this and hesitated to go in. He said 'Oh, come on in. There are gods here, too.' The story doesn't make much sense until you know that warming yourself at the stove is a Greek euphemism for defecation. Apparently, his friends came upon Heraclitus as he was relieving himself, and he said 'There are gods here, too. Don't be shy.'

Everything is full of gods. This is a very peculiar notion. What exactly does it mean? First, it's not really compatible with any conventional sense of piety. If there are gods in the outhouse too, then being divine is, well, not all that divine. Second, there's no necessity of referring to these omnipresent gods to explain any of the things that happen in the world because you've got the air, or the water, or the indefinite and the principle of change. So the gods fall out of the picture entirely.

Thus it was widely thought that these natural philosophers didn't believe in the gods of the city, that they were unbelievers in the conventional deities, because their accounts of nature didn't require the hypothesis of gods. They tried to give accounts of things that specifically excluded reference to gods and their influences, and they had a rather cavalier notion of what divinity was. This notion of divinity would encompass the high and the low, and it would seem to just refer to the cosmos and the natural principles.

It was very common for the Greeks to name the highest principle in any system "the divine," but that doesn't necessarily mean that they regarded it as a god in any conventional sense. The Greek natural philosophers would say air is divine, or water is divine, or the indefinite is divine, but they would always hasten to add that the indefinite has no interest in human affairs. It's totally uninvolved with human things, and, in fact, it doesn't even have a mind.

So, they used the word divine in a very loose sense. You could almost say they were just appeasing public opinion, because although it sounds very pious on the surface to say there are gods everywhere, when you start scratching the surface, you realize that if there are gods everywhere, that natural substances and forces are gods, and that these gods care nothing about human affairs, that is not, strictly speaking, atheism. But from the point of view of the defenders of the various local religions, it is the practical equivalent of atheism, for it undermines piety and belief in the gods of the city.

XENOPHANES

Xenophanes was born in Colophon near Ephesus in Asia Minor around 570 BCE. Like many of the early Greek philosophers, he wrote in verse. Based on the fragments that have come down to us, his primary interest was religion, which he viewed in terms of natural philosophy.

Xenophanes mocks the Greek gods for being anthropomorphic and culturally relative:

> Mortals believe that the gods are born and have human clothing, voice, and form. (DK 21B14; Curd, p. 26)

> Ethiopians say that their gods are flat-nosed and dark, Thracians that theirs are blue-eyed and red-haired. (DK 21B16; Curd, p. 26)

> If oxen and horses and lions had hands and were able to draw with their hands and do the same thing as men, horses would draw the shapes of gods to look like horses and oxen to look like oxen and each would make the gods' bodies have the same shape as they themselves had. (DK 21B15; Curd, p. 26).

If there are truly divine beings, surely they do not vary from time to time and place to place. Thus the gods we hear about in myth cannot be real.

Xenophanes also asserts that gods are good, which is something that no pious believer would deny. But then he argues that if the gods are good, the Greek myths can't be true, because they are filled with stories of the gods doing wrong.

> Homer and Hesiod have ascribed to the gods all deeds which among men are a reproach and a disgrace, thieving, adultery, and deceiving one another. (DK 21B11; Curd, p. 26).

> Give us no fights with titans, nor giants nor centaurs — the forgeries of our fathers — nor civil brawls in which no advantage is. But always to be mindful of the gods is good. (DK 21B1; Curd, p. 26).

If they're gods, you'd think they'd be above all that. We will encounter this argument again in Plato's *Euthyphro*.

Xenophanes did, however, believe there was a kind of god. But he would have to be totally unlike humanity: "God is one, greatest among gods and men. Not at all like mortals in body or thought" (DK 21B23; Curd, p. 26). Xenophanes disdained the Olympians for being obvious projections of Greekness, but his own god is just what you would expect of a philosopher: "All of him sees, all of him thinks, all of him hears" (DK 21B24; Curd, p. 26). Which means he's just a mind, not a body. This is the perfect god for people who lead the theoretical life and fall down wells in the process. Xenophanes' god is just the divinization of the activity of theorizing.

Although Xenophanes' god has no body, he sets all of nature in motion. How? Xenophanes insists he does it "without effort . . ." Of course, philosophers love to do things with as little effort as possible. This is why leisure is so important. Instead, god moves the world through thinking: ". . . he shakes all things with the thought of his mind" (DK 21B25; Curd, p. 27).

However, it's fairly clear that Xenophanes doesn't think that god is concerned with human affairs. He is not the kind of god that anybody but a philosopher could really find much in common with. The gods of the Greek philosophers were *improvident*. They didn't exercise any concern toward human affairs. In particular, they didn't exercise any concern for *moral* matters. The gods of the philosophers don't have any moral commandments for men. They are purely theoretical gods divorced from the whole realm of practice and human affairs.

ANAXAGORAS

Anaxagoras was born around 500 BCE in Clazomenae. He came to Athens and was a teacher of Pericles, who was the great statesmen of Athens in the fifth century BCE.

He was reputed to claim that the sun, which most people thought was a god, was just a big burning rock. And he was pretty much correct about that. But the fact that he thought the sun was a great big burning rock made the Athenians think he was impious. He clearly didn't believe in the gods of Athens, and so they put him on trial for impiety, and he was exiled from the city. He died near Troy in the city of Lampsacus in 428 BCE.

Anaxagoras was the first philosopher that the Athenians ran out of town for impiety. Socrates claimed to have read his work, and there are many ancient testimonials to the effect that Socrates was in some way a student of Anaxagoras at one period in his life. Socrates in Plato's *Apology*, says, 'You take me for Anaxagoras? Don't you know the difference between me and Anaxagoras?' He was dogged by the reputation of having studied Anaxagoras' teachings, although he might never have known Anaxagoras personally.

What Anaxagoras believed is very obscure. If you want to explain why there are different kinds of things, his answer is different kinds have always existed, albeit in the form of microscopic "seeds," as he puts it. One wonders just how many kinds of seeds there are. Are the seeds like the elements of the periodic table? Are there seeds of natural stuffs like wood and bone? Are there seeds of animal and plant species? Are there seeds of artificial kinds like pens and cups? How do microscopic seeds explain visible kinds? They are basically brought together and amalgamated into a sufficient size that they rise above the threshold of visibility and we can see them.

This is not atomic theory. The early Greek philosophers believed that ultimate reality is an undifferentiated stuff that it takes on forms, whereas Anaxagoras believed that the *forms* of everything were just as fundamental as the stuff, and the emergence of specific things into the world and their passing away could be explained simply in terms of them rising above or falling below the threshold of visibility, becoming amalgamated up to the size of something you can see and dissolving back into their microscopic constituents.

Anaxagoras believed that this process of coming into being and passing away was actuated by a cosmic principle which you can call the vortex: a great spinning, cosmic whirlpool that moves everything around, causing seeds to glom on to one another and get larger or get broken up and get smaller. What sets the vortex spinning? Anaxagoras says *nous*, or Mind. Mind, however, is just the most finely divided kind of matter. Thus Anaxagoras is a complete materialist.

In a sense, Anaxagoras anticipates Plato, because he doesn't really explain the forms of things; he just presupposes that the forms are already there, but we can't see them. The vortex imparts motion, which through necessity causes things to rise to visibility and to collapse back into invisibility. At the root of it, of course, is what he calls Mind, but Mind is in fact indistinguishable from matter.

Socrates was terribly interested in the theories of Anaxagoras as we'll see. There's one particular passage that is fairly useful in explaining as best we can what Anaxagoras is up to:

The rest have a portion of everything, but Mind is unlimited and self-ruled and is mixed with no thing, but is alone and by itself" ["The rest," I guess, means all the other little seeds that are out there.] For if it [Mind] were not by itself but mixed with something else, it would have a share of all things, if it were mixed with anything. For in everything there is a portion of everything, as I have said before. Things mixed together with it would hinder it, so that it would rule no thing the same as it does by being alone and by itself.

Mind is set up on its own pulling the strings, getting everything going. It's not mixed in and dissipated in its power amongst all the things of the cosmos.

For it [Mind] is the finest of all things and the purest. [It's matter. Fine, pure matter.] And it has all judgment about everything and the greatest power. And Mind rules all things that possess life—both the larger and the smaller. And Mind ruled the entire rotation, so that it rotated in the beginning. At first it began to rotate from a small area, but it rotates over a greater range and will rotate over a greater one. And Mind knew all the things that are being mixed together and separated off and separated apart. And Mind set in order all things, whatever kind of things were to be—whatever were and all that are now and whatever will be—and also this rotation in which we are now rotating the stars and the sun and the moon, and the air and aither that are being separated off. This rotation caused the separating off. (DK 59B12; Curd, pp. 56–57)

The "rotation" refers to a vortex that starts in a small place, and it gets larger and larger, drawing all the little seeds into it, which somehow produces the visible world. We will encounter this idea of the vortex in Empedocles as well. It also features prominently in the *Clouds*. At the root of the vortex is a material force that Anaxagoras calls *nous*, or Mind.

EMPEDOCLES

Empedocles was a rough contemporary of Anaxagoras. He was born in Acragas, Sicily around 492 BCE. He was a very active politician in his home city. He was also a physician and a philosopher who wrote in verse. The poem of Empedocles survives in some fairly substantial fragments. He was a rather striking figure. He went about dressed as a king in purple robes, a golden diadem, and bronze shoes. He claimed to be a god and a prophet:

> I go about among you, an immortal god, no longer mortal, honored among all, as it seems, wreathed with headbands and blooming garlands. Wherever I go to the flourishing cities, I am revered by the men and women, and they follow together in tens of thousands inquiring of the path to profit, some in need of prophecy, while others, pierced for a long time with harsh pains, ask to hear the voice of healing for all diseases. (DK 31B112; Curd, pp. 61–62)

Empedocles believed he was a god because the wisdom he attained exalted him above the merely human. But this makes one suspicious about the philosopher's piety. Just as the image of god you get in Xenophanes sounds suspiciously like a philosopher, you also have philosophers going around and claiming 'We are gods. We have become divine through the activity of philosophizing.' Eventually Empedocles' fellow citizens tired of his antics and drove him into exile. According to Diogenes Laertius, he leapt to his death in the crater of Mount Etna, hoping that people would think that he had ascended to the gods.

Despite Empedocles' religious pretensions, he was a natural philosopher. There are six basic principles in Empedocles' system: the four elements—earth, air, fire, and water—and two principles that cause the elements to move around and get reorganized. Those principles are love and strife. The four elements are the material stuff out of which everything is made. Then the question is: How do they get rearranged? What causes the processes of transformation? Love is the force that brings everything together, and strife is the force that disperses everything: the forces of integration and disintegration.

Like Anaxagoras, Empedocles speaks of a "vortex" that is apparently one of the stages by which the world we experience emerges from the six principles:

> When Strife had reached the lowest depth of the vortex, and Love comes to be in the middle of the whirl, at this point all these things come together to be one single thing, not at once, but willingly banding together, different ones from different places. As they were mixed, myriads of tribes of mortal things poured forth, but many contrariwise remained unmixed while they were mingling—all that Strife still held back aloft. For it not entirely completed its blameless retreat from them to the furthest limits of the circle, but it remained in some of the limbs where from others it had withdrawn. (DK 31B35; Curd, p. 67)

Empedocles also offers an account of how organisms emerged from the six basic principles. First, separate organs emerged:

> By her [Love] many neckless faces sprouted, and arms were wandering naked, bereft of shoulders, and eyes were roaming alone, in need of foreheads. . . . [In this situation, the members were still] single-limbed [as a result of the separation caused by Strife, and] they wandered about [aiming at mixture with one another]. (DK 31B57-58; Curd, pp. 68-69)

These *disjecta membra*, these bits of bodies, just float around, until love draws them together into composite organisms.

> But when divinity was mixed to a greater extent with divinity, and these things began to fall together, however they chanced to meet, and many others beside them arose continuously. (DK 31B58; Curd, p. 69)

But most of these organisms were monstrous:

Many came into being with faces and chests on both sides, man-faced ox-progeny, and some to the contrary rose up as ox-headed things with the form of men, compounded partly from men and partly from women, fitted with shadowy parts. (DK 31B61; Curd, p. 69)

These monsters, of course, failed to survive. But, after a long enough period of random collocations of body parts, harmonious combinations emerged that could actually survive. Thus Empedocles offers an account of the origin of living things through random combination and environmental selection. The process is driven entirely by natural necessity, and there's no need to refer to gods at all.

DIOGENES OF APOLLONIA

Diogenes of Apollonia was a slightly older contemporary of Socrates. His teachings are mentioned in Plato's *Phaedo*. He frequented Athens, so his teachings were widely known. His ideas are especially relevant to Aristophanes' depiction of Socrates in the *Clouds*:

And in my opinion, that which possesses intelligence is what people call air, and all humans are governed by it, and it rules all things. For in my opinion, this very thing is god, and it reaches everything and arranges all things and is in everything. And there is no single thing which does not share in this. But no single thing shares in it the same way as anything else, but there are many forms both of air itself and of intelligence. For it is multiform—hotter and colder, drier and wetter, more stable and possessing a sharper movement, and unlimitedly many other alterations are in it both of flavor and of color. (DK 64B5; Curd, p. 94)

Air is plausible as the ultimate stuff of reality, because it's something you can imagine taking on any number of different forms, especially if you look at clouds and see how fluid they are and how they take on shapes. Air can also become dense and opaque or refined and clear. This is probably why Anaximenes chose air as his ultimate stuff as well.

Like Anaxagoras and Empedocles, Diogenes of Apollonia also makes use of a vortex to explain natural processes:

> Air is the element. There are unlimited worlds and unlimited void. The air by being condensed and rarified is generative of the worlds. Nothing comes to be from or perishes into what is not. The earth is round and is supported in the center (of the cosmos) and has undergone its process of formation through the rotation [the vortex] resulting from the hot and the solidification caused by the cold. (DK 64A1; Curd, p. 95)

Take it or leave it. The fragments have an oracular quality because, for the most part, the arguments and observations that supported them have been lost.

Natural Philosophy in General

The main characteristic of the natural philosophers was the quest for a non-theistic, non-mythological explanation for everything. You don't need gods to explain the cosmos. You can explain it in terms of natural necessity. Not design. Not will. Not choice.

Another characteristic is that, although they make reference to gods or divine principles, their gods are entirely improvident. They have no concern with human affairs. Either they're mindless principles, or if they're minds, they are unconcerned with merely human affairs. In any case, they're improvident gods. They might get the vortex spinning, but that's it.

A third common feature is that they're entirely unconcerned with moral or practical issues. The whole point of early Greek natural philosophy is, in a sense, to rise above the practical and to understand what nature is. There's an implicit assumption here that nature is *not* moral. If you look out into the natural world, you discover just natural forces moving around by necessity. You do not discover any right or wrong, any moral law written into nature.

So, what does one do with the gods and morality? If something is excluded from the realm of nature, it is placed in a different realm. It is placed in the realm of convention or custom. And what happens at this time is the concepts of Greek *nomos* or *dike*, which can be translated as "law" and "justice" or "right," lose their primitive meaning of "the way of things," and *nomos* and *dike* become treated as conventions, as things that exist by the agreement of human beings. They're cultural things.

The things that happen by nature are amoral, and the things that happen by convention include the realms of the mythological gods and morality.

A fourth characteristic of these early Greek philosophers of nature is that they regarded nature as *good*. If anything's good, it's going to be nature. Not morally good, because morals are matters of convention. Good in an extra-moral or super-moral sense: worthy of respect. If anything's worthy of true respect, it's nature. Conventions are not worthy of any respect. They're contemptible. The main reason for this is that nature is unchanging.

What does that mean? Everything's changing around us: the weather, the seasons, etc. But the patterns of nature never change. The underlying causes of natural phenomena are eternal, unchanging principles, whereas human conventions and customs change over time and from place to place, and there's no apparent underlying order. They're *relative* to time and place. Well, what do you want to bank on? Things that never change or things that are always changing, always in flux?

The ancient Greek natural philosophers thought that what's unchanging is best, and what changes is contemptible. Therefore, the realm of convention—the realm of human things, if you will—was regarded by these people with a certain amount of disdain. Ordinary human beings were regarded as contemptible, because they're caught up in the things that change, that are unimportant, that just flow along. Morality, because it's merely a matter of convention, was regarded as somewhat contemptible as well.

THE SOPHISTS

The purely theoretical natural philosophers laid the foundations for a school of thought that was almost entirely practical in its orientation: the sophists. The sophists accepted the basic metaphysical framework of the natural philosophers, especially the distinction between nature and convention and the value judgments they made about that distinction. They regarded nature as good and convention as contemptible.

When you turn your attention to human affairs with that distinction in mind and ask yourself 'How should we live?' the answer is: 'We should live by nature, not by convention.' How does nature manifest itself in a human being? What's the most natural thing about us, as opposed to the merely conventional or customary?

The most natural thing about us is our desires. The mind is not the most natural, because the mind is so plastic and heavily stamped with convention. Thus the body is more natural than the mind. The most natural thing about the body is our desires. You find that desires are invariant from human being to human being. We all need to eat. We all need to sleep. We all have our little lusts.

The sophists taught that we need to live by nature, not by convention. To the sophists, living by nature meant to satisfy your desires as best you can. The sophists believed that all men desire wealth and power. Since politics was the path to wealth and power in ancient Greece, they taught politics. Since public speaking was the path to political power, whether they lived in an aristocracy or a democracy, the sophists taught rhetoric, including techniques to "make the weaker argument the stronger." The weaker argument is weak in truth, but it can be made stronger not by increasing its truth, but by increasing its persuasiveness. It is a form of swindling known to this day as the art of "sophistry."

Sophists regarded morality, religion, and all conventional scruples as contemptible. Thus you need to free yourself from these things as much as possible. However, if you want to persuade your fellow citizens, you also need to know how to exploit morality, religion, and other conventions as much as possible, in order to gain power over other people. We'll see all this when we look in the *Clouds*.

ANTIPHON

Antiphon the sophist was a younger contemporary of Socrates. He was the author of the treatise *On Truth*, only fragments of which survive. Antiphon very nicely encapsulates the attitudes of the sophists, showing their dependence on the Greek natural philosophers. The inner connection between sophistry and natural philosophy is one of the topics that is brought up in the *Clouds* and dealt with in a very comical way.

Antiphon claims that justice is entirely conventional. That's a teaching of the natural philosophers, too. When they looked at nature, they didn't see any right and wrong. They just saw natural processes borne along by forces of necessity:

> Justice is a matter of not transgressing the laws prescribe in whatever city you are a citizen of. A person would make most advantage of justice for himself if he treated the laws as important in the presence of witnesses and treated the decrees of nature as important when alone and with no witnesses present. For the decrees of laws are extra additions, those of nature are necessary; those of the laws are products of agreement, not of natural growth whereas those of nature are the product of natural growth not agreement. (DK 87B44; Curd, p. 105)

Antiphon says the best way to live is to give due regard to the conventional laws when there are witnesses around and to follow our natural desires whenever he can get away with it:

> If those who made the agreement do not notice a person transgressing the prescriptions of laws, he is free from both disgrace and penalty, but not so if they do notice him. But, if contrary to possibility, anyone violates any of the things which are innate by nature, the evil is no less if one notices him and no greater if all observe. For he does not suffer harm as the result of opinion, but as a result of truth. (*Ibid.*)

If we transgress the laws of nature, it doesn't matter if there's a witness there; we're still going to suffer the consequences.

Not only does Antiphon make a distinction between the decrees of nature and the decrees of convention, he holds that conventions are hostile to nature: "This is the entire purpose of considering these matters: that most of the things that are just according to the law are established in a way which is hostile to nature" (*Ibid.*).

That's really true. Just think of all our natural impulses and how conventional notions of right and wrong are an impediment to satisfying them. Conventions regarding property get in the way of the satisfaction of natural needs. If I'm hungry, and I don't have any money, I'm out of luck according to our ruling conventions. If I am forced to steal to feed myself, the police will come after me to enforce these conventions. By their very nature, conventions limit the satisfaction of natural desires, and the sophists thought that's bad.

It's bad because nature's the only thing with any real dignity or worth. We shouldn't give convention that much concern. We have to respect it only insofar as conventionally-minded people might see us and have us thrown in jail. But if they're not around, then we should follow the decrees of nature.

Antiphon goes on:

> For laws had been established for the eyes, as to what they must see and for what they must not, and for the ears, as to what they must hear and what they must not, and for the tongue, as to what it must say and what it must not, and for the hands, as to what they must do and what they must not, and for the feet, as to where they must go and where they must not. (*Ibid.*)

You can't look at pornography. You can't listen in on other people's phone conversations. You can't say anything you'd really like to say. You can't put your hands just anywhere you might want to put them. And you can't go by foot or plane or automobile anywhere you want to go. He's enumerating in rather nauseating detail.

"And for the mind, as to what it must desire and what it must not" (*Ibid.*). Convention gets inside our minds and shapes who we are. There are conventional-minded people who would never consider doing anything even slightly naughty or untoward because they have the whole of society embedded in their heads monitoring them and making them feel guilty for even thinking about things that are unconventional. This is a frustration of the liberty of nature, which would have us follow our desires wherever they lead us.

Antiphon continues:

> Now, the things from which the laws deter humans are no more in accord with or suited to nature than the things which they promote. Living and dying are matters of nature, and living results from what is advantageous; dying from what is not advantageous. But the advantages that are established by the law are bonds on nature, and those established by nature are free. (DK 87B44; Curd, pp. 105–106)

So, if we live by the necessities of nature, we're free. If we live under the bonds of convention, we're not free. Freedom is just living in accordance with our natural desires, and what we've lost through our conventional laws is our natural liberty.

Antiphon goes on: "And so, things that cause distress, at least when thought of correctly, do not help nature more than things that give joy. Therefore, it will not be painful things rather than pleasant things which are advantageous" (DK 87B44; Curd, p. 106).

This is another element of the sophists' teaching. They define what's good or evil in terms of pain and pleasure. They're hedonists. You're going to see this in the *Clouds* very clearly when you hear the Unjust Speech. Right and wrong are just equivalent to pleasure and pain.

"For things that are truly advantageous must not cause harm but benefit, but the things that are advantageous by nature are among these . . ." (*Ibid.*). Then there's a lacuna here, unfortunately; a papyrus wasn't complete. We're left to wonder.

"But according to the law, those are correct who defend themselves . . ." (*Ibid.*). Here's what the law tells us to do, and this is interesting: "The law tells us to defend ourselves after suffering and are not first to do wrong" (Ibid.). We have to wait until we've been aggressed against before we can defend ourselves with the law. We hear this all the time. 'But the stalker hasn't done anything yet! We can't send the police. Wait until the person actually attacks you, and then we can send the police.' That's what the law-abiding citizen has to put up with. But that's not good according to nature.

"For those who do good to parents who are bad to them . . ." (Ibid.). Society tells us to honor our parents, even if they're monsters. But nature doesn't.

"And you also follow the law, he who permits others to accuse him on oath but do not themselves accuse on oath" (Ibid.). Antiphon is referring to informants who tattled on others. A law-abiding citizen doesn't go around tattling on his neighbors. Instead, he sits around and waits until his neighbors tattle on him. Only then can he defend himself.

"You will find most of these cases hostile to nature. They permit people to suffer more pain when less is possible and to have less pleasure when more is possible and to receive injury when it is not necessary" (Ibid.). Unfortunately, the laws deter the law-abiding more than the lawless, so naturally, law-abiding citizens will suffer more than if they had been willing to take justice into their own hands.

"Now, if some assistance came from the laws for those who submitted to these conditions and some damage to those who do not submit but resist, obedience to the laws would not be unhelpful" (Ibid.). Unfortunately, that's not the case. The laws often don't benefit those who submit to the laws and punish those who don't.

Antiphon continues:

> But, as things are, it is obvious that the justice that stems from laws is insufficient to rescue those who submit. In the first place, it permits the one who suffers to suffer and the wrongdoer to do wrong, and it was not at the time of the wrongdoing able to prevent either the sufferer from suffering or the wrongdoer from doing wrong. And when the

case is brought to trial, there is no special advantage for the one who has suffered over the wrongdoer. For he must persuade the jury that he suffered and that he is able to exact the penalty. And it is open to the wrongdoer to deny it. . . . However convincing the accusation is on behalf of the accuser, the defense can be just as convincing. For victory comes through speech. (*Ibid.*)

This is a pretty bleak view of human society. It's bleak, but it's actually terribly accurate. So what's the solution? The solution is to not be so damn law-abiding and instead to pursue your advantage by all the tools you have available. One of the most important tools is the art of speaking. But if somebody's going to do you harm, you have to be willing to do him harm before he does harm to you. Otherwise, you're going to be a victim. It's a very tough-minded, "shoot first" philosophy for a lawless, low-trust world.

Pythagoras

I wish to end with Pythagoras, who is something of an outlier because he melded elements of natural philosophy with the initiatic mystery religion of Orphism. Pythagoras was born on the island of Samos around 570 BCE. After traveling to Egypt and Babylon in search of wisdom, he eventually settled in Croton in Southern Italy, where he created a school of philosophy that functioned as a religious sect and a political party that gained enormous influence. After around two decades, the people of Croton rose up against the Pythagoreans, killing some and driving out the rest. Pythagoras went into exile and starved himself to death, but his sect persisted for centuries.

Pythagoras believed in the immortality and transmigration of the soul. He also held that embodied existence was suffering. But if your soul is lucky enough to enter a human body, then you have a chance to escape embodied existence, but only if you get ahold of the teachings of Pythagoras.

The path to liberation is to purify your soul as much as possible of any connection to or admixture with the body. The best way to do this is by engaging in intellectual activities that strengthen the soul. The best kind of intellectual activities are those that have the least to do with anything practical. So, that would include science and mathematics.

Pythagoras was really the founder of mathematics as a theoretical activity. Beforehand, geometry was literally what the word means, which is "earth measuring." That's surveying. He turned geometry into a purely theoretical discipline. The purpose of this was to separate the soul as much as possible from the body, so that when the body died the soul would no longer be caught in the endless cycle of birth, rebirth, and suffering.

Now, this all sounds very Buddhistic, and the Orphic mystery religion of the time taught very similar things. Pythagoras was in a sense one of the first "gurus" of the West. He offered a religious worldview combined with spiritual exercises designed to bring about the salvation of the soul. These spiritual exercises involved study. They also involved asceticism, self-discipline, and self-denial.

Pythagoreans would give up their attachments to worldly things. They would live together in little colonies. They would give their property over to the group for its maintenance. And they would practice vegetarianism. They would swear off sex and any of the other pleasures of the flesh, because the pleasures of the flesh were considered rivets that keep the soul attached to the body and enmeshed in suffering.

The Pythagoreans became the model for every initiatic spiritual movement from Freemasonry to Dianetics. Every Pythagorean started with the most basic teaching. Those who passed were allowed to study higher-level teachings. Each successive class was smaller than the one before it. Thus only a select few learned Pythagoras' ultimate "esoteric" teachings. They were well-kept secrets, because we know almost nothing of them today, except for the idea that the two ultimate principles of the world were the limited and the unlimited.

We will recognize elements of Pythagoreanism in the *Clouds*: Socrates' Thinkery is like an ashram. His students practice asceticism. They study pure mathematics. And students have to undergo a process of testing and initiation, although Socrates botches it rather badly.

In the *Clouds* Socrates is shown to be a kind of combination of all the pre-Socratic schools, because Aristophanes thinks there's an inner harmony of these pre-Socratic schools, even though on the surface they're radically different. In particular, Aristophanes wishes to show that the doctrines of natural philosophy lead to sophistry, and sophistry leads to bad social consequences.

Aristophanes' treatment of Pythagoreanism in the *Clouds* is somewhat different, however, because practicing Pythagorean asceticism merely makes Socrates and his students unhealthy looking. But a far more important plot element of the *Clouds* hinges on the *failure* of Socrates to practice Pythagorean esotericism, i.e., measures to vet students and maintain the secrecy of his teachings.

Aristophanes' *Clouds*

"The Thinkery, a likeness of death, teaching Whirligig and Bamboozle, 'back to nature' without families, without the old paternal gods, and without *nomoi* (not paying back money owed and using unusual forms of words)..."

—Thomas Prufer[1]

Socrates was 46 or 47 years old when Aristophanes' *Clouds* premiered in March or April of 423 BCE at the festival known as the Greater Dionysia.[2] At this festival, Athens put on fifteen plays funded by donations from wealthy citizens. There were nine tragedies, consisting of three trilogies, each trilogy written by the same tragedian. Both Sophocles' *Oedipus* trilogy and Aeschylus' *Oresteia* were premiered at various Greater Dionysia. They also put on three satyr plays which were light-hearted treatments of mythical topics, written by the same playwrights who authored the tragedies. Finally, there were three comedies. Awards were given for the best tragedy trilogy, the best comedy, and the best satyr play.

The *Clouds* came in dead last in the competition. Interestingly enough, there was another play in the competition that very year that also parodied Socrates. It was by a playwright named Ameipsias. Only a few lines have survived from this play, but we know that it was voted either first or second place over the *Clouds*. Two years later, in 421 BCE, another comedy on Socrates, this one by Eupolis, was premiered. Aristophanes, of course, has gotten the last laugh, because the other plays have perished.

The plot of the *Clouds* is very simple. Strepsiades is a country

---

[1] Thomas Prufer, "A Note on *King Oedipus, Clouds, The Defense of Socrates, Phaedo*," unpublished typescript.

[2] All quotations from the *Clouds* are from *Four Texts on Socrates*, trans. Thomas G. West and Grace Starry West (Ithaca: Cornell University Press, 1984), and will be cited parenthetically in the text.

gentleman who makes a living tilling his land outside Athens. Strepsiades has married the niece of Megacles, whose name could almost be translated as "Big Shot." She was the niece of Big Shot from a wealthy urban family. Naturally, she has all kinds of expensive tastes.

Their son Pheidippides is a cross between the country gentry and the citified aristocracy. His name itself reflects that. Pheidippides is a compromise between his mother's desire to give him a classy aristocratic name (it has the root word for horse in it) and his father's desire to name him after an old-fashioned virtue. Thus Pheidippides means "thrifty horseman," which is a very strange concept, because keeping horses is quite expensive.

Pheidippides' desire to have horses and chariots and other expensive accoutrements has put his father in great debt. His father is forced to mortgage his land to spoil his son. He's very much an indulgent father. But the time is coming to pay off his debts, and he's trying to figure a way out. So, the old man decides to try something new-fangled. He wants to send his son to the Thinkery, which is a school run by Socrates. He has heard that in the Thinkery Socrates teaches how to "make the weaker speech the stronger."

The weaker speech is the *morally* weaker speech. To make the weaker speech the stronger means to make the morally weaker speech *more effective in persuading people*. It's morally weak but persuasively strong.

To induce Pheidippides to go to the Thinkery, Strepsiades asks Pheidippides to swear an oath that he will do his father's bidding. But when he finds out what his father has in mind, he breaks the oath immediately, because he doesn't want to go to the Thinkery at all. In the course of the *Clouds*, Pheidippides is corrupted, but it is clear from the very start that he's not the most honorable lad.

It's interesting that Strepsiades only knows a little bit about the Thinkery by reputation, even though it's right next door, but his son actually knows the names of Socrates and Chaerephon. Again, the son is a liminal figure, straddling the country gentry and the urban elite. The fact that he knows Socrates' and Chaerephon's names indicates that they themselves too don't quite fit into normal society either. Imagine the Thinkery as a little run-down building off to the side of the stage.

In Xenophon's *Memorabilia* Socrates says:

> Just as another is pleased by a good horse or a dog or a bird, so I myself am even more pleased by good friends, and if I possess something good, I teach it and I introduce them to others from whom I believe they will receive some benefit with a view to virtue. In reading together with my friends, I go through the treasures of the wise men of old which they wrote and left behind in their books, and if we see something good, we pick it out and we hold that it is a great gain if we become friends with one another.[3]

In the last sentence, the first two uses of "we" refer to Socrates and his friends, but the last use of "we" refers to Socrates and his friends and the wise men of old. Socrates and his friends are already friends with one another, but they become friends with the wise men of old through reading their books.

This really does refer to a kind of Thinkery, where Socrates and his friends get together to study philosophy. So, there's some reason to think that the Thinkery is not just Aristophanes' invention. Socrates inherited a house from his parents, and the Thinkery was probably Socrates' little run-down house.

Since Pheidippides refuses to go to the Thinkery, Strepsiades goes in his stead. Strepsiades is initiated into the Thinkery and educated there, but he's just too stupid, so he flunks out. He's finally forced to send his son. But this time he's successful in persuading Pheidippides to go to the Thinkery.

Pheidippides goes to the Thinkery and turns out to be a better pupil than his father. He learns how to make the weaker speech the stronger, becoming a rather shameless little S.O.B. in the process. His father *fêtes* him with a graduation dinner, and in the midst of the dinner they quarrel about poetry, the son beats up his father, and the father rushes into the street and asks his

---

[3] Xenophon, *Memorabilia*, trans. Amy L. Bonnette (Ithaca: Cornell University Press, 1994), I.6.14,

neighbors—whom he has wronged—to be witnesses to his plight. Then the son proceeds by means of argument to persuade his father that it's just to beat him.

But when Pheidippides tries to persuade his father that it's just to beat his mother as well, the old man snaps, and he won't hear another word. Instead, he calls to his slaves for help. One of the slaves takes up a rustic implement, a hoe, and climbs onto the roof of the Thinkery. He breaks the roof tiles, then Strepsiades sets the whole building ablaze. Socrates and his students are forced to flee for their lives. And that's the end of the comedy.

THE *CLOUDS* AS PHILOSOPHY

There's a lot of dirty language, funny jokes, and slapstick in the *Clouds*. But it would be a mistake to think that this is pure silliness, because the *Clouds* is really a philosophical work. In fact, in the play itself, the spokesman for Aristophanes calls it his "wisest play" (p. 137). I would argue even more strongly that it's the first fully extant philosophical work that we have in the Western tradition.

Many people who comment on the *Clouds* simply treat Aristophanes as a poet, a terribly reactionary poet. There's no question that he was an old-fashioned reactionary. He hated all the new-fangled things that were going on in Athens at the time and fought against them by mercilessly parodying them in his eleven surviving comedies, which are magnificent.

At the same time, Aristophanes is not what you could call a mindless conservative or reactionary in the sense that he simply defends the old ways because they're old. He's a new kind of defender of tradition. Aristophanes seems to regard the ancient ways as good, but not just because they're ancient. He appeals to another principle to argue that the ancient ways are good. He appeals to nature.

But this is very strange, because before Aristophanes, both the natural philosophers and sophists who appealed to nature were contemptuous of human conventions, especially long-standing, refined human conventions like traditions.

If Aristophanes is appealing to nature to validate tradition, he must have a very different conception of nature. It's very easy to believe that man has no nature when you see how plastic human beings are, how amazingly adaptable they are to all sorts of situations, how amazingly corruptible they are, how amazingly perverse they are. There doesn't seem to be any intrinsic limit to human behavior. It's very easy to think man is just conventions all the way down, or historically evolved traditions and practices all the way down, that there's nothing natural about us. But Aristophanes believes in human nature.

The second thing that's extraordinary about Aristophanes' appeal to nature is that he has the notion of what's *right* or *just by nature*, whereas the pre-Socratic natural philosophers and the sophists had no conception of what's right or just by nature. Their only conception of right was purely conventional, and they didn't think that convention really mattered.

So, Aristophanes represents the first thinker in the philosophical tradition to appeal to a notion of *natural right* based on human nature. It's on the basis of his understanding of human nature, and of what's right by nature, that he comes to a defense of the traditions of Athens.

Now, there are many reasons to believe that he's not entirely a defender of Athenian tradition. In a number of his plays, it's clear that he thinks that the gods have to be overthrown. That's clear even in this play.

In the contest between the Just Speech and the Unjust Speech, the Just Speech loses, yet the Just Speech is supposedly the speech that Aristophanes is most in sync with. It represents the conservative party in Athens at the time. Yet, Aristophanes—who is the playwright and thus has some control over what happens in his plays—contrives to have the Just Speech, his own side, lose. Why does he make the Just Speech lose?

The Just Speech loses because Aristophanes thinks that the traditions of Athens have weak points that must be changed in order to preserve the Athenian way of life as a whole. Every serious conservative thinker—Edmund Burke is an excellent example—recognizes that an institution or practice that doesn't have the capacity to change under new circumstances, does not have the capacity to conserve itself. To conserve old Athens, Aristophanes thinks it necessary to change old Athens, just up to the point that the weaknesses are eliminated. We're going to see what he thinks the weaknesses of the traditional position are. But, on the whole, he is still a conservative thinker.

INTRODUCTION TO THE THINKERY

When Strepsiades first points towards the Thinkery, he says, "That is a Thinkery of wise souls. In there dwell men who by thinking persuade one that the heaven is a stove, and it is around us, and we are charcoal. When someone gives them money, they teach him how to win both just and unjust causes by speaking" (p. 119).

The claim that heaven is a stove and that we're charcoals is a typically goofy, Strepsiadean misunderstanding of natural philosophy. This is one of the first things you notice about Strepsiades. He just doesn't understand science or natural philosophy. Whenever he hears a proposition of natural science, he translates it into something that's familiar to him, and what's familiar to him are practical considerations and bodily functions. So, we hear a great deal about farting in this play because apparently Strepsiades is quite familiar with that. We hear a great deal about food because, again, that's something that ranks high in his list of priorities. And ovens, charcoal, kneading pans, measures for barley, and so forth. They're all things that he finds intelligible.

Strepsiades has no idea of nature, i.e., of a non-human world, The idea of an objective world that you know scientifically, not through the categories of human concerns and practical interests, is entirely foreign to him.

Strepsiades doesn't know the names of the thinkers in the Thinkery. "I don't know their names precisely. Pondering thinkers, noble and good men . . ." (p. 128). It's interesting that this phrase "noble and good man" (*kalos kagathos* is the Greek) can be translated as "gentleman," if you don't want to do it literally, like the translators here.

Strepsiades thinks the guys over in the Thinkery are gentlemen, and this is an indication of his social class. He's an uneducated man, a rustic, a country farmer, and even though he has money and the men in the Thinkery have none, Strepsiades thinks they are somehow higher on the social scale.

Pheidippides' reaction is entirely different, and this shows how in some ways he thinks of himself as on a higher social level than his father because of his inheritance from his mother. He says, "Ugh, villains, I know. They're boasters, pale, shoeless men that you're speaking of and among them that miserably unhappy Socrates and Chaerephon." Socrates, indeed, was famous for going around shoeless.

Strepsiades continues, "It's said that they have two speeches: the stronger, whatever it may be, and the weaker. Of these speeches, the weaker wins, they say, although it speaks the more unjust things. So, if you learn this Unjust Speech for me, I wouldn't give anyone back even an obol of those debts that I owe because of you" (p. 120).

This is the plan. Strepsiades has to go himself in place of his son because his son is a sportsman. He doesn't want to spend his time slaving away indoors and lose his tan and get out of shape. So, Strepsiades has to go in his son's stead.

Strepsiades piously prays to the gods before he goes off to the Thinkery. There are people who will pray to God before they stick up a bank. They see no contradiction in praying for success at being a scoundrel.

Strepsiades knows himself to the extent that he knows he's old and slow. He doesn't think that he will be able to handle the subtleties of the Thinkery's program. As it turns out, Strepsiades has a far more accurate assessment of his own character than the people he meets.

Strepsiades approaches the Thinkery and bangs on the door. The student inside dresses him down as a crude buffoon because he caused a thought to miscarry. This is an allusion to Socrates, who claimed that he followed his mother's profession as a midwife, but he served as a midwife of ideas, helping them to be born.

The student says, "I can't tell you what's going on in here because these things are mysteries. You're not initiated." Strepsiades says, 'Well, okay. I've come to you to be a student.' "Well, I'll tell you then, but you must believe that these things are mysteries." Obviously, the Thinkery is not very discerning about with whom it shares its secrets. Then the student explains what Strepsiades had just interrupted.

A flea had jumped from Chaerephon's head to Socrates' head after biting Chaerephon on the eyebrow. Apparently, the Thinkery and its inhabitants are dirty and infested with vermin. This incident, however, does not prompt them to do something practical, like wash. Instead, it is an occasion for theory. They immediately began to speculate how many feet a flea can leap. But they decide not to measure it in terms of human measurements, our notion of feet, because that's our convention that we're imposing upon nature. They want to know how many feet a flea can leap in "flea feet," because that's nature's own measure.

There's a notion of objectivity here, of peeling away human categories and seeing nature as it is. They want nature to tell its story in its own language.

This is how they do it. They take some wax, melt it, and dip the flea's feet in the wax. Then after the wax cools, they have little slippers which they measure—with obviously very tiny instruments—to gauge the size of the flea's foot. Then they calculate how many flea feet the flea can leap. This is obviously absurd, but there's a serious point to it.

The next topic they discuss is how gnats hum. Do they hum from their anuses or from their mouths? A complex theory is presented that gnats actually hum through their anuses. Socrates is unkinking and plumbing the anuses of gnats, which is very delicate work. Strepsiades is terribly impressed: "Then the gnat's anus is a trumpet! Oh, thrice blessed for intestinal insight! How easily would a defendant escape the penalties if he thoroughly knew the intestines of the gnat!" (p. 122).

Then the student mentions how Socrates was recently robbed of a great notion on the courses of the moon by a lizard. Socrates was peering up at the moon, making astronomical observations, and a lizard crapped on him from the roof. This may be an allusion to the story of Thales looking at the heavens and falling down a well.

Then the student talks about how Socrates contrived to get their barley for their last meal, because not only is the place infested with bugs, they are also extremely poor and hungry, and they have to steal food to get by. The student says Socrates "sprinkled fine ash on the table, bent the meat spit [apparently they didn't need it for meat], and then taking it as a compass he made away with the cloak from the wrestling school" (p. 122).

Apparently, Socrates spread ash on a table top to create a surface on which he could draw; then using a compass, he did some sort of complex geometrical proof, and while the people were gawking at Socrates' geometrical acumen, he somehow stole a cloak from the wrestling school and pawned it to buy food.

This is very interesting, because Aristophanes is hinting that there's a connection between the activities of natural philosophers, who are concerned about things like geometry and astronomy, and the dishonest activities of sophists. It's a goofy connection, but he wants us to ponder what the underlying connection might be.

Then the student admits Strepsiades into the Thinkery, and he's aghast at how skinny, undernourished, and pale they are. He notices that there are some students who are looking down at the earth

> **STREPSIADES**: But why ever are these over here looking down at the earth?
> **STUDENT**: They're investigating the things beneath the earth.
> **STREPSIADES**: Then it's vegetable bulbs. (p. 123)

This is the first thing that comes to mind, right? Investigating things under the earth? Aha! Must be turnips! These are practical things under the earth, and that's all that Strepsiades thinks in terms of. Then he tries to give them advice about where to find good vegetables, and of course they're not interested in that. They're delving to Erebus under Tartarus. They're delving into the secrets of the underworld.

Apparently, they're bent over, so their heads are to the ground and their rear ends are pointing to the sky. And Strepsiades says, "then why is the anus looking to the heavens?" And the student says, "it itself, by itself, is being taught astronomy."

This phrase "it itself, by itself" is in Plato's *Phaedo*. It's the term that's used to refer to the "Forms": the eternal exemplars of the things that we see around us, the Form of cup or animal or chair. Later scholars argue on the basis of ambiguous testimony from Aristotle that Socrates didn't have a theory of Forms. But assuming that this phrase is being used in the same way as in the *Phaedo*, this is very good evidence that Socrates himself spoke of Forms, because this text was written long before Plato's dialogues, even before Plato was born. So, the theory of Forms may not be Plato's creation that he foists on Socrates. There's reason to believe it's something Socrates himself thought up.

Then the student says, "Well, go inside so he won't happen upon us." "Not yet! Not yet! Let them stay so I can share a little matter of mine with him." I think this may be an allusion to a prominent theme later in the play, which is buggery. But the student says, "No, they have to go inside. They can't take the air for very long." Their health is very delicate, you see.

Then Strepsiades looks around and sees instruments for observing the heavens and instruments of geometry. The word "geometry" literally means "Earth measurement," and so Strepsiades immediately thinks, "Oh, for land allotments!" For dividing up the Earth amongst people, i.e., surveying, which is the origin of geometry. The student says, 'No, we're not measuring the earth around here. We're measuring the *whole* Earth. All of it.' Anaximander, the first student of Thales, was renowned to be the first man who created a map of the whole earth. So, this is very consistent with the early Greek thinkers. Strepsiades, however, thinks measuring the whole Earth is simply an allotment of the earth to the Athenians, which he praises as a popular measure.

The students show Strepsiades the map, and they point to Athens, and Strepsiades says, "I don't believe that's Athens. Where are the law courts? Where are the judges?" These are the things that are foremost on his mind because he's got a lawsuit pending. Again, he wants to see the world drawn to the scale of his concerns. Drawn to an objective geometric scale, the law courts don't show up, but drawn to the scale of his concerns they would.

And then he says, "Well, where are the Spartans, our enemies?" The student points to another dot, and Strepsiades says, "So close? Can't you move them a little further away?" Again, by the scale of human priorities, you would draw Sparta far away, but by the objective scale of geometry you just have to put it where it is.

So, there's a conflict here between two basic ways of looking at the world. Strepsiades looks at the world through the lens of practical human concerns, whereas the pre-Socratic thinkers in the Thinkery have stepped outside the human perspective on things. They've put aside all their human concerns, and they're trying to see the world as it is in itself and measure it according to its own scale. Those are two very different perspectives on how to see the world.

If you sit outside the human condition and take up an objective, scientific perspective on things, you tend to find that the human condition is the last thing you worry about. Scientific naturalists tend to think that the language of science is the only objective language. What about everything else? Well, it's poetry; it's politics; but it's not objective. It's all rhetoric. Which is exactly the position of the ancient sophists. That it's all rhetoric; it's history; it's convention all the way down. We've made up our nature, and we can remake it at will. There is no human nature. The only nature is non-human nature.

Socrates first appears in this play floating aloft in a basket. This is a wonderful device for indicating how he's divorced himself from the human condition and the human point of view. He's floating above the Earth. Strepsiades coaxes him down out of his basket. Socrates doesn't want to come down at first, and he refers to poor Strepsiades as a mere "ephemeral one." Socrates is interested in the things that *are* and the things that *always will be*. He's interested in the laws of nature. Strepsiades is just a human being. He's going to be dead pretty soon. He's ephemeral. Natural law isn't, so Socrates is concerned with nature.

This is the basis for the natural philosophers' contempt for convention. Conventions change from time to time and from place to place, but the laws of nature, as the ancient Greeks understood it, do not change at all.

Socrates says he treads on air and contemplates the sun, and

Strepsiades says, "So, you're looking down on the gods from a perch?" The "looking down on" here has a dual meaning. It can mean literally looking down from above, but it can also mean holding the gods in contempt. Both of those meanings are there, because it's very clear that Socrates is an atheist.

Then we get a passage that sounds like any number of pre-Socratic fragments: "I would never discover the matters aloft correctly except by suspending mind and subtle thought and mixing them with their like, the air. If I considered the things from below on the ground, I would never discover them. For the Earth forcefully pulls to itself the moisture from the thought. The same thing happens also to watercress" (pp. 124–25).

My first reaction to this is "What?" It sounds weird, but this was early science, which combined wild analogies and a very mechanistic understandings of how things work. Thought is moist. If it dries out, then you can't think. Or Heraclitus thought that dry souls were the best and wet souls were the worst. So, there was a debate. Is the dry or the wet soul the better soul? The categories just don't seem to apply. It sounds like people tripping on acid.

Strepsiades then announces what he wants to learn: "Teach me the one of the two speeches. The one that pays nothing back. Whatever fee you set, I swear by the gods to pay you" (p. 125).

I don't know about you, but if somebody said that to me, what's the first thing that would come to mind? What's peculiar about that declaration? 'Teach me the speech that pays nothing back, and I swear that I'll give you whatever fee you demand.' Put it this way: if you go to a credit agency because your bills are in a shambles, I don't think any of these agencies will take you on without first securing payment in advance. If you say, 'I'm sorry, I'm $100,000 in debt. I have all these credit cards that I haven't paid. Help me out and then bill me,' it's not going to work. The first thing a practical person would see is this contradiction. If he wants to learn how to cheat, I'm not going to trust him to pay the bill later. I want the payment up front.

But what's the first thing that Socrates fastens on? It's the fact that he swears an oath by the gods. Socrates has a deaf ear for practical considerations and immediately focuses on the fact that

Strepsiades swears an oath by the gods. He says, "What gods indeed will you swear by? For, first of all, we don't credit gods." And Strepsiades says, "Well, what do you swear with? Iron coins . . . ?" The very idea of disbelief in gods doesn't occur to him. Strepsiades understands the idea of not giving god any credit in terms of money.

Strepsiades literally doesn't know what it means to be an atheist. Later on, when he promises not to recognize the other gods, he says, 'I promise and if they should come up to me, I'll just ignore them.'

Socrates says, "I'll teach you divine matters plainly."[4] He also asks, "Do you promise to associate in speech with the Clouds, our daimons?" (p. 125). He just said that we don't credit any gods here, but you have to promise to associate in speech with them. There's some reason to believe that associating with the gods *in speech* is all Socrates' religiosity amounts to. Today, we might call this "lip service."

When Strepsiades goes into the Thinkery for his instruction, Socrates refers to the Clouds as the "Queen of All," the ruler of all. After Strepsiades comes out of the Thinkery, Socrates does not ever mention the Clouds. Instead, Strepsiades swears an oath to fraud, queen of all. If the Clouds are queen of all, and fraud is queen of all, and there's only one queen, then we have to conclude that the Clouds are fraud.

This would make sense of the locution "to associate with them in speech." The divinity of the Clouds is a fiction for Socrates. The natural philosophers would deify natural forces. 'Yes, yes. We don't believe in the gods of the city, but we believe that water is divine.' People would think, 'Are these people just condescending to us? Are they just playing with us? Are they divinizing something which they don't think is divine for public consumption?' There was a sense that the early Greek philosophers were entirely disingenuous about their professions of religiosity. And Socrates is, in a very subtle way, being shown to be that disingenuous here.

---

[4] As we will see in Plato's *Euthyphro*, Euthyphro the soothsayer and enthusiast makes a similar promise.

But what's interesting is that the Clouds actually play a role in the play. Socrates associates with them in speech, but after he starts ignoring them, they still perform a function in the play. The Clouds are real *daimons*, even though Socrates believes they are mere fiction, mere fraud. And the question then is: What are the Clouds? What do they represent?

I want to suggest, at least as a preliminary interpretation, that the Clouds represent what you could call "wisdom from nature" or "wisdom according to nature," a wisdom that derives from following nature. For Socrates in the *Clouds*, wisdom from nature means simply natural philosophy, which is atheistic and amoral.

But it's very interesting to note that Aristophanes himself also indicates that he's a follower of the Clouds. In fact, Aristophanes is one of the Clouds, because when Socrates and Strepsiades retire into the Thinkery, there's a choral interlude. The lead Cloud in the chorus steps forward—it's called the *parabasis*, which literally means "stepping forward"—and gives a speech to the audience. And it's very clear that the lead Cloud is speaking on behalf of Aristophanes, which is very peculiar.

Socrates goes through a little initiation ceremony to make Strepsiades part of the Thinkery (p. 126). He sits Strepsiades down on a couch, puts a wreath on his head, and sprinkles him with flour from a can. It's a parody of the initiations of the mystery religions, which were adopted by certain schools of philosophy like the Pythagoreans. Socrates treats the initiation as a farce, but at least there's some nod in the direction of treating the Thinkery as a religious organization, at least on the surface. They at least go through the forms of a religious initiation while paying lip service to the Clouds.

THE INVOCATION OF THE CLOUDS

Then Socrates begins an invocation of the Clouds. "O, master and lord! Measureless air who holds the Earth aloft in bright aether and august goddesses, Clouds, the thunder and lightning, arise! Appear, O ladies, aloft for the thinker!"

The chorus offstage begins to chant, and the chorus slowly files in dressed as clouds. All the actors in Greek plays were men, even the ones playing women's roles. So, a group of men dressed as women who are Clouds would file in. They would probably wear white, flowing robes and masks to cover the fact that they had beards. They filed in slowly, chanting.

If anyone's ever seen Japanese Noh theater, this is probably what the Greek plays were like: extremely static, hieratic, slow-moving. You have to be a real connoisseur or you go crazy watching this stuff, because nothing ever seems to happen. For me, it's like watching baseball. It's two minutes of action crammed into three hours. Imagine them in very formalized poses, like Egyptian reliefs, tip-toeing in.

Socrates characterizes the Clouds as, "The heavenly clouds, great goddesses for idle men, who provide us with notions and dialectic and mind and marvel-telling and circumlocution and striking and seizing" (p. 128).

The Greek word for "idle men" is the root of the word "scholar." It just means idle lay-abouts, good-for-nothings. These idle men include, first of all, those who talk about notions and dialectic and mind. Those would be the natural philosophers. But also there are marvel-tellers (people who tell tall tales, including, perhaps, religious tales), circumlocutors (literally people who talk around topics), and strikers and seizers (smash and grab artists). These are the sophists. So the sophists and the natural philosophers are nourished by the Clouds.

These people are nourished by the Clouds because they base their worldview on nature. In the *Clouds*, Aristophanes is trying to display the underlying identity of the natural philosophers and sophists, who look quite different on the surface. Both groups, however, have essentially the same atheistic and amoral conception of nature.

Socrates continues:

> Then don't you know, by Zeus, that they [the Clouds] nourish most of the sophists, Thurian diviners, practicers of the art of medicine, idle-long-haired-onyx-ring-wearers, song modulators of circling choruses, men who are imposters about the things aloft. Idle do-nothings are nourished too because they make poetry and music about these Clouds. (p. 129)

Aristophanes is talking about the bohemian counter-culture of his time. This includes what we would call the New Age crowd today: astrologers, spiritual healers, channelers. "Thurian diviners" try to see the future. "Practicers of the art of medicine": medicine wasn't considered much of a science at the time. It was more akin to magic and faith-healing. "Idle-long-haired-onyx-ring-wearers" are probably the fashionably degenerate youth that Socrates was accused of corrupting. The "song-modulators of circling choruses" and those who "make music and poetry" about the Clouds refer to the artists of Athens, which would include Aristophanes himself.

What do all these people have in common? They are all unconventional. What does unconventionality have to do with the Clouds? The Clouds represent knowledge of nature, which leads to the breakdown of convention.

Surprisingly, Aristophanes claims that even superstition is nourished by the Clouds, i.e., by atheistic and amoral natural philosophy. How could this be the case? The decline of traditional religion and morals opens up a space for new religions and morals. But what would prompt their emergence? Could it be nature? Could the natural philosophers and sophists be wrong that nature teaches us to be atheistic and amoral? Could nature—particularly human nature—prompt us to create religions and morals?

It is worth noting that, although Socrates denies the gods of the city, the Clouds appeal to them in their choral ode. The Clouds represent knowledge of nature, but unbeknownst to Socrates, nature has a place for conventional gods. This lesson is made clear at the end of the play.

KNOWLEDGE OF HUMAN NATURE

What the natural philosophers, the sophists, and the "New Age" counter-culture of the day have in common is a certain critical distance from the reigning conventions. Aristophanes returns to the conventions of the city and embraces most of them, but he maintains some critical distance from them. The step that he takes outside the conventional viewpoint is made possible by an appeal to nature.

It's possible for people to criticize conventions of society "within" convention by stepping back from one convention and using another one basically as a lens for criticism. But you can't really take the whole of society into view that way. You're always "inside" it and depending on it. If you're going to take the whole of the human world into your view, you have to find a perspective outside of it, from where you can see it.

It's much easier to draw a map of a building if you can step back from it and see the whole contour of it, than if you're wandering around inside, trying to figure out how the whole thing fits together. So, if you're going to have a holistic understanding of the nature of human things, you'll need to have a standpoint outside of the human world from which to see them.

Nature provides that standpoint. This is why people are constantly trying to get to what's natural. We want to know what's permanent and what's not. Because if you remain entirely within the realm of convention it's very easy to mistake things that are merely conventional for things that are natural. People do that all the time. People visit different cultures and suddenly realize things that seemed entirely natural to them really aren't natural. They're "second nature," meaning that they're deeply embedded conventions.

One of the things that's interesting about the Clouds, too, is that they take on the shapes of things, and they reveal the natures of people.

Strepsiades says "They're like spread out wool, not women, by Zeus, not at all. They don't look like women. They look like big balls of wool. These have noses!" (p. 29). Socrates is famous for his big Karl Maldenesque nose, so the Clouds have taken on the shape of Socrates' nose. Then Strepsiades goes through a list of how the Clouds reveal people's inner nature by taking on their shapes (p. 30).

This shows that the Clouds have an insight into human character, and later on the Clouds make it very clear that they have grave reservations about Strepsiades' fitness for studying at the Thinkery. Socrates doesn't have such reservations, though, and this is a very important issue.

Socrates has merely token secrecy measures. He has a token

interview and a token initiation to get into the Thinkery. But these miserable tokens don't work. Socrates has absolutely no sense that Strepsiades is not the right kind of person to initiate into the secrets of nature, even though he has ample opportunity to determine this before he takes him into the Thinkery. Socrates is just a terrible judge of character.

But the Clouds aren't. What the Clouds represent is, in a sense, knowledge not just of nature in the non-human sense, but also knowledge of *human nature* as well. But Socrates is unaware of human nature. The Clouds represent wisdom derived from nature, but it's possible to derive wisdom about human beings from a study of nature too. Socrates is a natural philosopher who looks away from the human things to huge things like planetary bodies and tiny things like gnats and fleas but completely leaves out the realm of the middle where we live. We're middle-sized things. Socrates has no interest in that.

Socrates' conception of nature is much narrower than the conception of nature represented by the Clouds. So, in a sense, the Clouds are wiser than Socrates because they have a much more expansive notion of what nature is. In fact, when you get right down to it, Socrates is a fool in this play. He's the butt of humor because he behaves in a foolish way. Why does he behave foolishly? Because with all of his scientific knowledge, he has no knowledge of human nature, and therefore he does not act prudently.

THE NON-THEISTIC UNDERSTANDING OF NATURE

Socrates goes on to explain how the Clouds are the only goddesses, and all the others are drivel. "And what about Zeus?" Strepsiades asks. Socrates replies, "What Zeus? Don't babble. Zeus doesn't even exist" (p. 131).

Then Strepsiades says, "Who makes it rain then?" Because, of course, Zeus was the one who was supposed to make it rain. Socrates says that the Clouds make it rain. When have you ever seen rain without Clouds? But if Zeus makes it rain, then you'd think he could make it rain any time whether there are Clouds or not. Strepsiades finds that rather convincing.

'Then who makes it thunder?' Strepsiades asks. And Socrates

says, 'The Clouds make it thunder when they roll around and crash into one another up in heaven.' Strepsiades finds that interesting.

But then he says, "Well, who moves the Clouds around? Isn't that Zeus?" Socrates says, "No, they're borne along by necessity." "When they are filled up with much water and are compelled to be borne along by necessity, hanging down full of rain, then they heavily fall into each other, bursting and clapping."

"And who is it that compels them be borne along?" Strepsiades asks. "Is it Zeus?" And Socrates says, 'Not in the least. It's the ethereal vortex. The vortex causes things to happen.' Anaxagoras, Empedocles, and Diogenes of Apollonia held that a great cosmic vortex sets the rest of the cosmos in motion. It is the beating heart that sends everything else coursing around.

Strepsiades thinks, "Vortex? I hadn't noticed that Zeus doesn't exist and that instead of him Vortex is now king." The Greek word for vortex is *dinos*. And a form of Zeus is *dio*. Now *dinos* could be understood as the diminutive form of *dios* or the offspring of *dios*. So poor Strepsiades thinks that *dinos*, meaning vortex, is really the son of Zeus, that Zeus has been ousted by his own son, and there's a new king of the gods.

Of course, this is perfectly consistent with Greek mythology, because Zeus ousted his father who ousted his father before him. So Strepsiades immediately took the notion of a vortex, which is just a natural force, and turned it into another god. This is the pattern of Strepsiades' thinking. He really can't conceive of a non-theistic notion of nature.

Then, of course, Strepsiades wants to know about thunder. Socrates says, "Well, have you ever eaten some stew and gotten gas from it and it rumbles through your belly?" And Strepsiades says, 'Yes, indeed. Yes, indeed. That's happened to me many times.' Then follows a whole scatological routine. Socrates is trying to sap sublimity and majesty from heavenly forces by explaining them away on the analogy of the lowest of human things, namely intestinal gas and farting.

Then Strepsiades gets to the thing that really concerns him here. 'What about the thunderbolt? Because isn't it the case that Zeus smites perjurers with his thunderbolt?' That's what really concerns him because, of course, he's going to lie. He's going to go to court and be sworn in—the equivalent of putting his hand on the Bible by swearing an oath to Zeus—then he's going to lie to weasel out of his debts. Before doing this, however, he wants to know if Zeus is going to punish him.

Socrates says that the thunderbolt is caused by purely natural phenomena. Dry wind gets clogged up in the Clouds, then the Clouds are swollen up, and they burst, and the wind rushes out of the Clouds very quickly and is ignited by the swiftness of the force, so you get the thunderbolt. Of course, it's very clear that the lightning falls on the guilty and the innocent alike. Zeus sent lightning down to smite one of his own temples! Lightning hits oak trees. Oak trees don't perjure themselves. They did nothing wrong. Clearly, there's no Providence here. It's just natural, random phenomena.

Strepsiades is enormously relieved by this, because now his last scruple has been hung. He doesn't have to worry about Zeus, so he feels that he can now go forward with his plan to cheat his way out of his debts.

STREPSIADES ENTERS THE THINKERY

Then the Clouds address Strepsiades, and they say, 'Okay, old man, you're going to have to give up everything: food and sleep and friends and so forth and wine and gymnastics and fun. Then you'll have to study.' They're not sure that he's capable of it, and they're right. Socrates says, "Now, won't you believe in no god but ours? This Chaos [meaning the vortex] and the Clouds and the Tongue" (p. 133). This is their trinity: the Chaos, the Clouds, and the Tongue, meaning the art of speaking.

Then Strepsiades goes through a long list of things that he promises to do and what he wants to become (p. 133). I always imagine these lists as like Gilbert and Sullivan patter songs. Finally, he goes into the Thinkery

But the Clouds deliver a few prophecies. This is very important. The Clouds prophesy about the future of human behavior, which shows an understanding of human nature and also of the way society works. They know that what goes around comes around. Socrates doesn't.

Strepsiades says, "I don't want anything great. I just want to get out of my debts." And the chorus responds with the Delphic utterance, "Then you'll get what you yearn for since you have no desire for great things" (p. 134). That could mean that he'll get small things, but it could also mean bad things. All oracles utter such purposely ambiguous statements.

Then the Clouds say, "I think you're going to need blows" (p. 135). You're going to need a little bit of beating to get this into your head. Of course, that foreshadows what happens to him later at the hands of his son.

Finally, there's a last little bit of slapstick. As Strepsiades goes to the Thinkery, he acts like he's going down into the underworld. So, he takes off his cloak because you enter the underworld stripped. He says, "Put a honey cake in my hand" and they go down into the cave.

This is a *katabasis*, the descent into the underworld which is an image that you get in the beginning of Plato's *Republic*. *Katabasis* literally means just "going down." In the context of the Greek, it refers to stories of descent into the underworld, and so the Thinkery is a kind of underworld, which brings to mind how it's described at the very beginning. It's a Thinkery of wise souls, the shades, the souls of the dead—or the barely living.

Strepsiades goes into the Thinkery, then the first choral interlude takes place. During the interlude, an indeterminate stretch of time passes, during which Strepsiades is being educated. When the choral interlude ends, Socrates and Strepsiades emerge from the Thinkery. Then we see what Strepsiades has learned.

STREPSIADES FLUNKS OUT

It hasn't gone well. First Socrates bursts out of the Thinkery swearing an oath: "By Respiration, by Chaos, by the Air." The usual places of gods in his oath are occupied by three natural forces. Socrates then rants about a particularly bad student who is "rustic . . . resourceless . . . dull . . . and forgetful." Then he calls this student to come out. And out comes Strepsiades.

Socrates then quizzes Strepsiades on what he has learned. He begins with a rather academic issue, poetic meters, which the practical-minded Strepsiades mistakes for ways to measure grain. Strepsiades has no patience for such matters, because all he wants to learn is "The most Unjust Speech," i.e., sophistry. But Socrates insists that there are all sorts of theoretical prerequisites before one can learn the Unjust Speech.

Then Socrates wishes to talk about the gender of words. Language is the paradigm of "convention," but languages slowly evolve over time and are filled with inconsistencies. Socrates, being a rationalist, wants to make language more logical. But poor Strepsiades does not want to quibble and hair-split about words. He asks in exasperation, "Why am I learning things that we all know?" (p. 144). Socrates says, "For nothing, by Zeus!" This is the theorist's contempt for practical concerns. We're learning this for nothing. That's what's so good about it.

Finally, Socrates forces Strepsiades to crawl under his flea-ridden blanket and come up with a thought, or he's going to be booted out of the Thinkery. The first thing Strepsiades comes up with is how to get out of his lawsuit. He says, "I have an idea. I'll hire a witch to charm the moon out of the sky by capturing its reflection in a mirror, and then I'll put it in a little feathered box. Then the lunar months won't change, so I won't owe the interest on my loan" (p. 146). Socrates thinks that's pretty good. It's not great, but it's an attempt.

But the next thing Strepsiades comes up with is really quite good. He says, "How about when they write out an indictment of me, I take a glass lens and stand a little way off and reflect the sun and burn the indictment off the book." Socrates thinks that's a great idea! It's applied science, science applied to mischief. This encapsulates the whole thesis of the *Clouds* about the relationship of natural philosophy and sophistry.

The connection between the investigation of nature and the collapse of morality is the death of Zeus. Only when Socrates shows that we don't need the gods to explain nature does Strepsiades feels completely comfortable behaving badly. Science causes morality to collapse by undermining religious sanctions for moral behavior.

The third thing Strepsiades comes up with, however, is quite shocking, and it leads to his immediate expulsion from the

Thinkery. Socrates asks, 'What if you get indicted? What will you do next?' And Strepsiades says that he'll run away and hang himself. That way they can't bring him to trial. It would work, of course, but it seems self-defeating.

Why is this argument the last straw for Socrates? After all the stupidity he's endured with Strepsiades, you'd think that this wouldn't be any worse. But for some reason, the idea of not preserving one's life seems especially offensive to Socrates. Socrates seems to put a premium on self-preservation.

That's very different from the Socrates you get in Plato, who doesn't put a premium on self-preservation but on doing the right thing. The idea of giving up one's life for anything seems entirely irrational for Socrates in the *Clouds*. Apparently, he values nothing more than his own skin.

THE DEBATE BETWEEN THE JUST & UNJUST SPEECHES

Once Strepsiades has been expelled, he turns to the Clouds for help. The lead Cloud, who speaks for Aristophanes, advises Strepsiades that the only way out of his ruin now is to send his son to the Thinkery. The Clouds also tell Socrates that he had better take advantage of his good fortune right away, because "somehow such things are wont to turn in another direction" (p. 148). The Clouds, in short, are displaying both knowledge of and concern for human affairs.

This is out of character as far as Socrates and other natural philosophers were concerned. They did not believe in the gods of the city, and the natural forces they deified are non-human and unconcerned with human affairs. At best, they are mere gods of the philosophers. At worst, they are an attempt to hoodwink the public. But in neither case would such gods behave as they do here.

Thus, Aristophanes is putting forth a new conception of natural philosophy, which seeks to understand human nature as well, and not just desires, which even the sophists appealed to, but the realm of human affairs that the sophists and natural philosophers classified as ever-mutable conventions.

Pheidippides is finally forced to go into the Thinkery to learn how to make the weaker speech the stronger. But before he goes into the Thinkery, Socrates says, "I'm not going to tell him myself which of the speeches [the Just or the Unjust] is the best. I'll let the speeches teach him." Socrates claims that he is not teaching anything. The arguments themselves are doing the teaching.

Then actors personifying the Just and the Unjust Speech come out of the Thinkery and have a debate.

The Just Speech says:

> I will speak then of the ancient education as it was established when I was flourishing, speaking the just things and when moderation was believed in. First, it is needful that no one hear a boy muttering a sound. Next, that those from the same neighborhood walk on the streets here in good order to the cithara teachers lightly clad in a group even if the snow came down like barley meal. Next again, he used to teach them to sing a song by heart standing with their thighs apart. "Pallas, terrible sacker of cities" or "A far-reaching shout," pitched to the harmony that their fathers handed down. If anyone was ribald or added any modulation of the sort they use nowadays . . . he would be thrashed and beaten with many blows as one who had effaced the muses. (p. 154)

So, children are to be seen and not heard. They're to learn patriotic songs. They're to march around in little formations lightly clad so they won't get soft and effeminate. If they try to change the songs handed down from the past, they'll be thrashed for effacing the muses. It sounds like boot camp. This is the old-fashioned education, and it's supposed to produce the virtues the Greeks prized: moderation, courage, piety, and so forth.

> It was needful for the boys to keep their thighs covered while sitting at the gymnastics trainer's so as to show nothing cruel to those outside. Next again, when they've stood up they had to smooth the sand back again and be mindful not to leave behind an image of puberty for their lovers. (pp. 154–55)

The Just Speech has a fascination with the genitalia of pubescent boys. He's fascinated with the ancient Greek institution of pederasty. He's a little more fascinated by it than might seem appropriate.

> At that time, no boy would anoint himself below the navel so that dew and down bloomed on their private parts like fruit. Nor would he make up a soft voice and go to his lover, he himself pandering himself with his eyes. Nor was it allowed to him at dinner to help himself to the radishes, nor to snatch dill or parsley from his elders, nor to eat relishes, nor to giggle, nor to cross his legs. (p. 155)

The Unjust Speech simply mocks the Just Speech as old-fashioned and silly. The Unjust Speech has a sense of progress, that things are getting better and better, whereas the Just Speech has a sense that things are getting worse to the extent that we depart from the old ways. So, the Unjust Speech makes fun of things that are old-fashioned throughout.

The Just Speech says, "Yes, but these are the things from my education which nurtured the men who fought at Marathon," Athens' "Greatest Generation" who beat the Persians. 'We might have been square, but we were very tough back then.' The Just Speech then accuses the Unjust Speech: "But you teach them how to bundle themselves up in their cloaks right away. So then I'm ready to choke whenever someone at the Panathenaea who ought to be dancing holds his shield in front of his haunch . . ."

The point is that today the youth are soft. They're bundled up in their cloaks so they won't catch the sniffles. They don't know the proper warrior dances.

And so the Just Speech says finally to Pheidippides, "In view of these things, lad, be bold and choose me, the stronger speech. You'll have knowledge of how to hate the marketplace and keep away from the baths and to be ashamed at shameful things and to be inflamed if anyone mocks you." An aristocratic disdain for commerce and a strong sense of honor are parts of the old-fashioned education.

"And to stand up from your seat for your elders when they

approach." Old-fashioned respect.

> And not to misbehave towards your own parents and not to do anything shameful that would tarnish the statue of awe. And not to dart into a dancing girl's house lest you be broken off from your good fame by being hit with a fruit by a whore for gaping at the things there. And not to talk back to your father at all and not maliciously to remind him, by calling him Iapetus at his age, when he nourished you as a nestling.

Sexual continence and family values.

Of course, the Unjust Speech says, 'You'll be a goody two-shoes. People will think you're just a baby.'

And then, in a passage that is beautiful in some ways as well as funny, the Just Speech says:

> Yes, but you'll pass your time in the gymnasium, sleek and flourishing, not mouthing prickly perversities in the marketplace like they do nowadays. And you won't be dragged into court over a greedy, contradicting, shystering, petty affair. Rather you'll go down to the academy and run under the sacred olive trees with the moderate youth of your own age. You'll be crowned with a wreath of white leaves smelling of yew and of leisure and of the white poplar shedding its leaves and in the season of spring delight whenever the plane tree whispers to the elm. But to do these things that I tell you and pay mind to them you will always have a sleek chest, bright complexion, large shoulders, slender tongue, large buttocks, small penis.

This brings us to a strange notion. The Greeks left us statues of mature men with large buttocks and tiny penises. This was considered the height of attractiveness.

The Just Speech continues: "If you pursue what we do nowadays, first you will have a pale complexion, small shoulders, narrow chest, big tongue, small buttocks, big haunch, long decree." Then he says if you listen to the Unjust Speech you'll end up with bad pederasty. He condemns pederasty, but it's apparent he's fascinated with it at the same time.

Now let's examine the Unjust Speech. When the two speeches first come out the Just Speech begins by insulting the audience. He calls them mindless and corrupt, whereas the Unjust Speech flatters them and says, 'No, they're wise.'

Now let's look at the Unjust Speech's refutation of the Just speech. First, he says that he won't let you wash in warm water because that makes people soft. The Just Speech says, 'In our days, the men took cold baths. And yet, who is the toughest of them all? Isn't it Heracles? Well, the Greeks called hot springs the "baths of Heracles." You've never seen a cold bath of Heracles, have you? No? Well, there you are then. If Heracles is the toughest of all, and he took warm baths, then who are you to say that cold baths are necessary to build good character?' That's the first refutation.

It's very important to note that the Unjust Speech asserts that he wants the Just Speech to go first. This is because he can't make a speech on his own. He has to wait until the Just Speech speaks and then he picks holes in what the Just Speech says. He's parasitic on what the Just Speech says.

The next argument is this: the Just Speech says that you shouldn't hang around the marketplace. That's a bad thing to do. But if you look at Homer, isn't Nestor, the wisest of the Greeks, an orator, a man of the public place, the marketplace? Yes? Well, there you go then.

Then the next argument is this. It's against the idea of being moderate. The Unjust Speech says moderate men don't flourish. Nice guys finish last. Villains get ahead. Moderation also denies one pleasure. The sophists were hedonists. Their great appeal was to offer a life of pleasure. "Would they deprive you of boys, women, *kottabos* [a drinking game], relishes, drinking, boisterous laughter? But what is living worth if you are deprived of all these things?"

"Well then, from here I go on to the necessities of nature." Here we have this notion of necessity. "What if, through the necessities of nature, you have sex with a married woman and you're caught? What do you say to the husband? Well, if you listen to me, you'll say, 'Didn't Zeus get bested in love? Who are you to be any better than Zeus?'" The Unjust Speech appeals to the example of the gods, but the Greek gods are notorious for doing bad things.

The last thing the Unjust Speech deals with is the issue of buggery. To the ancient Greeks, passive anal homosexual intercourse was considered to be dishonorable. Yet, of course, it happened all the time. On the one hand, it was strictly a bad thing. But on the other hand, it was a very common bad thing.

The Just Speech has condemned buggery, thus the Unjust Speech responds, 'Where do all the politicians come from?' The buggered. 'What about all the tragedians?' Well, they were buggered too. 'What about the public advocates?' They were buggered. Then he says, 'What about the audience here?' And you can imagine the Just Speech looking out into the audience and saying, 'Well, he was. And he was. And he was!' Of course, everyone's laughing. 'They're all buggered! You debauchees!' Then he takes off his cloak and deserts to the other side. He's been bested.

THE WEAKNESSES OF THE JUST SPEECH

Aristophanes is basically on the side of the Just Speech. Yet, at the same time, he recognizes that the Just Speech has weaknesses, which cause him to lose to the Unjust Speech. By analyzing those weaknesses, we can construct a stronger defense of Athenian tradition.

First of all, the Just Speech doesn't know the art of rhetoric, the art of persuasion. Persuasion is an art, which means it is morally neutral. You can persuade people of good things as well as of bad things. So, it's foolish to allow scoundrels to practice rhetoric but not learn rhetoric oneself to fight them. The Just Speech doesn't know rhetoric because he begins by insulting his audience, whereas the Unjust Speech begins by flattering them, which is a clear sign of superior rhetorical skill.

Second, the Just Speech doesn't know how to defend what you could call natural inequality and natural authority. This comes out very clearly in relationship to the gods. Heracles takes warm baths, so why can't we? That's the question. Well, one could answer by simply saying Heracles was the offspring of a god, and you're not. So, maybe Heracles doesn't need to take as many pains to make himself tough as a mere mortal does. We're not on equal ground with Heracles. He's better than us. There's a natural inequality that exists there, and therefore we can't expect to act in the same way.

The same point goes for when he appeals to the example of Zeus. Yes, Zeus is a notorious philanderer. But Zeus is a god, and we are not. Hera is the goddess of the family, yet she also cheats on her husband just as the husband cheats on her. Zeus is the patron of the patriarchal family, yet he's also an adulterer which undermines the family. So, why shouldn't we all be adulterers too? Well, because Zeus is a god, and we're not.

The Unjust Speech basically says we should do as the gods do, not as the gods say. The gods don't practice marital fidelity, but they tell us that we should. Since we're not on equal terms with them, it's possible for them not to practice what they preach. Only if you're on equal terms with somebody is it right to object to their hypocrisy.

When you're a kid, and your parents say they want you to go to bed at nine o'clock, and you say, 'But *you* don't go to bed at nine o'clock!' The proper response is, 'I'm older than you, and I know what's in your interests, and that's that. So, you go to bed at nine o'clock. It's not equal between us.'

There's a natural authority that parents have over children or gods have over mortals. This authority is based on natural inequality. Parents are wiser than children, and gods are wiser than mortals. But the Just Speech doesn't have any way of defending that, and so as soon as these inequalities are pointed out, he just gives up. That's a deep flaw.

Aristophanes is pointing out that inequality is a lesson we need to learn from nature. Because of inequality, specifically the inequalities of wisdom but also the inequalities of age, there are inequalities of proper behavior. You can never treat your parents as equals, and they can never see you as equals. That's just the way things are. Even if you're much wiser or smarter or better educated, they always see you as a kid. There's an inequality there that can't be erased.

The third weakness is related to the second, which is that the Just Speech appeals to myth and to the poets to back up his education. Yet, the Greek myths were extremely bad sources of moral examples. Now, of course, you could say we are supposed to do as the gods say but not as they do. But still, it would be better to have better myths, better gods, gods that you could actually look up to, which the Greeks certainly couldn't do. So, the attempt to found morality on the Greek gods is a very foolish undertaking in Aristophanes' view.

The fourth weakness of the Just Speech is that he cannot tolerate human failure. This is highlighted by the whole issue of buggery. On the one hand, the Just Speech wants to maintain certain standards of sexual morality. He holds that certain things are dishonorable or shameful. Yet, as soon as he's confronted with the fact that people don't live up to his standards, his reaction is simply to abandon his standards.

Yet if you maintain high moral standards, it is inevitable that, given human nature, people are going to fail to meet them. Thus, one of the costs of maintaining high moral standards is having to be somewhat tolerant of human failings. Because if you have very high ideals, and you can't accept that people will fail to meet them, you will be forced to abandon your ideals.

The Just Speech has no tolerance for the fact that there is a gap between real and ideal human behavior, and, since he can't bring real behavior up to the ideal, he abandons the ideal and gives in to what is real. He lowers his standards because he can't abide any difference between what's ideal and what's real.

The fifth problem is that there is no room for pleasure in the Just Speech's worldview. The Just Speech waxes poetic about the old-fashioned virtues, but he doesn't try to show that old fashioned virtues have their pleasures too. He just says that if you don't comply, you'll be thrashed. But is there anything in virtuous behavior for me, besides just avoiding a thrashing? Pleasure is a powerful motivation. If virtue brings no pleasure, then pleasure becomes a powerful ally of vice.

If these five weaknesses cause the Just Speech to fail, then by correcting these weaknesses, we can offer a much more powerful defense of Athenian tradition. This defense is characterized by a knowledge of rhetoric, which puts it perilously close to sophistry, especially in the eyes of the undiscerning. It also appeals to nature, including pleasure, to guide human action, as opposed to appealing to the gods. This too is dangerous, because to the undiscerning it looks like natural philosophy.

THE CONCLUSION OF THE *CLOUDS*

When Strepsiades sends Pheidippides into the Thinkery, he tells Socrates to be sure to sharpen both sides of his son's jaw and both sides of his tongue. Of course, a two-edged sword is dangerous to whomever wields it, as Strepsiades soon discovers.

When Pheidippides comes out of the Thinkery, Strepsiades throws him a graduation party. They get into an argument about poetry, specifically about Euripides. The son wants to sing a song from Euripides on incest, and the father thinks that's shocking. Words are exchanged, then blows, and poor Strepsiades is beaten by his son. He rushes outdoors and asks for his neighbors to bear witness to this affront, not even thinking that he has undermined his neighbors' willingness to stand by his side by his willingness to cheat them. He's starting to realize that what goes around, comes around.

Then Pheidippides argues that it is right to beat his father: 'Isn't it right for the wise to beat the foolish?' 'Yes.' 'Well, I am wiser than you are, so I need to beat you for your own good.' The only inequality that Pheidippides can recognize is the inequality of wisdom. He doesn't recognize that there's an inequality built into the relationship of parents and children that has nothing to do with wisdom. Even if your parents are foolish, you owe them respect. But that's completely evaporated from poor Pheidippides. He has no respect for his father whatsoever. He only has respect for Socrates. Socrates truly has corrupted this youth.

But then Pheidippides proposes beating his mother as well. That really sends Strepsiades over the edge. Why? It could simply be love. It could also be chivalry. But the fact that the son wanted to sing a song about incest might have suggested to Strepsiades that this is what he really had in mind. But even though it is not exactly clear what taboo Pheidippides has violated, he has gone too far. Strepsiades refuses to hear anymore. We discover that the Tongue has power only as long as people are willing to listen.

First, Strepsiades turns to the Clouds and reproaches them for recommending that he send Pheidippides to the Thinkery. The Clouds respond that Strepsiades himself is responsible, because he wanted to cheat his creditors. When Strepsiades reproaches them for not warning him, the Clouds reply "We do this on each occasion to whomever we recognize as a lover of villainous affairs, until we throw him into evil so that he may know dread of the gods" (p. 174). The Clouds, in short, are teaching Strepsiades a moral lesson. Ultimately, they are on the side of the ancestral gods and moral goodness. Contrary to the natural philosophers, nature is not on the side of atheism. Contrary to the sophists, nature is not on the side of immorality.

Then Strepsiades tries to enlist Pheidippides in taking revenge against Socrates. Pheidippides, however, refuses to do "injustice" to his teachers. Leaving aside that this is actually a question of justice, it seems that in the Thinkery, there is at least some sort of "honor among thieves."

Strepsiades then exhorts Pheidippides "Have awe before ancestral Zeus!" Zeus is the god not only of the law courts, but also of the patriarchal family. Strepsiades suddenly realizes that the Zeus he had to overthrow in order to cheat on his debts is the Zeus he needs to preserve his family.

Pheidippides asks if there really is a Zeus. Strepsiades responds "There is!" What he really means is, 'There *must* be.' Zeus must exist, because the utility of Zeus is now apparent to him. Zeus is an important prop of the moral order. He must exist if the family and justice are to be preserved. To which Pheidippides replies, "Vortex is king, having driven out Zeus." Either he's mocking his father's stupidity by repeating his words, or Pheidippides doesn't really understand Socrates' teachings either.

Strepsiades then addresses the god Hermes for advice. He is probably speaking to a Herm, a block statue depicting the head and genitals of the god Hermes that typically stood outside of houses to ward off bad fortune. Strepsiades' Herm was probably set up to guard his family. Stepsiades imagines that Hermes tells him to burn the Thinkery to the ground, which he and his slaves immediately do, forcing Socrates and his students to flee for their lives. The end.

We're going to find many allusions to the *Clouds* throughout Plato's dialogues. So, the larger meaning of the *Clouds* will become clearer as we read Plato.

I will argue that the *Clouds* taught Socrates the necessity of turning away from studying non-human nature back towards understanding human things. Socrates was looking for wisdom by looking to nature, but he ended up a fool because he was searching for wisdom in the wrong kind of nature. He was searching for wisdom in non-human nature, in very large and very small things, and ignoring the human world. It's only by looking at human nature that you will learn what's right by nature, which will allow you to become a good judge of character and to regulate your actions prudently rather than foolishly.

The *Clouds* is the first work of what we call Socratic philosophy. But it's not Socratic. It's Aristophanean. The Socratic turn away from non-human nature towards human things and the turn away from theory-centered philosophy to moral-centered philosophy is already in the *Clouds*. This gave a very powerful impetus to Socrates to turn from being a pre-Socratic philosopher to a Socratic philosopher, or what I would call an Aristophanean philosopher. It's a turn towards what we can call a humanistic rather than a scientific approach to philosophizing.

Socrates attacks Aristophanes in the *Apology*, but what's most extraordinary about the Platonic dialogues are the open and silent tributes to Aristophanes that appear everywhere. Aristophanes was really the great teacher of both Socrates and Plato and the first philosopher of their type in Western history.

APPENDIX
Class Discussion About the *Clouds*

The next session of the class, which focused on Plato's *Theages*, began with a discussion of the *Clouds*.

GREG JOHNSON: Here's an interesting question: in the *Clouds*, Aristophanes shows how the earlier natural philosophers brought about the collapse of morality and society and therefore paved the way for the sophists. They brought about the collapse of morality by undermining religion. Zeus hurls thunderbolts at perjurers, and you'd never be a sophist if you really believed that Zeus would smite you dead with a thunderbolt. But once science relieved Strepsiades of fear of the gods, the way was clear for him to be a scoundrel, and it led to his corruption and the corruption of his son. So, science undermines morality by undermining religion.

But Aristophanes believes that there is a right and a wrong according to nature. Aristophanes could turn away from traditional religion and traditional morality without becoming a nihilist, because he believed that nature could teach morals. But when you look at the behavior of the Clouds, which personify this kind of wisdom according to nature, they take great pains to recognize, or at least pay lip service to, the gods of the city. But why do they need to recognize the gods of the city if one can appeal to nature to teach morals? What's the necessity of preserving the gods if you have an appeal to nature?

STUDENT: Would it be so you wouldn't be banished?

GJ: Well, that would be an external reason. You don't want to get your fellow citizens angry at you, so you go around paying lip service to their beliefs. But is there another reason besides that?

STUDENT: I don't think that the Clouds are that unlike the Olympian gods, since the Clouds trick Strepsiades and Socrates into doing wrong, and then they are punished.

GJ: And that's not unlike the Olympian gods who are constantly playing tricks on mortals and getting them to be hubristic and then punishing them.

If you look at the contest of the Just and Unjust Speech, one reason the Just Speech fails is his dependence upon the gods in order to back up his moral teachings. That shows that Aristophanes thinks appealing to the gods, at least in some cases, undermines morality. So, that would give even more force to the question. If Aristophanes regards the gods as such bad moral examples, why not dispense with them altogether? Why not toss them out and go directly to nature?

At the end of the play, Strepsiades embraces the gods of the city again. He embraces Zeus and Hermes, both in their roles as protectors of the family. But if Aristophanes could give a non-religious argument for respecting the traditional family, why appeal to Zeus and Hermes? All you'd need to do is teach Strepsiades and Pheidippides what is right by nature. Then you could dispense with the gods.

Let's just pretend that instead of Strepsiades and Pheidippides going to Socrates' Thinkery, they went into Aristophanes' Thinkery instead. And Aristophanes said, 'Look guys, Zeus doesn't exist, and vortex isn't king either, but you should pay your debts, and you should honor your father and mother and be a good guy because . . .' Couldn't you convince them? Couldn't you give them a good, solid, knock-down, iron-clad philosophical proof that certain things are right by nature?

STUDENT: Anarchy emerges. The son beats the father, and he's going to beat the mother. You have complete chaos.

GJ: But wouldn't that be the case only if the conventions were ignored and ridiculed but nothing else was put in their place?

Why is Aristophanes loath to completely substitute nature for the gods? Why wouldn't Aristophanes, if he were alive today, basically say, 'One of the purposes of public education should be to strip away all of people's religious superstitions and teach them the right way of living, which can be justified by a rational appeal to human nature'?

STUDENT: Religion is natural to man too.

GJ: So, you're saying that one of the things natural to us is having religious illusions? Not every religion can be true. So, even if you're a partisan of the truth of one, if you take it seriously, you must regard all the others as illusory, and you have to come up with some kind of explanation for why people are so prone to these illusions. It seems to be natural.

But still, lots of these illusions give rise to attitudes like slavery or widow-burning. Wouldn't you just want to get rid of those things? Sweep them away? Teach the Hindus and Muslims to respect women? Wouldn't that be a good thing?

Why would Aristophanes draw back from this conclusion? He seems to draw back from it.

STUDENT: He sees disbelief as corruptive of society.

GJ: But the old corrupters are amoral, and he's a kind of moralist. So, why not replace religious morals not with self-seeking and hedonism but with intelligent, rational morals? Wouldn't that be a great step forward in human civilization? What's to prevent that? What's to prevent us from progressing from religious superstition and an ethics based on religious taboos to a morality based on a rational understanding of nature?

STUDENT: Religion gives some people power over others.

GJ: Well, I think that would clearly be part of it, but I don't think Aristophanes is one of these people trying to hold power for himself.

STUDENT: You're going to tell us, right?

GJ: Well, I just want to see what comes up.

Let me raise this question: Can you imagine Strepsiades learning what's right by nature? Have you ever seen Strepsiades to be capable of learning anything by nature?

STUDENT: No. After being in the company of Socrates for a period of time, he learned nothing.

GJ: It's impossible for Strepsiades to have a non-theistic understanding of nature. As soon as he hears about the vortex, he just thinks that's Zeus' son who's overthrown him. And Pheidippides is apparently in the same boat.

Socrates is unaware of human nature and specifically the different types of men. There are some types who can never know what exists by nature or what's right or wrong by nature. And, therefore, if you ask how they know what's right or wrong, they learn it through religion.

However, the play also makes it clear that religions are fickle allies of morality. Put it this way: I think the average American who believes in Christianity is morally better than he would be if he didn't believe in anything. However, if he became too enthusiastic about the Bible, chances are he would be worse than a non-believer. This is one of the dangers. There's a lot of evil in the Bible: 'Go out and kill the Canaanites to the last man.' 'Well, okay. We have to go out and find the Canaanites and kill them!'

I know a professor who's a very Orthodox Jew, who claimed to follow all the laws. A friend of mine who was studying with him asked, 'Well, what about killing all the Canaanites? What if new neighbors moved in next door and you were to go over to give them a house-warming gift and discover Canaanite literature on their coffee table? What would you do?' He was appalled to face this question. He didn't know what he would do. In truth, he's better than his religion, because he wasn't an enthusiast. He was only following the good precepts, not the bad ones.

The capacity to distinguish between the good and bad precepts of religion presupposes, does it not, some sense of right and wrong over above what the religion tells you?

STUDENT: Convention is natural. If you are a student of human nature, you have to acknowledge convention.

GJ: You would have to acknowledge that they're natural, but you don't necessarily have to acknowledge that they're all good. One of the things that's very clear about the *Clouds*, again, is the recognition that the gods are just as much a source of morality as they are a source of corruption. One way the gods lead to moral corruption is the idea that you should do as the gods do, rather than do as the gods say. Zeus says, 'Honor your father.' Zeus himself overthrew his father. Zeus came from a pathological, dysfunctional family, yet he's the god of the family order. That works fine as long as you recognize that you're supposed to do as Zeus tells you but not do as Zeus does.

The way the Unjust Speech undermines the traditional moral teachings is to ask, 'Why not do what Zeus does? Wouldn't piety be doing as Zeus does? Zeus philanders, so you should too. And if you're caught in the act, you just jump up and say, "Who are you to go against the ways of Zeus?"' There's a recognition that religion is both an extremely powerful way of teaching morals to those who simply couldn't be guided by reason. Yet, at the same time, there's a recognition that religions themselves are somewhat ambiguous in their moral teachings and therefore they have to be carefully managed.

You could manage them and pick and choose among their moral teachings only if you already knew what's good or bad on the basis of nature.

STUDENT: Couldn't it be an obstacle also? Say you're taking a newborn baby and going through the stages of development. If the religion was there, wouldn't you be preoccupied teaching the child the precepts of the religion versus starting them off by teaching them this moral standard according to nature, this objective good?

GJ: But *can* you teach babies what's right according to reason and nature? Wouldn't you have to wait until they attain the "age of reason"? Freud deals with this issue in *The Future of an Illusion*. It's not in his own voice, but in the voice of his critic, whose criticisms are so powerful that Freud eventually changed his mind. In this book, the critic says to Freud, 'How can society afford to give up on the use of religion as a moral teacher and replace it with reason, given that reason does not fully develop until after a person's puberty? Would we be able to delay moral teachings until after puberty?' No. That would be an absolute disaster.

I believe Thomas Sowell said that every new generation of

children is an invasion of barbarians. Children come into the world amoral, selfish, and wicked. They torment bugs. They torment cats. They torment one another. Barbarians lack social skills, social graces, and a sense of right and wrong. The task of education is to civilize the barbarians before they overwhelm us.

If children are left to their own devices, they tend to be impulsive, egocentric, and driven by their feelings. They never learn to strategically suppress their desires, to think long-term about desire satisfaction. They become solipsistic and anti-social. You can't depend on them. They have a tenuous sense of obligation to others. These sorts of patterns are seen in under-socialized or under-parented kids. That is a concern if you're only going to educate your kids about right and wrong when they are 16 or 17. You're going to have uneducable kids, because they'll grow up impulsive and ruled by their desires.

STUDENT: Why can't you teach that to them secularly? Why does it have to be shrouded in religious convention? You don't walk out in front of the car. You can teach that secularly . . .

GJ: You can convince a person that those are good things, intellectually speaking, but unless they're taught that by habituation very early on it doesn't really stick, and that's a terrible problem. This is why inhibiting a child's impulsiveness early on is very good for him, because it gives him a very solid grounding of habit. Then later on he can understand why these are good habits to have, why it's good to be dependable or punctual. But if he has never gotten into the habit of being punctual, then even if you can teach him rationally why punctuality is a good thing later on it's still not going to be the kind of thing that sticks with him and can become the basis of a habit.

STUDENT: Aren't you giving religion a free ride? Religion can be used by tyrants.

GJ: But listen, we've looked at both sides of this issue. We've seen how religion can make you worse or better than the average untutored person. Now, let's look at the good side of it for the moral education of children. Of course, it can warp them and ruin them if it's done badly. So, again, it's got to be carefully managed. But there's a sense in which something like religious education seems indispensable for having a purchase on the minds of young kids.

For instance, most religions teach morals in the form of stories. Now, if you don't use parables from the Bible, you can at least teach them other moral parables, because these things can be grasped. Children don't need a general appreciation of the principles behind them. That can come later. But they need concrete, vivid illustrations of right and wrong behaviors and different consequences. Aesop's fables are great for this.

Religious education is ultimately education in the form of narratives, myths. And there are many other myths besides just religious narratives. Any human being, even with an IQ of 70, can follow simple stories. Narratives have an amazing capacity to cut across the divisions that exist between people in terms of intelligence and aptitude.

Now, the stories have to be carefully managed, and if you look at Plato's *Republic*, we learn about the myths that have to be gotten rid of, because they're bad examples.

STUDENT: You don't have to lie . . .

GJ: Has anybody here ever told his child the story of the fox and the grapes? Is that story true?

STUDENT: Of course not!

GJ: Then you lied! You lied to your child! Shame on you!
But Plato talks about the *noble* lie. False stories are not necessarily lies or invidious in a moral sense. You tell kids stories that are false all the time.

'Where do babies come from?'

What's crucially important to understand is that there's a teaching about the relationship of morality and religion implied in the *Clouds*. We will see the same ideas when we look at Plato's *Euthyphro*.

Plato's *Theages*

The *Theages* is a short Platonic dialogue that can be read as a response to Aristophanes' *Clouds*. In both texts, Socrates is approached by a country gentleman to educate his son. In the *Clouds*, the father is insistent, the son reluctant. In the *Theages*, it is just the reverse. In the *Clouds*, Socrates takes on the student and corrupts him. In the *Theages*, however, Socrates refuses to take on the student for fear of corrupting him. Like the *Clouds*, the *Theages* is a comedy, and as in the *Clouds*, by the end of the *Theages*, Socrates ends up the butt of the joke, despite his best efforts.

The subtitle of *Theages* is *On Wisdom*. Theages, for whom the dialogue is named, wants Socrates to teach him wisdom. But the wisdom Theages seeks is not the wisdom philosophers pursue. Indeed, philosophy is never mentioned here at all. Nature is never mentioned at all. The soul is never mentioned.

Aristophanes ultimately derives his wisdom from understanding human nature, and not just the nature of the body (even the sophists knew the body) but the nature of the soul and the kind of care it requires. This is also the foundation of Socratic philosophy. Ultimately, Socrates is all about the nature and care of the soul. Yet the soul is never mentioned here.

Socrates would never have a conversation about philosophy without mentioning nature or the soul. So, the *Theages* is not a philosophical discussion. Instead, it is a non-philosophical discussion between a philosopher, Socrates, and two non-philosophers: Demodocus and his son Theages.

The *Theages* displays how Socratic philosophers deal with non-philosophers. As we will see, the Socrates of the *Theages* keeps his philosophy close to his chest, unlike the Socrates of the *Clouds*, who all too readily shares philosophy with two non-philosophers, Strepsiades and Pheidippides, with amusing though ultimately disastrous consequences for all involved.

Who Was Theages?

Theages was an actual historical person who is mentioned

elsewhere in the Platonic writings. Theages is mentioned in Book Six of the *Republic*. Socrates is talking about the kinds of people who might be seduced away from the study of philosophy by politics, and how they might resist: ". . . some might be held back by the bridle that restrains our friend Theages—for he's in every way qualified to be tempted away from philosophy, but his physical illness restrains him by keeping him out of politics."[1] Socrates then immediately mentions what kept Socrates himself out of politics, namely his *daimonion*, which also plays an important role in the *Theages*.

Socrates knows Theages well enough to call him a friend. Although Theages is interested in philosophy, Socrates does not think he is drawn to philosophy by his very nature. In fact, Socrates thinks Theages is by nature more drawn to politics than philosophy. You can say that he has a political rather than a philosophical temperament, character, or soul. This is consistent with the Theages of this dialogue.

What keeps Theages from politics is his body. He's too sickly. But his sickly constitution does not prevent him from talking about philosophy. In fact, it predisposes him to intellectual pursuits. Theages, in short, sounds like the worst possible candidate for studying philosophy. He is not drawn to it by his soul but pushed toward it by his body.

The dramatic date of the *Republic* is 411 BCE, and the dramatic date of *Theages* is 409 BCE, two years later. If the Theages of this dialogue is the same one in the *Republic*, Socrates already knows him and has a pretty good idea that he is not a philosophical type. But in the dialogue, Socrates asks Demodocus, the father of Theages, to introduce his son. Does this imply that Socrates does not already know Theages? Or does it merely imply that Socrates wishes to conceal the fact that he already knows Theages from his father?

Theages was apparently dead by 399 BCE, because Socrates mentions that he is dead in Plato's *Apology*. Perhaps his illness killed him.

---

[1] Plato, *Republic*, trans. G. M. A. Grube, in Plato, *Complete Works*, ed. John M. Cooper (Indianapolis: Hackett, 1997), 496b, p. 1118

Theages' father Demodocus is a country gentleman. He's also wealthy and politically prominent. He might well be the general Demodocus mentioned by Thucydides in Book 4 of *The Peloponnesian War*. Socrates treats him with respect and deference.

A Chance Encounter

Socrates is apparently out and about, and Demodocus and Theages run into him by chance. Demodocus says, "Socrates, I have been needing to talk to you in private about some matters, if you have leisure, and even if you don't and your business is not very important, make some time for my sake."[2] This is important because it reveals that Demodocus doesn't know that Socrates *never* has any business, that he doesn't do anything practical, and he's always at leisure.

Socrates says, "Why, I happen to be at leisure in any case and, indeed, for your sake, very much so. If you wish to speak about something, you may."

Demodocus asks Socrates if he'd like to speak in private. We know that Socrates did speak in private, and of course in the *Clouds*, Socrates teaches in the privacy of the Thinkery. But Plato and Xenophon tried to dispel Socrates' shady reputation by emphasizing that he usually conversed in public. Demodocus suggests they go to the *stoa* or portico of Zeus the Liberator. The *stoa*, however, was a public place. It is also a shelter dedicated to a god, which is also in stark contrast to the Thinkery, where Socrates proclaims that Zeus doesn't even exist. The *stoa* is also an appropriate place for a non-philosophical conversation. And as we shall see, Socrates makes both reference to and use of the divine and quasi-divine throughout this conversation.

The *stoa* of Zeus the Liberator was erected in honor of Zeus' help in delivering the Athenians from the Persians. This hearkens back to the previous generation who fought off the Persians. They had been supplanted by this time by Pericles and other demagogues who had transformed Athens from a tough-

---

[2] Plato, *Theages*, trans. Thomas L. Pangle, in *The Roots of Political Philosophy: Ten Forgotten Socratic Dialogues*, ed. Thomas L. Pangle (Ithaca: Cornell University Press, 1987).

minded, independent little city-state into an empire. These two generations represent two different forms of life: Athens the old republic, small, self-contained, more concerned with its independence than anything else, versus the imperial Athens sprawling all over the Mediterranean, constantly grasping for new conquests and new taxes that eventually overstepped itself and was destroyed in the Peloponnesian War, which came to an end in 404 BCE, only five years after the date of this dialogue.

A QUESTION OF EDUCATION

It's clear that Demodocus is a farmer, and his understanding of how things grow is based on farming. He's trying to deal with how his son will grow—i.e., how his son has to be educated—and he's quite disturbed because his son keeps talking about wanting to become wise.

Demodocus says:

> Socrates, all living things tend to follow the same course—particularly man, but also the other animals and the plants that grow in the earth. It's an easy thing, for us farmers, to prepare the ground for planting, and the planting is easy too. But after the plants come up, there's a great deal of hard and difficult work in tending to them. It seems the same goes for people, if others have the same problems I've had. I found the planting or procreation—whatever you're supposed to call it—of this son of mine the easiest thing in the world. But his upbringing has been difficult, and I've always been anxious about him. (121 b-c, Smith)[3]

Demodocus is like the natural philosophers. He has an understanding of non-human nature from tending it, and he wants to apply his knowledge to the tending of human beings, namely his son. This is creating conflict, because his son does not want to be tended like a plant or livestock. He has distinctly human needs that are chafing against his father's tutelage. There's a conflict between father and son. The son, it seems, wants to become

---

[3] Plato, *Theages*, trans. Nicholas D. Smith, in Plato, *Complete Works*.

wise. So finally, the father has been led to the city to seek out a teacher for Theages, and he has come across Socrates.

Maybe Demodocus intended to come across Socrates. We don't know. As we have seen, Demodocus doesn't know Socrates well. But he certainly knows something about Socrates. Specifically, as we will see, Demodocus thinks Socrates is a sophist, or something in that camp.

Demodocus continues: "There are many things I could mention, but his current passion really scares me—not that it's beneath him, but it *is* dangerous. Here we have him, Socrates, saying that he wants to become wise" (121d, Smith).

Theages wants to become wise, yet the dialogue keeps philosophy (true philosophy) hidden. We have to understand Theages' idea of wisdom in that light. Theages wants wisdom understood in a popular way, not as Socrates understands it. As it turns out, Theages wants wisdom as understood by the sophists, who claim to make people wise in the ways of politics and persuasion.

Demodocus goes on:

> What I think is that some other boys from his district who go into town have got him all worked up by telling him about certain discussions they've heard. He envies them, and he's been pestering me for a long time—he's demanding that I take his ambition seriously, and pay money to some expert who'll make him wise. The money is actually the least of my concerns, but I think what he's up to is very risky. (121d, Smith)

If the account in the *Republic* is correct, Theages is already known to Socrates, although his father is unaware of this. This is analogous to the *Clouds*. Strepsiades doesn't even know who Socrates is, but Pheidippides knows his name. So, in both texts, the son is more urbane than the rustic father. Because his friends spend time in the city, Theages has learned of intellectual discussions and what they promise. Thus he wants to take part.

Demodocus is willing to grant that pursuing wisdom is somewhat noble. But he thinks it is also a very dangerous thing.

On this point he agrees with Strepsiades too. Strepsiades knows very little about the Thinkery, but he knows that it will teach him how do to wrong. Strepsiades, however, *wants* to do wrong, whereas Demodocus wants to avoid it and keep his son safe as well.

Demodocus says that money is no object. He apparently has a lot of money, and he's willing to spend it lavishly on his son. This also sounds like Strepsiades. Demodocus opposed Theages for a long time, but he's finally giving in, which is a sign of being an indulgent father. Of course, many indulgent parents tell themselves the story that Demodocus tells: "For a while I held him back with reassurances. But since I can't hold him back any longer, I think I'd better give in to him, so that he won't get corrupted, as he might by associating with someone behind my back" (122a, Smith). If you can't beat them, join them.

Demodocus continues:

> So, now I've come for this very purpose: to place this boy with one of those who are reputed to be "sophists." You have, therefore, shown up at a fine moment for us — you whom I would especially like to take counsel with when I am actually going to do something about such matters. (122a, Pangle)

Socrates replies, "Well, you know, Demodocus, they say that advice is a sacred thing, and if it is ever sacred, then it surely is in this case" (122b, Smith). Here Socrates appeals to the sacred. Socrates always appeals to the divine when talking with ordinary folks. This is a pattern that you find in the Platonic dialogues. He's speaking in the public language.

Socrates continues: "There's nothing more divine for a man to take advice about than the education of himself and his family" (122b, Smith). Here, Socrates is making claims about things he knows. Those who believe Socrates claims not to know anything, please take note. Why is education so sacred? Because education cultivates the soul, and that's the most important thing you can do.

DEFINING ONE'S TERMS

Socrates begins by defining the terms of discussion:

> First, then, let's settle what you and I intend to discuss. I might perhaps be taking it to be one thing, and you another, and then, after we'd discussed it a while, we'd both feel silly because I, the one giving advice, and you, the one taking advice, would be thinking about entirely different matters. (122c, Smith)

We don't want to seem too comic, in other words. Remember that in the *Clouds*, some of the funniest exchanges between Socrates and Strepsiades are based on equivocations. They think they're talking about the same thing, but they're really not. 'Let's talk about meters.' 'Yes, I haven't had any barley today. I'd like ten meters, please.' Socrates is taking some precautions to ensure that this old farmer knows exactly what they're talking about, so they don't misunderstand one another and become comical as in the *Clouds*.

Then Socrates urges another precaution: ". . . it occurs to me that this youth may desire not this thing that we suppose he desires but something else. And then again, we'd be even more absurd taking counsel about something else." So, not only do Socrates and Demodocus need to understand one another, they also need to understand what Theages wants. They can't just presume it. They'd better ask. Thus begins Socrates' discussion with Theages.

The name Theages can mean either "revering god" or "envying god." This is an interesting ambiguity. It's the very same ambiguity that you see in the battle between the Just and the Unjust Speech, because the Just Speech says we should revere the gods and the Unjust Speech says if you revere them you should act like them, which is to envy them. The Just Speech says, 'Do as the gods say.' This is piety. The Unjust Speech says, 'Do as the gods do.' This is blasphemy, but it can cloak itself in piety. The gods are bad, however, so imitating them is a path to moral corruption.

Of course, Theages is a historical figure. Plato did not coin his name. Thus this parallel to the *Clouds* may be a mere coincidence. Or maybe Theages' name inspired Plato to construct a response to the *Clouds* around Theages and his father.

WHAT IS WISDOM?

Since Theages wishes to become wise, Socrates asks him about the nature of wisdom, hence the subtitle of the dialogue: "Which do you call wise? The ones who *know* concerning the matter, whatever it may be, about which there are knowers, or the ones who *don't*?"

In other words, are wise people knowers or not knowers? Good question.

"The ones who are knowers," says Theages.

And Socrates replies, "What then, didn't your father teach and educate you on the things in which the other sons of gentlemanly farmers here are educated such as letters, cithara playing, wrestling and other kinds of contests?" Note that these are the same things that the Just Speech includes in his description of the education of young gentlemen.

> THEAGES: Yes, he has.
> SOCRATES: Do you still suppose, then, that you are lacking in some knowledge which it is fitting that your father look to on your behalf?
> THEAGES: I do.
> SOCRATES: What is this? Tell us so that we may gratify you.
> THEAGES: *He* [Demodocus] knows, Socrates, because I've often told him. But he says these things to you on purpose as if he didn't know what I desire. With other talk of this kind he battles against me and isn't willing to place me with anyone! (123a–b, Pangle)

The son is chafing at the father again. Theages thinks his father is playing dumb as a delaying tactic. Pretending not to know, of course, is a form of irony. But if people suspect you of it, it makes them angry. Irony, if undetected, protects you. Irony, if detected, actually endangers you. Socrates discovered this much to his chagrin, as indicated in Plato's *Apology*.

Socrates: "But the things you said to him before were said, as it were, without witnesses. Now, however, make me your witness and in my presence declare what this wisdom is that you desire." This is a pregnant passage. First of all, the talk of witnesses obviously alludes to Socrates' later trial. Second, things said with and without witnesses obviously correspond to public and private forms of conversation. Socrates had a bad reputation in Athens for being ironic, which means keeping his opinions to himself and a select circle of friends. Here, however, Socrates champions public discourse in front of witnesses. The apologetic intent is clear.

Then Socrates asks Theages if he wants the kind of wisdom that people who pilot ships have (steersmen, navigators). Theages says no. That's the piloting art, not the kind of wisdom he wants. But what about the art of the charioteer? Is this the kind of wisdom that he wants? Again, no.

Socrates is identifying wisdom with a kind of art, a kind of knowledge. This is highly questionable. In fact, Socrates is highly critical of just this idea. But Socrates is testing Theages. He wants to see if Theages is the kind of student he wants to take on, which is something that is conspicuously absent with the Socrates of the *Clouds*. All Strepsiades had to do was say, 'I'm here to be a student,' and he was accepted. There was no test. Whereas Socrates is testing a prospective student here, and he's asking him which kind of knowledge is wisdom.

So what's the right answer? Based on other Platonic dialogues, there's a fundamental difference of kind between wisdom and the sorts of skills and knowledge that Socrates mentions here. So Socrates is intentionally assuming a false premise. "What kind of knowledge is the wisdom you seek?"

The right answer is something like this: Wisdom isn't really knowledge, because wisdom is the ability to make *right* use of things, including knowledge. Knowledge isn't really wisdom because you can use knowledge foolishly. All Socrates' examples of knowledge (piloting, charioteering, medicine, music, gymnastic), can be used foolishly, and therefore they can't be wisdom. To be used well, they need wisdom to be added to them, which means that they're not wisdom.

But isn't wisdom some sort of knowledge, some sort of know-how? The Socratic-Platonic concept of wisdom is "the ability to make right use of all things." Isn't that a kind of knowledge, a kind of art? Fair enough. But one must clearly grasp that there is a difference in kind between wisdom and ordinary examples of knowledge or know-how. With ordinary knowledge, you can always ask: Is this knowledge used wisely? Ordinary knowledge needs the supplement of wisdom to steer it to good ends.

But you can't ask if wisdom is wise. So wisdom not only governs everything else according to the good, it also governs itself. Wisdom is necessarily and unconditionally good, whereas everything else is good only on condition of being used wisely. Now, if you want to call wisdom a kind of knowledge, for instance "knowledge of how to make right use of all things," this is fine as long as you understand that wisdom is different in kind from every other form of knowledge. All forms of knowledge require wisdom to direct them to the good, but wisdom is unfailingly good, thus it needs no supplementation. If wisdom is knowledge, it is no ordinary knowledge.

In the *Theages*, wisdom and ignorance are being opposed to one another. And wisdom and knowledge are being identified. But that's really not the way to look at it, because wisdom is not equal to knowledge. The clearest way to appreciate this fact is to ask: What's the opposite of wisdom? Foolishness. Folly. And the opposite of knowledge is ignorance. So, even if you're not sure if wisdom and knowledge are the same thing, the difference becomes clear if you ask if folly and ignorance are the same thing. Are ignorant people fools? Are foolish people ignorant? Not necessarily. It's possible to be very knowledgeable and still be a fool. For instance, Socrates in the *Clouds*.

It is also possible to have a certain amount of wisdom and still be ignorant. Interestingly enough, in the *Clouds*, Strepsiades actually shows more wisdom than Socrates. Remember when Strepsiades leaves the Thinkery after being expelled. He goes to Pheidippides and tries to get him to go into the Thinkery in his place. Then Strepsiades swears Pheidippides to secrecy before informing him that Zeus doesn't exist. Strepsiades realizes that

Zeus' nonexistence could have terrible consequences if widely known. So he's not going to just tell it to just anybody. He's not going to tell Pheidippides unless he promises not to blab it around. Old Strepsiades may be dumb; he may be ignorant; but he's no fool.

So ignorance and wisdom can go together, just as folly and knowledge can go together. So wisdom is not equivalent to knowledge, and folly is not equivalent to ignorance. But in the *Theages*, the underlying assumption is that wisdom and knowledge are the same and that folly and ignorance are the same. Socrates, of course, knows better than this. But he's trying to see if Theages can grasp the difference.

This is how Socrates teaches throughout the Platonic dialogues. Plato teaches by indirection. His philosophy is not explicitly stated in any of the dialogues. He says this in his *Seventh Letter*. If that's the case, why read his dialogues if he does not present his philosophy there? Because the teaching isn't *stated*, but it is *implied*, and it's implied in this way. A problem is set up in the dialogue that begs for a certain kind of solution, and if you figure out what that solution is, that's Plato's answer. So, Plato forces you to find out what his teachings are. They're never stated directly, but they can be inferred if you find the solutions to the problems he sets forth.

THE BRUSH-OFF

Poor Theages is going to be running around this little exercise wheel a bit. But at a certain point, Socrates does the strangest thing. He tries to get rid of Theages. He has evidently decided that Theages is not a suitable student. But Theages won't go, so this Platonic response to the *Clouds* still ends on a comic note at the expense of poor Socrates.

Let's go back into the text. Socrates asks Theages if wisdom is equivalent to several arts: piloting, charioteering, medicine, music, and gymnastic. Theages says he doesn't want to learn any of these arts. Finally, at 124a, he makes clear the kind of wisdom he wants to learn, and it is an art: *the art that rules those in the city*, not the art that rules the sick or the art that rules the exercising or the art that rules singers and choruses, but the art that rules *all* people in cities. That's what he wants.

At this point, Socrates says, 'that would be a kind of controlling or ruling art. So, would you like to be a farmer, because farmers rule the threshers and the reapers and the harvesters and the sowers?' But Theages says that he doesn't want to be a farmer. If he did, he'd just stay down on the farm.

So Socrates asks about the art that rules "sawyers and borers and planers and turners," namely the carpenter's art? Theages doesn't want to do that either.

Then Socrates suggests that he wants to learn the art, "by which we have knowledge how to rule *all* these arts, as well as the farmers and the carpenters and all the public craftsmen and private non-craftsmen both women and men? Perhaps this is the wisdom you're seeking!" (124b, Smith). What he's asking is, 'Do you want a *comprehensive* art? The art that rules all the other arts.'

Now defining wisdom as a comprehensive art still presumes that wisdom is a kind of knowledge or know-how. Wisdom is a kind of comprehensive technical knowledge that rules the other arts. It puts all the arts in their place. But this comprehensive art still isn't wisdom, because we can imagine it being used for bad ends.

Still, though, this definition is getting closer to Plato's authentic idea of wisdom. For Plato, wisdom is the capacity to make right use of all things. It has two aspects: *right use* and *all things*. It's not wisdom if it doesn't have rightness or comprehensiveness. At least Theages grasps that wisdom is comprehensive. But there's no mention of the good here, and that's also crucial. Because to be truly wise in Plato's sense, you have to make *right* use of all things.

Tyranny & Wisdom

Then Socrates goes on the offensive. He gives a list of tyrants: Aegisthus, Peleus, Periander, Archelaus, and Hippias. These tyrants used the art of tyranny to rule over the other arts of the city.

Socrates: When someone wants to rule over all the peo-

ple in the city together, doesn't he want the same sort of rule as these people had—tyranny, and to be a tyrant?
THEAGES: Apparently.
SOCRATES: Isn't this what you claim to desire?
THEAGES: It seems so, from what was said.
SOCRATES: You rascal! So you want to be a tyrant over us . . . (124e, Smith)

Theages somewhat reluctantly agrees with Socrates here, and with good reason, for this argument is shameless sophistry. Theages has arrived at the idea that wisdom is a comprehensive art that rules over the other arts of the city. Socrates has established, at best, that tyranny is *one example* of a comprehensive art that rules over the other arts of the city. But he has *not* established that it is the *only* such art. Thus, he is wrong to accuse Theages of desiring to be a tyrant.

At this point, Socrates asks Demodocus if he is not ashamed of his unwillingness to send Theages to a school for tyrants. But if it is shameful to want to become a tyrant, then surely there is no shame in resisting Theages' desires. Then, using the language of the law courts, Socrates asks Demodocus to "deliberate about whom we should send him to and by means of whose company he might become a wise tyrant" (125a, Smith).

But here Socrates sneaks in something crucial. If wisdom and tyranny are the same thing, then it would be repetitive to talk about a "wise tyrant." But if it's meaningful to talk about a wise tyrant, that implies that you can have foolish tyrants as well. And if you can have a foolish tyrant, then being a tyrant is not equivalent to being wise. There's a distinction between wisdom and tyranny that's being sneaked in here.

Then Socrates quotes Euripides: "Tyrants are wise through keeping company with the wise" (125b, Pangle). So, tyrants are not wise in and of themselves, but wise derivatively by keeping company with wise people. Who are the wise? Sophists or philosophers.

Then the question is: *In what* are these people wise?
Socrates illustrates with a series of craft analogies.
Farmers are wise by keeping company with the wise. Wise in

what? Of course, wise in farming. A farmer becomes wise by keeping company with somebody who is already wise in the art of farming.

The next example is cooks becoming wise by keeping company with the wise. Who are these wise people? People who are already wise in the ways of cookery.

Then Socrates talks about wrestlers. Wrestlers become wise by associating with the wise, namely those who know the art of wrestling.

Then he asks Theages: If tyrants become wise by associating with the wise, what sort of wisdom do they have? What is the "tyrannic art"?

But Theages thinks that Socrates is just mocking him. After all, Theages is there so Socrates can *tell him* what the tyrannic art is. But Socrates, of course, does not teach by putting information into people, but by trying to draw it out of them.

But Socrates is being deadly serious and presses on: "Didn't you assert that you desire this wisdom by which you might rule over all citizens? If you did thus, would you be anything other than a tyrant?" (125e, Pangle). At this point, Theages pushes back against Socrates.

Theages says, "For my part, I would pray, I suppose, to become tyrant—preferably over all human beings and, if not, over as many as possible, and so would you, I suppose, and all the other human beings—or moreover, probably rather to become a god" (125e–126a, Pangle).

This seems like a rather shocking admission. But we have to be very careful here. Theages is saying that *everyone*, even Socrates, would probably want to be a tyrant, or even a god. This, he thinks, is common opinion, to which he will pay lip service ("pray"). But, he says, "This is not what I said I desire." Theages is willing to stand *against* what he sees as the popular desire to be a tyrant.

Theages would indeed like to rule over the city. "But not by violence, the way tyrants do. I want to rule over those who voluntarily submit. This is the way other people—men of good repute in the city—rule over other people" (126a, Smith). If wisdom is the ability to make right use of all things, then Theages' conception of wisdom is far closer to true wisdom than the tyrannic art. For tyranny is a comprehensive technical skill exercised without concern for what is right. But Theages wishes to acquire a comprehensive art of rule that is consistent with "good repute." Now having a reputation for goodness is not necessarily the same thing as being good. But Theages is still concerned with goodness, which makes him much better than a tyrant.

Theages wants to be a democratic statesman, a demagogue which means "leader of the people." Socrates gives the examples of Themistocles, Pericles, and Cimon. These were the leaders of the popular party in Athens that created Athens' great empire and eventually led it to ruin. Is this the kind of man Theages wants to become? "Yes, by Zeus, *that's* what I mean!" is Theages' reply (126a, Smith).

At this point, it is clear to Socrates that Theages isn't a bad lad. Nor is he stupid. But neither is he a philosopher. He simply wants to go into politics, and he has mistaken Socrates for a someone who can teach him political science and rhetoric.

How to be a Demagogue

Then Socrates asks Theages if, just as horsemen learn the horseman's art from other horsemen, doesn't he believe that a would-be demagogue should learn the demagogic art from other demagogues? "Or," Socrates adds, "do you believe you'll become wise in what these men do by associating with other people and not with the politicians themselves?" (126c, Smith). These other people, of course, are the sophists, who are paid teachers of political science and rhetoric, which is what Democdocus and Theages think Socrates is.

But then the conversation takes a comic turn, and as in the *Clouds*, Socrates is the butt of the joke. Theages says:

> I've heard, Socrates, about the arguments they say you offer, that the sons of the politicians are no better than the sons of the shoemakers. And I believe that what you said is really true, from what I've been able to see. So I'd be foolish if I thought that one of these men would give his wisdom to me, but wouldn't be of any help to his own

son, if indeed he could have been helpful to anyone else in these matters. (126d, Smith)

Socrates really has offered this very argument, for instance one finds it in Plato's *Alcibiades* I, the *Meno*, and the *Protagoras*. Socrates argued that the demagogues really don't have an art, because if they had an art, they would be able to teach it, and you'd think that they'd teach it to their own children first of all. Yet, the sons of Pericles and the rest turned out to be political ignoramuses. They didn't grow up learning how to be demagogues.

Apparently, this argument has gotten back to Theages. So Theages has caught Socrates contradicting himself. Socrates has been trapped by his own teaching, hoist by his own petard. Socrates isn't as clever as he thinks he is. Nor is Theages as dumb as Socrates takes him to be. This is a comic situation. Dry comedy, but comedy nonetheless.

Why is Socrates using an argument that he himself has rejected to persuade Theages to study with the demagogues? Obviously, because he doesn't want to take Theages on as a student.

When Theages catches Socrates in a contradiction, Socrates' response is as shameless as any sophist's. He simply ignores Theages' point and goes on the attack. He demands to know what Theages would do if he had a son who was pestering him to become a demagogue if he refused to study with the demagogues. But Socrates' demand presupposes the very assumption that Socrates himself has called into question, namely that the demagogues have an art that they can teach.

Socrates then suggests that if Theages does not want to study with the demagogues, he should take up with one of the gentlemen of Athens:

> ... we'll place you with any of the gentlemen in politics you want, of the Athenians at least, who'll associate with you without charge. You won't waste any money, and you'll also gain a much better reputation among the general public than if you associate with someone else. (127a, Smith)

The gentlemen are the older, non-demagogic faction in Athens, represented by Strepsiades and the Just Speech in the *Clouds*, by Demodocus in the *Theages*, and by Aristophanes' own political sympathies. They were conservative, elitist, antidemocratic, and anti-imperialist.

Socrates tries hard to sell Theages on the idea of studying with the gentlemen. First, Socrates says, they won't charge Theages for their teaching. Second, associating with them will bring Theages a better reputation, and it has already been established that reputation matters to Theages.

But Socrates remains silent on the most important question: If the demagogues can't teach the art of ruling to Theages, what makes Socrates think that the gentlemen can?

Theages' response to Socrates is again quite amusing. He says, "Well, then, Socrates—aren't *you* one of these gentlemen? If you'll agree to associate with me, that satisfies me, and I won't look for anyone else" (127a, Smith). Again, Theages has gotten the better of Socrates. After all, is Socrates going to deny that he is a gentleman?

CORRUPTING THE YOUTH

At this point Demodocus pipes up in support of Theages studying with Socrates:

> O Socrates, that's not a bad idea at all! And you would oblige me as well; for there's nothing I would consider a greater stroke of luck than if he were content to associate with you and you agreed to associate with him. Indeed, I'm even ashamed to say how much I want it! I beg you both: you—to agree to associate with this boy, and you—not to seek to associate with anyone other than Socrates. You'll thereby relieve me of a great load of worry. As it is now, I'm very afraid that he might fall in with some other person who'll corrupt him. (127b–c, Smith)

Socrates is shown as a corrupter of the youth in the *Clouds* and accused of corrupting the youth in his trial. But here's a father saying, 'Socrates, take on my son as your student because I don't want him to be corrupted.' The apologetic intention of this text is clear.

Theages is willing to study with Socrates, so Demodocus basically offers Socrates a blank check. But Socrates refuses his offer in a very diplomatic way, first heaping praise on Demodocus for wanting what's best for his son, then denying that he has the knowledge that Theages is seeking. Socrates says:

> ... if Theages here refuses to associate with the politicians and seeks some other men, who claim to be able to educate young people, there are a number of such men here: Prodicus of Ceos, and Gorgias of Leontini, and Polus of Acragas, and many others, who are so wise that they go from city to city and persuade the most aristocratic and wealthiest of the young men—who can associate with any of the citizens they want without charge—these men persuade them to desert the others and associate only with them instead, to pay a great deal of money up front, and, on top of that, to be grateful! It would be reasonable for your son and you to choose one of these men, but it wouldn't be reasonable to choose me. I know none of these magnificent and splendid subjects. I wish I did! (127e-128b, Smith)

Now, if Plato wanted to depict Socrates as a *really* nice guy, Socrates would have said, "Sure! Come aboard!" But, of course, Socrates *doesn't*. In fact, Socrates suggests that Theages would be better off studying with the sophists, the real corrupters of the youth. Which, in a way, does make Socrates a corrupter of the youth, albeit not by teaching but by his refusal to teach. Socrates doesn't seek to benefit everybody with whom he comes into contact. He keeps himself to himself.

EROS & THE DAIMONION

Interestingly, Socrates claims that the sophists have genuine knowledge which he himself lacks: "I know none of these magnificent and splendid subjects. I wish I did!" These subjects are political science and rhetoric. But Socrates does not deny knowledge altogether. He continues:

> I am always saying, indeed, that I know virtually nothing, except a certain small subject—love [the Greek is *ta erotika*, the erotic things], although on this subject, I'm thought to be amazing, better than anyone else, past or present. (128b, Smith)

This is what Socrates knows. He knows the erotic things. Now, Socrates is not boasting of sexual prowess. In Plato, *eros* is essential to understanding the nature of the soul. Thus knowledge of erotic things means knowledge of the soul. Socrates never explicitly mentions the soul in the *Theages*, but when he does talk about the soul, he uses this term *eros*.

Theages responds:

> Do you see, father, Socrates is, in my opinion, still not at all willing to spend some time with me since, for my part, I am ready if you are willing, but he says these things to us in jest. [He just treats this as a joke.] Because I know boys of my age and a little older who before they kept company with him were of no account, but since they started to frequent this man in a very brief time became manifestly superior to all those to whom they were previously inferior. (128b-c, Smith)

Then Socrates says, "Do you know, then, *what sort of thing this is*, child of Demodocus?"

Theages: "I do, by Zeus! That if you wish, I too shall become like those."

Socrates says, "No, good fellow, but it has escaped your notice *what sort of thing this is*. I shall explain it to you."

Again we have the phrase "what sort of thing this is." What's going on here? What does "this" refer to?

Theages thinks "this" refers to how people are improved by associating with Socrates. But that's not what Socrates meant, so he says, "No, good fellow, but it has escaped your notice what sort of thing this is." Socrates is clearly referring back to the previous topic, namely his knowledge of erotic things. Then Socrates tells us what his knowledge of erotic things is:

> I shall explain to you. For there is something demonic which, by divine dispensation has followed upon me beginning from childhood. [I don't think it begins from childhood, but let's put that aside for now.] This is a voice which, when it comes, always signals me to turn away from what I am going to do, but never urges on, and if one of my friends consults with me and the voice comes it's the same. It turns away and will not allow the action. To those things I will furnish you witnesses. (128d, Pangle)

Then Socrates talks about a number of people who have failed to heed his divine sign and have come to ruin. Basically, what he's saying is this: 'Theages, my divine sign has said not to take you on as a student, and I dare not disobey it, lest something terrible happen.'

This divine sign is Socrates' famous *daimonion*. A *daimonion* is a little *daimon*, and a *daimon* is a half-divine, half-mortal being that exists between the realms of gods and mortals. Socrates' *daimonion* is his guardian angel, if you will. Eros, if you read Plato's *Symposium*, is treated as a *daimon*, as something between the mortal and divine. Think of the classic images of Eros or Cupid as a winged baby with a bow and arrow, conveying the gifts of Aphrodite to mortals.

So what sort of thing is knowledge of erotics? How is it a *daimonion*, a divine guardian? Notice that Socrates is not identifying the *daimonion* with *eros* itself, but with *knowledge* of erotic things. Socrates's *daimonion* is his personification of his *knowledge* of the soul. Socrates never speaks openly of the soul here, as he does in the *Republic*. The *Republic* is a philosophical conversation, but the *Theages* is not. The *Theages* is a conversation with two non-philosophers, with a reject from the Thinkery and his father. So Socrates only speaks of the soul indirectly, under the guise of the *daimonion*.

The *daimonion* is not just a personification of psychological knowledge, but also of moral knowledge, of knowledge of right and wrong. What's good is what perfects the human soul; what's bad is what corrupts it. To know the nature of the soul, and the forces that move it, and what perfects it and what corrupts it, is to know the difference between right and wrong. That is moral knowledge.

How is Socrates' *daimonion* a *guardian* angel? Socrates' knowledge of the soul and morality allow him to make prudent decisions regarding himself and others. In the *Theages*, we see Socrates trying to rebuff a would-be student based on the judgment of the *daimonion*. Socrates thinks that Theages isn't suited for philosophy, that philosophy would corrupt him. Being a corrupter of the youth would be bad for Socrates too — bad intrinsically, no doubt, and also bad if his fellow citizens wished to take revenge.

Is knowledge of right and wrong innate in human beings? I would say yes and no. It's clearly innate if you understand it as a capacity that we can all develop. But it's not innate as something that's actualized. Because there are many people who don't know it. So, the issue is this: Theages does have this capacity to know the difference between right and wrong. Everybody does.

However, Socrates' refusal to consort with Theages is not based on the assumption that Theages can't know the difference between right and wrong, but simply that philosophizing is not going to help him make that distinction, that he's not the kind of person who can sharpen his moral insight by trying to discover the nature of the soul and what's right by nature. That's the substance of his judgment here.

Socrates' *daimonion* is a kind of sixth sense about human character. Knowledge of erotic things is knowledge of the soul. But the soul can take on many different forms. There are many different types of human beings. Socrates' capacity to act rightly, to act prudently, is based on his capacity to discern the different types of human beings and deal with them appropriately: to fit his speeches and deeds to the person with whom he is dealing. This is exactly what he's doing.

Why doesn't Socrates want Theages to become his own student? Because he thinks that Theages would probably be corrupted. So, in a sense, by refusing to take on this student, Socrates is refusing to corrupt him. The father is wrong to think that Socrates couldn't corrupt him. Socrates knows he can corrupt the youth. He knows that philosophy can corrupt the youth. He could make Theages a worse person by teaching him philosophy, but he chooses not to and sends him on his way. He realizes that even a sophist couldn't corrupt Theages as much as philosophy could. Of course, I think his preference clearly would be for Theages to study with the gentlemen, to be like his father. He doesn't linger too long on trying to persuade Theages to follow the demagogues.

The way Socrates talks about the *daimonion* in this dialogue is very interesting, and it gives a sense of his understanding of Theages. Theages is from the country, and it turns out that he is rather superstitious, so Socrates speaks of the *daimonion* as if he were telling ghost stories. "Those who followed it turned out well, but those who refused to listen to it came to ruin." He lays it on thick.

Theages' response is again very amusing. At the very end of the dialogue, after Socrates goes through a long story about all the people who have benefited or been harmed by listening to or not listening to his *daimonion*, Theages responds:

> To me, Socrates, it seems that we should do this: Make trial of this daimonic thing by keeping company with one another, and if it permits us this will be best. But if not, then at that time we shall immediately deliberate on what we ought to do. Whether we shall keep company with someone else or whether we will try to placate the divine thing that comes to you with prayers and sacrifices in whatever ways the diviners proscribe. (131a, Pangle)

Theages is a little bulldog. He's not going to let go of Socrates. He says to Socrates, 'Okay, Socrates, this is serious. But look, there are ways of managing these *daimonic* things. We'll test to see if I make any progress, and if I'm not then we'll try to placate it through magic.' He's very serious about this.

And Demodocus says, "Don't oppose the lad any longer in these matters, Socrates, for what Theages says is well spoken."

Socrates says, "But if it seems that that's the way it has to be done, then that's the way we'll do." That's the end of the dialogue.

Despite his best efforts, poor Socrates is not off the hook yet. He doesn't know what to do. He doesn't want Theages as a student. But he doesn't want hurt the poor lad's feelings, and his father's a fairly powerful man. He has to be diplomatic. But in the end, Socrates is just too nice and lets himself be bullied. We never know what the outcome of the story is. But it is genuinely funny.

THE *THEAGES* & THE *CLOUDS*

This dry little comedy is clearly a systematic response to a much bigger and juicier comedy, the *Clouds*. The *Clouds* presents Socrates as a corrupter of the youth, whereas in the *Theages*, Demodocus clearly thinks of Socrates as an alternative to the corrupters of the youth. In the *Clouds*, Socrates is shown teaching in the privacy of the Thinkery, which is a place of rank impiety, whereas in the *Theages*, he speaks in public under the stoa of Zeus the Liberator. Socrates also speaks piously of the gods of the city. When Socrates rejects Theages, he attributes his decision to the *daimonion*, presenting an act of discrimination as an act of piety. In the *Clouds*, Socrates is shown as reckless and undiscriminating in taking on students, but in the *Theages*, he is shown to be discriminating and diffident.

But the *Theages* also has a tragic dimension, for it shows how even an entirely innocent Socrates can end up framed as a corrupter of the youth. If Socrates speaks in public, naturally word will spread about his teachings and abilities. Naturally, students will present themselves. Socrates can do his best to choose only those students who will be helped by his teachings. But some unsuitable applicants, like Theages, won't take "no" for an answer. Thus Socrates can be strong-armed into taking students he doesn't want. In the *Theages*, Plato depicts Socrates as having noble intentions and taking serious precautions to make sure that philosophy does not go wrong. But, as we know, despite the best of intentions and efforts, ten years later, Socrates was on trial for his life.

In the *Theages*, Socrates says that the *daimonion* visited him from childhood on. I don't think that is true. If you look at the *Clouds*, there is no sign that Socrates has a *daimonion*, meaning a knowledge of human nature that allowed him to make prudent decisions. In the *Clouds* Socrates is naïve about human nature. He doesn't know the distinction between right and wrong. Thus, there was no voice that constrained him from corrupting Pheidippides.

The *Clouds* premiered in 423 BCE, and the *Theages* is set in 409 BCE, fourteen years after. I wish to argue that the *Theages* shows us what Socrates learned from Aristophanes. As we have seen, in the *Clouds*, Aristophanes presents a philosophical critique of pre-Socratic philosophy. Aristophanes' own philosophy is based on an understanding of human nature, which gives him natural standards of right and wrong. This is also a pretty accurate description of Socrates' own mature philosophy, which he personifies as the *daimonion*. Thus the Socrates of the *Clouds* has no *daimonion*, but the later Socrates does, precisely because of Aristophanes' philosophical influence on Socrates.

This is borne out by Plato's *Symposium*, which has a dramatic date of 416 BCE, about seven years after the *Clouds*. In the *Symposium*, Aristophanes and Socrates are depicted as good friends.

How could Socrates become friends with Aristophanes after the brutal parody of the *Clouds*? When someone makes a fool out of you, there are basically two ways you can respond: You can laugh at yourself or you can get angry. If you can laugh at yourself, that's a sign that you can take a certain distance from yourself, learn from your folly, and grow beyond it. In such a case, one can even come to be grateful to the person who made a fool of you. But if you're unable to laugh at yourself, then you are unable to be objective about yourself, which means that you have difficulty learning from your follies. Thus when somebody makes a fool out of you, naturally you are going to hate him.

In Plato's *Euthyphro*, the subject of our next chapter, Socrates speaks of his upcoming trial. He says that if the men who are trying him are able to laugh, the outcome is hopeful. But if they're not able to laugh, then the outcome is known only to the soothsayers. I suggest that Socrates is actually speaking about men who are willing or unwilling to laugh *at themselves*. Socrates makes fools out of people all the time in Plato's dialogues. If they are capable of laughing at themselves and rising above their folly, they can become Socrates' friends. But if they are unable to laugh at themselves, Socrates is going to make new enemies.

Not only did Aristophanes teach Socrates important philosophical truths, he also taught Plato how to write philosophy. Plato's dialogues are works of fiction. Many of them are plays. What kind of plays? Of the three ancient Greek dramatic genres — tragedies, comedies, and satyr plays — the Platonic dialogues are closest to comedies. Socrates even jokes around as he dies.[4]

Aristophanes taught Socrates wisdom by mocking him in a comic play, and Plato depicts Socrates making fools of his interlocutors in dialogue after dialogue. (The *Theages* is a major exception, for here Socrates ends up the fool.) For Socrates, confronting people with their folly is the beginning of wisdom. But nobody made a bigger fool of Socrates than Aristophanes, and nobody made him wiser.

---

[4] The neo-Platonist Olympiodorus the Younger (c. 495–570) claimed that after Plato's death, the plays of Aristophanes were discovered under his pillow. See Olympiodorus, *Commentary on the First Alcibiades of Plato*, ed. and trans. L. G. Westerink (Amsterdam: North-Holland Publishing Co., 1956), 2.66–72.

Plato's *Euthyphro*

The *Euthyphro* is one of eight Platonic dialogues set around the trial and death of Socrates. The *Euthyphro, Apology, Crito,* and *Phaedo* are the most famous. They are among Plato's most widely-read dialogues. Four other dialogues—the *Theaetetus, Sophist, Statesman,* and *Cratylus*—are also set in the days preceding Socrates' trial. These are among Plato's most difficult dialogues.

Euthyphro is important because not only is it part of the scene-setting for the trial and death of Socrates but also because, like so many of these other dialogues, it constitutes a response to Aristophanes' *Clouds*. All the Platonic dialogues we will read here respond to Aristophanes' *Clouds*. They don't entirely refute what the *Clouds* says about Socrates. But they at least indicate that there's more to Socrates than the Socrates of the *Clouds*.

Socrates underwent a philosophical development, and the Socrates of the *Clouds* is in some sense a true representation of Socrates at one time in his life. But the Platonic Socrates is also a true representation of Socrates at a later point in his life. The Platonic Socrates holds positions that are in many ways identical to the philosophical position of Aristophanes that you can tease out from between the lines of the *Clouds*. Socrates, when he becomes a mature thinker, is heavily influenced by Aristophanes.

The Background of the *Euthyphro*

What in the dramatic situation of *Euthyphro* reminds you of the *Clouds*? Father beating. Euthyphro is beating up on his poor old father by taking him to court.

Euthyphro's father caused the death of a man through neglect. The man who died was a hired laborer who had murdered a family servant or slave. And the father, the head of the household, had the criminal bound and thrown in a ditch, then sent somebody off to Athens to inquire about the proper course of action. But since he wasn't particularly concerned with the well-being of the murderer, the man died of neglect and exposure in the bottom of the ditch. The son, Euthyphro, was outraged that his father had brought about the death of this man and so decided to prosecute him for murder.

Now, this is an extraordinary act because in Ancient Greece, murder was not what we call a criminal offense. It was a civil offense, meaning that if you murdered somebody the state would not bring charges against you on behalf of the victim. The people who usually brought charges against a murderer were the family members of the victim. Of course, if the victim had no family, nobody would have cared about him, and you could quite easily get away with murder. Or if you murdered the whole family, you could quite easily get away with murder, because there would be nobody around to prosecute you.

This is a vestige of a pre-political kind of order that you find in places around the Mediterranean today: places like Albania, for instance, where the social units are little clans that are extremely rivalrous and fractious. Clan loyalty is the most important form of loyalty. They had very tenuous connections to anything larger than these extended families and groups. Therefore, if somebody kills a member of your group, it's up to the extended family to avenge them. This pre-political notion of right and wrong was embedded within the Athenian political system. They were not that far removed from that kind of clannish Mediterranean pre-political structure.

The prosecution by Euthyphro of his father is an especially odd thing because it violates the whole of what's considered the natural order of family life, which is that you take care of your own. If somebody in your family is murdered, then you prosecute. But if a member of your family murders somebody else, especially a stranger, and especially a stranger who murders somebody close to the family, then prosecuting him is a complete inversion of the proper order of things. It's proper to take care of one's own first and not proper to be concerned about some stranger before your own.

So, Euthyphro is doing something that seems wrong. And it's not just wrong in the moral sense. It's impious. Piety refers to, first and foremost, the respect that you owe the divine. But for the Greeks, the divine is at the root of historical traditions and institutions. The more ancient they were, the closer they were to the gods. Therefore, by extension, there was not only a piety towards the gods but piety towards any institution that was founded by the gods, including the family. Euthyphro, however, finds this ridiculous. Therefore, he's prosecuting his father for murder. Of course, this is analogous to father-beating.

SOCRATES INDICTED FOR IMPIETY

The dialogue begins with Euthyphro saying, "What is new, Socrates?" (2a). Which indicates that he knows Socrates already. Euthyphro knows a number of things about Socrates' character and reputation. First of all, he knows where he normally hangs out—at the Lyceum—and that he doesn't usually hang out where the dialogue is set, namely at the Porch of the King, a kind of covered walkway where the "king" or "*archon*," namely the official in Athens who presided over legal proceedings, held court.

Euthyphro says, 'Surely, you don't also happen to have some lawsuit before the king as I do, Socrates?' (2a). He has a sense that Socrates is not the kind of guy who would be involved in something political or legal. Again, it indicates that he has some knowledge of Socrates' character, at least some opinion about Socrates' character.

And Socrates says, "The Athenians don't call it a lawsuit, but an indictment" (2a). An indictment is something that's handed down by the state for crimes against the state. And piety, which for us is an entirely private issue, was for the Greeks a very public issue.

The state wouldn't prosecute you for murder, but they would prosecute you for being impious. Why? Because religion to the ancient Greeks was largely civil religion, meaning that religion was central to the city-state. A person who somehow undermined religion was considered a traitor. The gods were there to protect the city, and religious rituals were instituted to ensure the gods continued to protect the city. If you got in the way of that, it would be like getting in the way of any other government policy.

The Greeks were not necessarily concerned with your private *opinions* about the gods. Concern with the right opinion is called *orthodoxy*. "*Orthos*" means right, and "*doxa*" means opinion. But they were concerned with what is called *orthopraxy*: having the right practice. That meant you were considered a pious person if you took part in the publicly instituted rituals of the city.

Xenophon says that Socrates was extremely scrupulous about maintaining all the proper public respects due to the gods. Thus, he should not have been convictable of impiety. But Socrates is really being accused of bringing in new gods and undermining belief in the old gods, and this has to do with opinion. Because he's accused of bringing in new gods and undermining belief in the old gods, he's being accused of corrupting the youth.

Euthyphro says, 'It's an indictment? What are you saying? Someone, as is likely, has brought an indictment against you, Socrates, for I won't charge you with doing it against another' (2b). Again, he thinks he knows that Socrates would never do wrong to another person although he could be wronged by others. This, of course, is a Socratic principle that's defended in the *Gorgias*: that it's always better to suffer wrong than to do it.

Euthyphro also indicates that he knows all about Socrates' *daimonion* (3b). So, again, there's a general familiarity with Socrates.

Socrates explains why he's in trouble. A young fellow named Meletus has brought an indictment against him on the charges of impiety. Socrates says: ". . . he asserts that I am a maker of gods, and on this account—that I make novel gods and don't believe in the ancient ones—he had indicted me . . ." (3b).

The description of Meletus is fairly detailed and interesting (2b). He has long straight hair. He's not quite full-bearded. He has a hooked nose. All of these characteristics would be meaningful to the Greeks who had strong beliefs in physiognomy, which is the idea that you can read people's character from their appearances. A hooked nose was not considered noble, like a Roman nose. It was seen as a sign of a vexatious and nasty nature. Just think of birds of prey. Not quite full-bearded indicates that he is somewhat feminine in the view of the Greeks. Long hair was foppish. The overall picture is of a foppish, effeminate, vexatious, and false character.

But Socrates claims that what Meletus is accusing him of is no trivial matter. Socrates really does believe that you must carefully oversee the education of the young. He says:

> He [Meletus] alone of the politicians appears to me to begin correctly. For it is correct to take care of the young first so that they will be the best possible, just as a good farmer properly takes care of the young plants first and after this the others as well. (2d)

Here Socrates likens child-rearing to agriculture, which bring to mind Strepsiades in the *Clouds* and Demodocus in the *Theages*.

> And so, Meletus is perhaps first cleaning us out, corrupters of the young sprouts, as he asserts. Then, after this, it is clear that when he has taken care of the older ones, he will be the cause of the most and the greatest good things for the city. At least that is the likely outcome for someone beginning from such a beginning. (2d–3a)

Now, there's a little bit of sarcasm there. I don't think Socrates really believes that Meletus' intentions are all that good. But there is an indication that Socrates agrees in principle with the idea that you should be very concerned with the upbringing of the young, and you should clean out the corrupters. His real quarrel is not with cleaning out corrupters so much as the accusation that he himself is one of the corrupters of the youth.

This, again, is an indication that Socrates is willing to make knowledge claims about things like education. Here he's saying it is good to be concerned with rearing the young right from the very beginning. Every time you find a knowledge claim by Socrates, it has something to do with education or the nature of the soul. The connection, of course, is that education properly done is the cultivation and care of the soul. Socrates *knows* a lot when you actually look at the knowledge claims he makes, but they're always claims about the soul and its proper tendance.

In the *Theages*, Socrates says he's stupendously knowledgeable about erotic things and that, of course, refers to the soul. In the *Theages*, he identifies his *daimonion* with his knowledge of erotic things. So, the *daimonion* is a way of personifying Socrates' knowledge of the human soul.

Euthyphro thinks he knows immediately what Socrates means when he says he's been accused of being a corrupter of the youth or a maker of gods. "I understand, Socrates. It's because you assert that the *daimonion* comes to you on occasion. So, he has brought this indictment claiming that you are making innovations concerning the divine things" (3b). For the Greeks and the Romans, making innovations in political and religious matters is tantamount to treason. This is an indication of the incredibly conservative nature of all traditional societies.

EUTHYPHRO THE ENTHUSIAST

Euthyphro goes on and says, 'He's obviously going to slander you in court before the many' (3b). Then he says that he is in the same situation as Socrates:

> Whenever I say something in the Assembly concerning the divine things, predicting for them what will be, they laugh at me as if I were mad. And yet of the things I have foretold I have spoken nothing that is not true. Nevertheless, they envy us all who are of this sort. But one should not give any thought to them but should confront them. (3c)

Euthyphro claims also to have a power to predict the future and to know divine things. Euthyphro is what you would call a diviner. He's a soothsayer. He claims to be able to know the future. He also claims to know what the gods want.

In the *Cratylus*, which is one of the dialogues associated with the trial and death of Socrates, Euthyphro is mentioned too. He is described as an *enthusiast*. An enthusiast is a person who claims to know the divine. In eighteenth-century English, the term *enthusiasm* referred to claiming knowledge of divine things. A religious enthusiast claimed to know the will of God. So, Euthyphro is an enthusiast and a soothsayer. This is his profession and his claim to fame. He thinks it sets him apart from—and above—the rest of humanity (5a).

Before every important decision, the ancients would consult a soothsayer. They looked for omens and auspices in the flight of birds or the entrails of slaughtered animals to ensure they did the right thing at the right time.

But apparently Euthyphro wasn't taken very seriously as a diviner. Or maybe he predicted or recommended things that the Athenians did not want to hear.

Many of the people who appear in the Platonic dialogues are attested to in other historical sources. But we don't know of a historical Euthyphro outside of Plato, so he could be an entirely fictional character. The name "Euthyphron" means "straight thinker." There's something appropriate about that name. Although his arguments go in a circle, there's something clumsily straightforward and earnest about the way he thinks.

Euthyphro's piety is really the grossest form of impiety. How does he justify beating up his poor old father in court? Basically, he says, 'The gods do it':

> Human beings themselves believe that Zeus is the best and most just of the gods, at the same time that they agree that he bound his own father because he gulped down his sons without justice, and that the latter, in turn, castrated his own father because of other such things. (5e–6a).

In sum: because the gods beat their fathers, so should I. That's not piety in any conventional sense.

But, of course, Euthyphro claims to know what piety is better than the general public. Euthyphro claims to have knowledge of the gods. Not just an opinion or a likely story. He claims to know precisely what they want. His knowledge of the gods leads him to *imitate* the gods—not to do as they *say* but to do as they *do*. There's something vain and hubristic about Euthyphro.

Euthyphro is a straight thinker in the sense that he's not a very subtle thinker, so when he looks at what the gods do, he thinks 'I should do the same.' He doesn't grasp the subtlety that maybe the gods get to do things differently *because they're gods*. In that sense, Euthyphro is just as clueless as the Just Speech in the *Clouds*, who doesn't know how to defend piety toward the gods once it's pointed out that the gods do bad things.

LAUGHTER & WISDOM

Euthyphro says, 'Socrates, they're just envious of you. We should pay no heed to these people. We should just go confront them.' And Socrates responds:

> My dear Euthyphro, being laughed at is perhaps no matter. For in fact, the Athenians, as it seems to me, do not much care about someone whom they suppose to be clever, unless he is a skillful teacher of his own wisdom. But their spiritedness is aroused against anyone who they suppose makes others like himself, either from envy, as you say, or because of something else. (3c–d)

This "because of something else" is interesting. Socrates never says what it is, but what could it be? Yes, the Athenians might get angry at skillful teachers because of envy, but they might have other reasons as well. Envy is a shameful motive. Could the "something else" be more noble? For instance, the desire to preserve the youth from corrupters, a motive that Socrates regards as noble? Socrates is not as willing as Euthyphro to dismiss the motives of his accusers.

Euthyphro goes on, "That's why I do not at all desire to try out how they are disposed towards me in this regard" (3d). Euthyphro has counseled Socrates to be confrontational, but here he shows himself to be conflict averse. Euthyphro doesn't want to know what the masses think of him. He says that they laugh at him, but he doesn't want to know what they would do, if he really annoyed them, which means that although he does show up to the assembly occasionally, he apparently doesn't do it very often. He's not very eager to try their patience. Euthyphro is prudent about this.

Socrates says, "Perhaps *you* seem to make yourself available only infrequently and not to be willing to teach your own wisdom" (3d). They're not mad at Euthyphro, because he doesn't show up very often.

> But I fear that *I*, because of my philanthropy, seem to them to say profusely whatever I possess to every man, not only

without pay, but even paying with pleasure if anyone is
willing to listen to me. (3d)

Socrates had a reputation for always being in public and saying
whatever he thinks. Of course, the fact that Socrates seemed very
candid could be deceptive. Socrates could, of course, be prudently silent about a lot of things.

Socrates continues:

So if, as I was saying just now, they were going to laugh at
me as you say they do at you, it would not be unpleasant
to pass the time in the law court joking and laughing. But
if they are going to be serious, then how this is going to
turn out is unclear except to you diviners. (3d–e)

So, Socrates is confirming here that Euthyphro sees himself as a diviner.

This is a really pregnant passage. When Socrates goes on trial, he plans to do what he's been doing for years. He's going to make fools out of his accusers. There are two reactions you can have when somebody makes a fool out of you.

First, if you can laugh at yourself, which means that you can see your own folly. It is a sign that you can take a step back from yourself, see yourself as you are, and get beyond the humiliation. You can understand and improve yourself that way. I think that is what happened with Socrates and Aristophanes. Aristophanes made a fool out of Socrates in the *Clouds*. But Socrates could laugh at his own folly. Because of that, he could get beyond it and become wiser.

In Plato's *Symposium*, which takes place eight years after the premier of the *Clouds*, Socrates and Aristophanes are shown as friends. That shows that Socrates is capable of befriending someone who made a fool of him. Why? Probably because he was indebted to him in some sense.

If you are behaving foolishly, and someone brings that to your attention, that is a good thing, because folly is bad, thus you want to be rid of it as quickly as possible. So if somebody shows you to be a fool, you should thank him and become his friend. Of course, it's tough love. It's hard to live down.

This brings us to the second possible reaction. Serious people can't laugh at themselves when shown to be fools, even if they really are being foolish, and even if abandoning their folly would be the best thing for them. Instead, they just get angry at whoever points out their folly, thus they persist in being fools. For instance, Anytus, one of Socrates' accusers, is depicted being worsted by Socrates in Plato's dialogue *Meno*. Anytus is not the kind of guy who can laugh at himself, so he became Socrates' enemy. Socrates in the *Apology* admits he made lots of enemies that way.

So, if Socrates is tried by men who can laugh at themselves, the trial will go well. But if they are not the kind of men who can laugh at themselves, the trial will go badly. This means that Socrates is bound and determined to make fools of the jurors. Socrates claims that this activity is philanthropic, because it can lead people to wisdom. But to the casual observer, Socrates must look like a real jerk.

SOCRATES BECOMES EUTHYPHRO'S STUDENT

Euthyphro then explains the lawsuit that has made his family indignant. Socrates says:

> But before Zeus [Zeus, of course, is the patron of the family, the patron god of fathers], do you, Euthyphro, suppose that you have such precise knowledge of how the divine things are disposed and the pious and impious things, that, assuming that these things just as you say, you don't fear that by pursuing a lawsuit against your father, you in turn may happen to be doing an impious act? (4e)

Euthyphro replies, "No. There would be no benefit for me, Socrates, nor would Euthyphro be different from the many human beings if I didn't know all such things precisely" (5a). This is his hubris.

So, Socrates says, 'Well, Euthyphro, in that case I should become your student, because I'm being charged with impiety, and you know better than anybody else what piety is. So, if you teach me what piety is, then I can march into that law court, and I can show Meletus that he's wrong to think that I am impious. So teach me, Euthyphro, what piety is so that I may better myself and get out of this lawsuit.'

Euthyphro, of course, is flattered by this. He doesn't catch the sarcasm here. Socrates doesn't think Euthyphro is an expert on divine things. Socrates says 'Let me be your student.' But his real intent is to teach Euthyphro a lesson, namely that he doesn't know what piety is. Therefore, he should be very careful about pursuing this suit against his father, lest he genuinely anger the gods. Because if Euthyphro doesn't know what the gods want, maybe he should just follow the customary views about the gods. Thus Socrates takes a father-beater and turns him back into a dutiful son, which is exactly the opposite of what the Socrates of the *Clouds* does with Pheidippides and Strepsiades. In the *Euthyphro*, Socrates straightens out a corrupted youth.

Euthyphro agrees to teach Socrates. Then Socrates asks:

> . . . tell me now, before Zeus, what you just now strongly affirmed plainly. What sort of things do you say the pious and the impious are, concerning murder and concerning other things? Or is the pious itself the same as itself in every action? And again, isn't the impious opposite to everything pious, for it itself is similar to itself and has one certain *Idea* in accordance with impiety? Everything, that is, that is going to be impious. (5c–d)

That's a mouthful, but he's talking about the "Ideas" or "Forms." We don't have to say too much about Forms, because not too much is said about Forms in this dialogue. Basically, a Form is a model, in Greek *paradigm*. It functions like this. Say that you want to identify certain acts as pious. Honoring your mother and father is a pious act. Attending religious festivals is a pious act. Not taking a god's name in vain is a pious act.

But what is it about these acts that makes them pious? They differ in all sorts of ways. But we think they are all the *same*, insofar as they are pious. What is this common element that makes them all pious? If we can isolate this element, then we would have a *Form* or *model* of piety.

In other Platonic dialogues, these Forms or Ideas are given a much more developed metaphysical status. But for our purposes here, the Form or Idea is really a verbal *definition* of what piety is. This definition allows you look at particular acts and distinguish the pious from the impious ones. It's a universal definition of piety, as opposed to particular examples of piety.

There's an idea known as the Socratic fallacy: If you can't define something verbally, you don't really know what it is. I don't think that Socrates believed this. In fact, Socrates believed that you can't arrive at an abstract, verbal definition of piety unless you *already* know what piety is in a non-abstract, pre-verbal manner. So Socrates would never claim that you don't know what piety is until you define the term. But he uses this false premise against Euthyphro.

Socrates argues that if Euthyphro can't give a definition of his special notion of piety, then he doesn't know what piety is any better than anyone else. Therefore, he should follow the common understanding of piety and stop prosecuting his father.

THE FIRST ATTEMPT AT A DEFINITION

Socrates asks Euthyphro: 'What's the Idea of piety? You say you know it better than anybody. If you know better than anybody, say it. Say what it is.' Euthyphro replies:

> . . . the pious is just what I am doing now: to proceed against whoever does injustice regarding murders or thefts of sacred things, or is doing wrong in any other such thing, whether he happens to be a father or mother or anyone else at all; and not to proceed against him is impious. (5d–e)

Euthyphro offers as "proof" of this definition that Zeus beat his father, and his father beat his father before him, so there's nothing wrong with Euthyphro beating up his poor old father in court.

But Socrates objects that Euthyphro has merely given an *example* of piety, whereas Socrates was asking for the *Idea* of piety itself. Then Socrates reformulates this request for an Idea.

> **SOCRATES**: Do you remember that I didn't bid you to teach me some one or two of the many pious things, but that *eidos* [Idea] itself by which all pious things are pious? For surely you were saying that it is by one *Idea* that the impious things are impious and the pious things pious. Or don't you remember?
> **EUTHYPHRO**: I do.
> **SOCRATES**: Then teach me whatever this *Idea* itself is so that by gazing at it and using it as a pattern, I may declare that whatever is like it among the things you or anyone else may do, is pious, and that whatever is not like it is not [pious]. (6d–e)

Socrates doesn't want to remain on the level of examples. He wants to move up to an Idea of piety, which is what all pious acts have in common, in virtue of which they are pious acts.

PIETY IS DEAR TO THE GODS

Euthyphro then gives his first real definition of piety: ". . . what is dear to the gods is pious, and what is not dear is impious" (6e). Piety is what the gods like. Impiety is what they dislike.

Socrates' response is quite good. Don't the gods have battles amongst themselves? What are they quarreling about? They're not quarreling about weights and measures and other things that can be answered simply. Instead, they're battling about what's just and noble, what's right and wrong, what's pious and impious.

So, if what's pious is what's dear to the gods, wouldn't that mean that adultery is both pious and impious? It's pious because it's dear to Zeus, who's always committing adultery, but it's impious because it's not dear to Hera, who's always trying to prevent Zeus from committing adultery. Which means that the same thing can be both pious and impious, and that can't be true.

A good definition of piety would be something that allows you to distinguish pious and impious things, whereas, on this account, the same things are both pious and impious. So, this cannot be a correct account.

PIETY IS DEAR TO ALL THE GODS

The next definition Euthyphro gives is that "the pious is what all the gods love, and . . . the opposite, whatever all gods hate, is impious" (9e). If the gods agree that something is dear to all of them, that is a pious thing. And if the gods agree that something is not dear to all of them, that is an impious thing. Whatever the gods can't agree upon is neither pious nor impious.

Socrates doesn't even touch the major problem with this idea, which is that the gods most vehemently disagree with one another over the most important moral issues, which would thus be neither pious nor impious.

Instead, Socrates raises a different problem, and here the text gets kind of dense. Rather than go through it line by line, I'll just give you the gist of the argument. Are good things good because we *think* they are good? Or do we *think* things are good because they *are* good?

The first view is what you could call a *subjective* value theory. The subject imparts value to things. We like them, therefore, they become likeable. Whereas the other view can be called an *objective* value theory, which is that things are good in and of themselves, and it's only because they are good in and of themselves that we then think that they are good. That is, if we're thinking properly.

Euthyphro thinks that what's pious is pious in and of itself, that it's *objectively* pious. Therefore, what's *dear* to the gods can't be the definition of what's pious. It is just a description of the gods' *subjective reaction* to pious things. But it leaves unclear what they are reacting to. What are the objective marks of pious things that the gods are looking at? That's what a true definition would include. If we can arrive at this definition, then we don't even need to consult the gods. We can just identify pious things on our own.

SOCRATES OVERTHROWS THE GODS

Socrates is making a revolutionary point. Socrates is upholding a standard of right above what the gods believe. There are objective goods. These objective goods are objective even to the gods themselves. The gods now have something above them to look up to: what is right and wrong in and of itself.

If we know what is objectively right and wrong, we have a standard by which we can judge the gods themselves. If there are objective goods that the gods do not recognize, then the gods are mistaken or the gods are immoral.

Socrates uses this kind of argument in the *Republic* to begin sweeping away the whole pantheon of Greek gods, because they're all bad. His assumption is that if anything is a god, then it must be good. Since the gods of the Greeks are not good, they cannot be true gods.

That is a radical position. It implies that Socrates really doesn't believe in the gods of the city. It implies that he is bringing in a new divinity, something that's more deserving of piety than the gods themselves: an objective notion of good, what's *right by nature* rather than *right by opinion*. What's right by nature stands even above the gods. In a sense, then, Meletus' indictment is correct.

What makes the gods worthy of piety? Obviously, the gods must be good. The gods must earn our respect by submitting to the same objective moral laws that we do, and if they don't earn our respect, we don't owe them any piety. Indeed, we have to conclude that they aren't real gods. Because real gods must be good gods.

After Euthyphro talks about father-beating in Zeus' family, Socrates utters a pregnant line:

> Is this, Euthyphro, why I'm a defendant against the indictment: that whenever someone says such things against the gods, I receive them somehow with annoyance? Because of this, as is likely, someone will assert that I am a wrongdoer. (6a).

Socrates is annoyed whenever he hears evil acts attributed to the gods, for he believes that the gods cannot commit evil acts. He continues:

So, now, if these things seem so to you too, who know well about such things, it is certainly necessary, as is likely, for us to concede them as well. For what else shall we say, since we ourselves also agree that we know nothing about them? But tell me before the god of friendship [Zeus], do you truly hold that these things have happened this way? (6b)

Socrates says "we know nothing" about the gods. Socrates could be using the "royal we" here, but I think he's referring to "we Greeks." We Greeks—except for you, Euthyphro, who know so much—know nothing about the gods. But the Greeks *think* they know all kinds of things about the gods. If we know nothing about the gods, that implies that everything that we *think* we know about the gods is not knowledge, i.e., that it's false. The gods of Athens are swept clean away with this single line. It's somewhat understated, but the implication is quite clear.

EDUCATING EUTHYPHRO

Socrates is an unbeliever in the gods of the city. Yet in the very next line, he invokes Zeus as his witness. This is very much like Aristophanes in the *Clouds*, who, on the one hand, has a notion of what's right by nature over and above conventional views but at the same time gives lip-service to the gods of the city. But why do that if you have access to an objective standard of what's good?

The answer is pretty much the same for Socrates as it is for Aristophanes: because not everybody is improved by pushing aside the conventional religion. Euthyphro is a wonderful example of a man made worse by his unconventional views.

Euthyphro thinks he is better than the many. He's thrown aside convention, but that has made him into a father-beater and a vain fool. Socrates is deflating Euthyphro's attempt to think unconventionally and moving him back to the conventional thinking. Why? To make him a better man, a better son, a better citizen. However, in other Platonic dialogues, Socrates encounters people whom he tries to free from the grip of convention. Why? Because he sees they would be improved by that. It really depends on the individual character and situation.

There are two sources of moral guidance. On the one hand, there's conventional opinion, and on the other hand there is what's right by nature. Usually they teach the same things, of course, but for different reasons. Between them is a no man's land with no moral guideposts at all. Most people who begin to think critically will depart rather quickly from convention in the direction of what's right by nature. Unfortunately, they don't always make it to the other side. They just end up wandering around in no man's land without any kind of moral guidance whatsoever, and when they occasionally step back into the realm of ordinary life, they screw everything up, like Euthyphro is doing.

Euthyphro has enough intelligence, intellectual curiosity, and self-confidence to step outside of convention. But he doesn't have the wherewithal to get across the wasteland and find some other source of moral guidance. Therefore, his life is morally unmoored, and his behavior is destructive, both of his family and himself. Socrates is bringing him back to the conventional view of things. He's clipping his wings a little bit. Euthyphro tried to soar like an eagle, but Socrates thinks he's better off as a little barnyard fowl.

Now it is important to understand the circumstances here. Socrates would not be sticking up for Euthyphro's father if he thought he were a monster. But Euthyphro's father did not just pick a random stranger and kill him intentionally. He let a murderer die while trying to do justice. But this does not matter to Euthyphro, because his mind lacks nuance. It's straight thinking rather than subtle thinking. It's not that Euthyphro is caught up in his head, it's that he is caught up in one little part of his head.

If Euthyphro's father were a monster and Socrates knew that, then Socrates might be having a very different conversation, trying to persuade Euthyphro that just because he's your father doesn't mean that he shouldn't be prosecuted. In Plato's *Gorgias*, Socrates not only argues that criminals ought to be punished but that they have a *right* to be punished for their own good, and if we don't punish them, then we're denying them their rights. Because true punishment improves the soul.

In Book I of the *Republic*, Socrates takes the idea that what's right is helping your friends and harming your enemies, which is a very conventional notion, and completely overturns it. He asks, 'But what if your friends are bad men?' Helping your friends who are bad men would be helping them be bad. Helping your father to be a bad man would be helping him to be bad. Euthyphro is not that subtle, but Socrates would be able to make that distinction, and if Euthyphro's father were truly a bad man, Socrates would probably be urging Euthyphro to prosecute, because there would be a clear instance of the conventions about what's right being out of whack with what's really right.

PIETY IS TENDING THE GODS

After Socrates makes it very clear that piety is not what is dear to the gods, individually or collectively, he then establishes to Euthyphro's satisfaction that piety is a form of justice. But which form? How is piety different from other kinds of justice? Euthyphro answers: ". . . that part of the just is reverent as well as pious which concerns the tendance of the gods, while that which concerns the tendance of human beings is the remaining part of the just" (12e). Later, Socrates suggests and Euthyphro agrees that this concept of piety is a kind of "commerce" between gods and mortals (14e). But what do the gods get out of this? Euthyphro asserts that we can't improve the gods. They don't *need* anything from us. So, what kind of commerce is this? Euthyphro replies:

> I also told you a little while ago, Socrates, that to learn precisely how all these things are is a rather lengthy work. [Namely, how things are with the gods.] However, I tell you simply that if someone has knowledge of how to say and do things gratifying to the gods by praying and sacrificing, these are the pious things. (14a–b)

But this attempt at a definition just amounts to more examples of pious things.

THE TRUE DEFINITION OF PIETY

Euthyphro then continues, ". . . and such things preserve private families as well as the communities of cities. The opposites of the things gratifying are impious, and they overturn and destroy everything" (14b). I wish to argue that this is actually the true definition of piety as far as Socrates is concerned.

Socrates says:

> You could have just told me much more briefly, Euthyphro, if you wished, the main point of what I was asking. But you are not eager to teach me, that is clear. For you turned away just now, when you were at the very point at which, if you had answered, I would have already learned piety sufficiently from you. But as it is—for it is necessary that the lover follow the beloved wherever he leads—again what do you say the pious and piety are? Isn't it a certain kind of knowledge of sacrifices and praying? (14b–c)

Socrates says, "You turned away just now when you were at the very point at which if you had answered I would have already learned piety sufficiently from you." This indicates that Socrates has a pretty good idea of what piety is. Euthyphro almost got there but then turned away at the last minute. So Socrates is being disingenuous when he says, 'Teach me piety, O wise Euthyphro!'

But what has Euthyphro turned away from at the very brink of giving a definition of piety? Let's look again at what Euthyphro says, subtract the things that Socrates clearly rejects, and see what's left.

> However, I tell you simply that if someone has knowledge of how to say and do things gratifying to the gods by praying and sacrificing, these are the pious things. And such things preserve private families as well as the communities of cities. The opposites of things gratifying are impious, and they overturn and destroy everything. (14b)

Socrates rejects the idea that piety is a matter of doing what's gratifying to the gods because it is equivalent to defining the pious as what's dear to the gods. So, if we cross that out, what remains is "such things preserve private families as well as the communities of cities." And *that*, I think, is exactly what Socrates believes piety is.

Again, if Socrates does not believe in the gods of the city, why does he pay lip-service to them? Part of it is simple self-interest, namely, to avoid prosecution for impiety. But beyond that, Socrates thinks that religion preserves private families and cities. It's a source of social cohesion and a tool of moral and political education. People can be made better by belief in false gods.

Now, the gods were not *created* to perform this role. But no matter how belief in the gods comes about, given sufficient passage of time, socially destructive religious beliefs will be discarded and socially constructive ones will be strengthened. For instance, religious groups like the Shakers that practiced complete celibacy have become almost extinct. Why? Because their form of piety does not preserve families and cities. Whereas forms of religion that say 'Be fruitful and multiply' tend to survive. This is just a naturalistic view of the sociological function of religion, even religions that aren't true. They can't *all* be true. But they maintain themselves to the extent that they are consistent with the overall health of a society. This is the extent to which Socrates thinks that piety is a valuable thing.

However, Socrates is also quite able to recognize aspects of traditional religions that aren't conducive to the preservation of the family. How can he recognize that? Because he has a higher standard to look to: the standard of natural right. So, on the one hand, he's willing to tinker around with — erase, reform, censor, whatever you want to say — certain aspects of the traditional religion that lead people to behave badly. But, on the other hand, he's completely willing to keep all those aspects of the traditional religion that make people better than they otherwise would be. From the point of view of natural right, this is what makes piety good.

This is pretty much the view of the *Clouds*. This is why the Clouds, who represent wisdom derived from nature, recognized the gods of the city. Socrates didn't then. But now he does.

EUTHYPHRO GIVES UP

The next definition of piety is actually attempted by Socrates. Socrates says, "Piety, Euthyphro, would be a certain form of commerce for gods and human beings with each other" (14e). And, again, he asks, 'What do the gods get from it?' And Euthyphro says that the gods get what is dear to them. They get praise, gratitude, sacrifices, etc. But Socrates notes that they've already rejected the idea that the pious is what's dear to the gods. So the argument has come around in a circle.

Then Socrates says, 'Alright, Euthyphro. One more time from the top':

> SOCRATES: Then we must consider again from the beginning what the pious is, since I will not voluntarily give up out of cowardice until I learn it. Do not dishonor me, but apply your mind in every way as much as possible and tell me the truth now. For if in fact any human knows, you do, and like Proteus you must not be let go until you tell. For if you didn't know plainly the pious and the impious, there is no way that you would ever have attempted to prosecute an elderly man, your father, for murder on behalf of a hired man. Rather, as to the gods, you would have dreaded the risk that you would not do it correctly, and, as to human beings, you would have been ashamed. But as it is now, I know well that you suppose that you know plainly the pious and the not pious, so tell me, Euthyphro, best of men, and don't hide what you hold it to be.
>
> EUTHYPHRO: Some other time then, Socrates, for now I am in a hurry to go somewhere, and it is time for me to go away.

What Socrates says here is: 'Euthyphro, if you *don't* know what the pious is better than anybody else, then you would *not* prosecute your father. You would never dare risk it. But since you're prosecuting your father, I know that you must know.'

But, of course, Euthyphro has now come to the realization that he *doesn't* know any better, and he's left to draw the conclusion that maybe he *shouldn't* risk prosecuting his father. And so he makes a hasty exit. But apparently, he's not sticking around the law court, so maybe he has decided not to pursue the lawsuit against his father.

Then Socrates says,

> Such things you are doing, comrade! By leaving, you are throwing me down from a great hope I had: that by learning from you the things pious and the things not, I would be released from Meletus' indictment. For I hoped to show him that I have now become wise in the divine things from Euthyphro and that I am no longer acting inadvisedly because of ignorance or making innovations concerning them and especially that I would live better for the rest of my life. (15e–16a)

He's pouring on the sarcasm, but Socrates is satisfied that he already knows what piety is. It is pretty much the conventional notion of piety. The Greeks were not concerned about whether people actually held correct opinions about the gods. They simply wished to preserve religious institutions that sustained the state and the family. Socrates is all for that. But at the same time, he's maintaining his intellectual liberty to think otherwise about the gods based on his understanding of what is right by nature.

Like the *Theages*, the *Euthyphro* is a lovely response to the *Clouds*. The *Euthyphro* depicts Socrates behaving exactly the opposite of the Socrates of the *Clouds*. And he's doing so on the basis of the very philosophy that we can draw from the *Clouds*. Beyond that, the *Euthyphro* is a comic drama, although much shorter and drier than the *Clouds*. Thus the *Euthyphro* is another tribute to the Aristophanean influence on the formation of Socratic philosophy.

Plato's *Apology*

In Plato's *Apology of Socrates*, Socrates doesn't say he's sorry. The word "apology" here means "defense." Thus a better translation would be *Defense of Socrates*. The *Apology* is a defense of Socrates in three senses. First, it is a defense *by* Socrates. Second, it is a defense *of* Socrates, a self-defense. But Socrates is not just defending himself. He's also defending philosophy.

As a self-defense speech, the *Apology* failed, and Socrates was executed. As we shall see, from a logical point of view, the *Apology* also fails to defend Socrates. In fact, if read carefully, the *Apology* is an admission of Socrates' guilt. We'll see how the *Apology* fares as a defense of philosophy.

The *Apology* is a marvelous text, and there's good reason to think that the basic arguments were actually made by Socrates, because Plato was present at Socrates' trial. He wrote and circulated this text not long after Socrates' death. We would probably have heard from contemporary accounts if it fundamentally falsified what Socrates said. There's also another *Apology of Socrates* by Xenophon which has a number of similarities, although it's a much shorter text, and most of it is a report on Socrates' trial, not a representation of the speech itself.

The *Apology* is an artfully crafted text. Like all of Plato's texts, it has different layers of meaning. The original speech undergoes a kind of poetic transformation or fictionalization. It not only reports the gist of what Socrates said to the jury, it also teaches a larger philosophical lesson about the relationship of philosophy to political life. How does philosophy justify itself to the city, i.e., to the public at large, most of whom are not philosophical?

This is an issue, because philosophy is an unusual thing. Aristophanes' *Clouds* shows just how odd and questionable philosophy seems from the point of view of ordinary human beings, how it seems both comical and destructive. Therefore, philosophy needs to give an account of itself. This is especially true in ancient Greece, because the ancient Greeks had a tendency to put philosophers on trial.

Socrates was the third major philosopher who was put on trial by the Athenians. The first was Anaxagoras, who is mentioned in the *Apology*. Anaxagoras was a teacher of Pericles. He was a foreigner, a political insider, and had a reputation for atheism and impiety. He was brought up on essentially the same charges as Socrates. Anaxagoras, who was from Clazomenae, quit Athens and was not seen there again. The Athenians also ran the great sophist Protagoras out of town. Unfortunately, poor Protagoras died when his ship sank leaving Athens, denying the world of any more Protagorean teachings.

How to Read the *Apology*

I'll let you in on the big secret. To the question, "How can philosophy justify itself to the city?" the answer of the *Apology* is: It can't. At least, it can't justify itself *as philosophy*. The clearest indication of this fact is just how systematically deceptive and sneaky Socrates is in his defense speech. Socrates is lying. But Socrates is *forced* to lie, given the nature of his audience and the nature of the life that he's trying to defend.

Socrates was tried before a jury of 500 Athenian citizens chosen by lot. There was no separate judge. There were officials of the court who conducted the proceedings, but judge and jury were one and the same. The jurors could have been just about anybody. They were definitely his peers.

The accusers made their speeches first. There were three accusers: Meletus, Anytus, and Lycon. Then Socrates gave his defense speech. Then the jury voted on whether to convict or not. They voted to convict. Then the leader of the accusers, Meletus, got to propose a penalty. He proposed death. Then Socrates was allowed to propose a counter-penalty. Then the jury voted again on what penalty to accept. Then Socrates got to say a few last words, no matter what the outcome was. We have only Socrates' portions. None of the accusers' speeches have come down to us, but we know the gist of their accusations.

At the start, Socrates says that after hearing his accusers, he can't believe what he has heard. They spoke so persuasively that he didn't even recognize himself. Yet Socrates knows himself, and he knows that the accusations are completely untrue.

Now Socrates will speak in precisely the opposite way. Instead of speaking falsehoods in a clever way, he's going to speak nothing but the truth, and he's going to do it in a way that you would expect from a man who is a foreigner to law courts. He's going to do it in a bumbling, halting fashion, because he's not a professional speaker. He's not a clever speaker at all.

Socrates says of his accusers, "They're not ashamed that they will be immediately refuted by me in deed" (17b). Socrates is alerting us to the fact that sometimes deeds can refute speeches. This is a general principle for reading all of Plato's dialogues.

Jacques Derrida accuses Plato of "logocentrism," which means focusing on words, the Greek word for which is *logoi*. But actually, if you read Plato's dialogues, they're not logocentric at all, because all of the *logoi*, all of the speeches, have to be read in relation to all of the *deeds* that are narrated. The meaning of the Platonic text comes about as the total effect of the speeches and the deeds working together. So, you have to look at what's done as well as what's said.

Socrates begins by saying that he is not a clever speaker. But in the very act of saying that he's not a clever speaker, he is demonstrating that he is a master of rhetoric. Imagine Senator Blowhard stands up and gives a long, eloquent, artfully crafted speech. Then Senator Leghorn stands up and says, "Well, you know, I can't compete with Senator Blowhard's high-flown phrases and fancy intellectual justifications, so let me tell you what my momma used to say." Then he presents his argument in a folksy, down-to-earth manner.

This is one of the oldest tricks in the rhetorician's book: pretending to be a non-clever speaker, just a plain-spoken, ordinary guy speaking from the heart, saying the first things that come into his mind, unfiltered and thus entirely sincere. It's a kind of *jiu-jitsu* move, turning your opponents' strengths into weaknesses and your weaknesses into strengths, throwing him by highlighting how slick and clever he is, making the audience think, "I'm being bamboozled by the first guy, but this clumsy, plain-talking bumpkin's going to tell it to me straight."

Socrates portrays himself as naïve. He's just arrived at the law court. He's foreign to their ways. By contrast, Strepsiades in the *Clouds* is quite knowledgeable of the law courts but completely out of place when he arrives at the Thinkery. Socrates is by now an old man like Strepsiades. Just as Strepsiades arrives at the Thinkery and announces himself as he would at the law courts, Socrates arrives at the law court and says, 'I am foreign to the way of speaking here, and I will speak as I have always spoken.' Which would be the way of the Thinkery. That's a nice comic reversal.

THE OLD & NEW ACCUSERS

Then Socrates makes a distinction between two sets of accusers: the first accusers and the later accusers. The first accusers are characterized as follows:

> They got a hold of the many of you from childhood, and they accuse me of persuading you—although it is no more true than the present charge—that there is a certain Socrates, a wise man, a thinker on the things aloft, who has investigated all things under the earth, who makes the weaker speech the stronger. (18b)

This is clearly a reference to the *Clouds*, where Socrates is introduced floating in a basket, investigates the underworld, and makes the weaker argument the stronger. Later he says, 'I don't know their names unless one of them happens to be a comic poet' (18d). Then, later on, he explicitly refers to Aristophanes and the *Clouds* (19c). So, the old accusers really are just Aristophanes, although we know of at least two other plays mocking Socrates, one of which premiered at the same time as the *Clouds*. Socrates is arguing that Aristophanes, not he, has corrupted the youth with the *Clouds*, giving Socrates a bad reputation entirely without justification.

Socrates will first refute the old accusers, principally Aristophanes. He claims this will be difficult, because he can call no witnesses (18d). Of course, that also makes it impossible for any witnesses to contradict him. Then he'll refute the new accusers, Meletus, Anytus, and Lycon.

Socrates speaks only to Meletus here, because Meletus was

the mouthpiece of Socrates' accusers. After the Athenians regretted killing Socrates, they put Meletus on trial and executed him. Anytus and Lycon were exiled.

FALSE & TRUE DEFENSES OF PHILOSOPHY

Before Socrates begins refuting the old accusers, he says, "let this proceed in whatever way is dear to the god" (19a). Socrates is portraying himself as pious, because he's been charged with impiety. This brings us back to the *Euthyphro*. It's very interesting to compare Socrates' views in the *Euthyphro* about piety with his professions of piety here in the *Apology*.

If you look at the *Euthyphro* and raise the question "Is Socrates pious?" you can say yes and no. You can say yes, Socrates is pious, in the minimal sense that the Greeks accepted which is that he was orthopractic. He prayed, swore oaths by the gods, and attended the festivals. He went through the motions with everybody else. That was good enough as far as the Greeks were concerned.

But one could ask if Socrates was pious by a more rigorous standard, namely: "Did he *believe* in the gods of the city?" There are some subtle indications that he didn't. He says that he can't believe that the gods would do anything bad. But that virtually eliminates all of the stories that the Greeks told about the mischievous Olympians. He also says that we know nothing about the gods, which implies that what we *think* we know about the gods really isn't knowledge, which is equivalent to saying that the Greek views of the gods are false. So, he's very impious in that sense.

But then there's another sense in which he's even more pious than those who believe in the gods, because he believes that anything divine would have to be good. True divinities would have to measure up to an objective standard of what is right. He believes in an objective, natural right which is above the gods themselves and serves as a criterion by which you can judge them good or ill. Socrates regards what is right by nature as worthy of the highest form of respect or piety. So, in a sense, he's even more pious than the most pious Greeks, because he believes that no gods can do bad things. He thinks it's impious to say that the gods do evil.

Socrates is quite quick to reject the notion of piety that Euthyphro offers: the pious is what is dear to the gods. He thinks that's a preposterous notion. However, in the *Apology*, Socrates invokes what is "dear to the god" (19a), a standard of piety that we know he himself rejects. Socrates is not being entirely forthright or honest. He is accommodating how he speaks to public opinion.

Now let's skip forward to after Socrates has been found guilty, but before he's condemned to death. This is his speech where he proposes a counter-penalty to death. Socrates suggests that his service to Athens be recognized by giving him free meals at public expense for the rest of his life (36d). Such meals were a public honor, so this suggestion predictably outraged many jurors. Socrates could not pay a fine, because he had no money. But some of his friends put up the money for a fine, so that's the counter-penalty that he ends up actually proposing.

Socrates wouldn't accept exile. He wouldn't accept prison. Nor would he accept just remaining silent about philosophy.

> Perhaps, then, someone might say, "By staying silent and keeping quiet, Socrates, won't you be able to live in exile for us?" It is hardest of all to persuade some of you about this. For if I say that this is to disobey the god and that because of this it is impossible to keep quiet, you will not be persuaded by me, on the ground that I am being ironic. And, on the other hand, if I say this even happens to be a very great good for a human being—to make speeches every day about virtue and the other things about which you hear me conversing and examining both myself and others—and that the unexamined life is not worth living for a human being, you will be persuaded by me still less when I say these things. (37e–38a)

This is a rich passage, but what he's basically saying is this: 'Look, I've tried to persuade you that philosophy is a good thing because it's dear to the gods.' Namely, Socrates claimed that he began to philosophize because heard that the oracle of the god

Apollo at Delphi said no man was wiser than Socrates. Of course, this story presupposes that Socrates *already* had a reputation for wisdom, so it can't be the real beginning of his philosophical quest. Moreover, Socrates says he *disbelieved* the oracle and began to question people philosophically in order to *disprove* the oracle. Yet he presents this as the height of piety. But wouldn't true piety lead him to *believe* the oracle, not try to *refute* it?

SOCRATIC IRONY

Socrates told the jurors that he philosophized in service to the god Apollo. But they didn't believe him.

Socrates was not believed because he has a reputation for being "ironic." Now, for the ancient Greeks, irony is a kind of dissimulation, a kind of dishonesty, a kind of phoniness in which a person pretends to be less than he is, or to know less than he does. For a Greek of noble aspirations, irony was considered the only forgivable vice. The highborn cultivate irony to protect the feelings of their inferiors, which lessens resentment between the classes, thus stabilizing the social order. Thus in aristocratic societies, it is considered bad taste to flout one's superiority in front of one's inferiors. For instance, one does not flash one's wealth in front of people whom it might make feel envious.

The same goes for other forms of superiority. If you're smarter than somebody, you don't use big words to make him feel inferior. If somebody is uneducated or lacks a certain cultivation of taste, you don't try to dazzle him by showing that you are more educated or have better taste.

Socrates is ironic in the Greek sense but not to hide his wealth or social superiority, which he lacked. Instead, he tries to hide his intellectual superiority. That means he talks down to people. He pretends to know less than he really knows.

But magnanimity only works if people don't know you are practicing it. Unfortunately, Socrates has gotten a reputation for irony. Thus the jurors dismiss Socrates' story about his mission from Apollo as simply a condescending deception. To add insult to injury, if people know that you're being ironic with them, it implies that you think they are inferior, which they resent.

Socrates has told the jury a story about how philosophy is dear to the gods. We know from the *Euthyphro* that Socrates rejects that definition of piety. The trouble is, though, that nobody believes him when he says it, because they think he's being ironic. So at this point Socrates is saying, in effect, 'Well, you didn't believe the story about Apollo, so here's the unvarnished truth: "The unexamined life isn't worth living." You'll like that even less.'

WISDOM MAKES LIFE WORTH LIVING

The *real* reason Socrates pursues wisdom is that wisdom makes life worth living. None of the good things in life are necessarily good *for* us unless we have the wisdom to use them properly. Without wisdom, the best you can hope for is to luck out, in other words, to be in a fool's paradise. But most people have no such luck. Thus most unwise people end up suffering needlessly.

Indeed, for Socrates, one is better off dead than a fool. For Socrates, wisdom is primarily practical wisdom, and practical wisdom dwells in us as virtue, which is the harmonious order of the soul. Folly dwells in us as vice, the corruption of the soul. Socrates famously declared that he would rather suffer wrong—including unjust execution—than to do wrong.

To do wrong corrupts one's soul, i.e., it makes one vicious. Suffering wrong, however, does not corrupt us. No matter what your enemies do to you, they can't make you into a bad person. They can kill you, but they can't make you into a monster. Only you can do that, by doing wrong. For Socrates, there are worse things than death, and one of them is villainy.

Is Socrates sacrificing his life for philosophy? I would say that he's sacrificing his life for the sake of his soul. He's willing to die because he's not willing to live under just any old conditions. He's not willing to live in a condition where his soul is corrupted.

The only vice Socrates is willing to stoop to is irony. He's willing to lie. But there are two kinds of lies. One is a lie you tell somebody else, and the other is a lie you tell yourself, which corrupts your soul. Whatever Socrates is willing to do, he's not willing to lie to himself.

Socrates also believes deception can be used as a tool for helping other people, so he doesn't necessarily believe that by deceiving people he's corrupting their souls. For instance, in the *Euthyphro*, Socrates persuades Euthyphro using false premises: 'Euthyphro, if you can't define piety, you don't know what it is.' Well, that's really not true, but Euthyphro believes it, and Euthyphro is better for having been purged of his hubris that he knows what piety is better than anyone else.

This, in a nutshell, is the political predicament of philosophy. Philosophy cannot persuade the vast majority of human beings that it is a worthwhile activity because, in effect, it says their lives aren't worth living without it. No one wants to hear that. So Socrates is forced to tell a more appealing falsehood about philosophy, namely, that it is dear to the god Apollo. But this isn't persuasive either, because he has a reputation for irony.

HOW SOCRATES GOT A REPUTATION FOR IRONY

How did Socrates get a reputation for being ironic? We have to look back to the *Clouds*. The Socrates of the *Clouds* doesn't have any irony at all. He openly declares that the gods of the city do not exist. Thus when Socrates presents philosophy as a mission from Apollo, many of the jurors simply conclude that he is having them on.

It is ironic (in the modern sense of the word), that Socrates probably learned to be ironic (in the Greek sense) from the *Clouds*, since the reputation he gained from the *Clouds* probably made his irony ineffectual.

After Socrates has been condemned, he says, "the sign of the god [his *daimonion*] did not oppose me when I left my house this morning nor when I came up here to the law court, nor anywhere in the speech when I was about to say anything, although in other speeches it has often stopped me in the middle while I was speaking" (40b). So Socrates admits that sometimes he does not say everything that he thinks.

What's the connection between the *daimonion* and Socrates' ability to moderate his speeches?

Socrates has no *daimonion* in the *Clouds*. Nor does he exercise moderation in his speeches. But if you look at what he says in the *Theages*, that his *daimonion* is identical with his knowledge of eros, and if you look at the *Symposium* and *Phaedrus* where the knowledge of erotic things is identified with knowledge of care of the soul and character, then you realize that Socrates' *daimonion* refers to his ability to divine the nature of people's characters and to accommodate what he says to the person he is speaking to, which is a skill he lacks in the *Clouds*.

Socrates is forced to give a dishonest defense. He's been accused of being interested in natural philosophy (investigating things below the earth and above the heavens). He's been accused of teaching how to make the weaker speech the stronger. There's reason to think that these charges might have been true at one time, but by the time he came to trial, they weren't true of Socrates anymore. He had changed.

If Socrates were to give an honest defense, he would say, 'Yes, but.' 'Yes, you're right. The Socrates of the *Clouds* is a bad guy. But I am no longer the same Socrates. You mistake me for an earlier incarnation of myself.' But given the way attention spans work, the only thing most people would remember is the frank admission of guilt but not the explanation of why it is no longer the case. They'll hear the 'yes,' but most of them won't listen to what comes after the 'but.'

Socrates can't give an honest defense of his life. So he has to dishonestly defend his entire life against the charges. He just issues a blanket denial that he's ever investigated nature; he gives a blanket denial of ever teaching the art of speaking. He admits that he makes people angry, but that's not what he's on trial for. He's saying, 'I haven't done any of the things you've accused me of, but I do realize that I've really, really irritated a lot of you, and a lot of you hate me.'

SOCRATES VS. THE NEW ACCUSERS

Socrates spends a lot of time refuting the charges as they are posed in the *Clouds*. Then he turns to refuting the present charges, which are not formulated in terms of "he investigates nature and makes the weaker speech the stronger," but instead formulated as "Socrates does not believe in the gods of the city, he invents new gods, and corrupts the youth." For his refutation of those charges, he first assimilates those charges to the charges in the *Clouds*, then he denies them. But when he deals with the charges of the actual indictment, he deals with them in a rather slippery way. He issues a series of "non-denial denials."

Socrates states Meletus' accusation:

> Socrates does injustice and is meddlesome by investigating the things under the earth and heavenly things, by making the weaker speech the stronger and by teaching others these same things. It is something like this. (19b–c)

Now, that's not exactly Meletus' charge. Diogenes Laertius has quoted the actual indictment:

> Socrates breaks the law because he does not recognize the gods recognized by the city, and because he introduces other new divinities; and he breaks the law because he corrupts the youth. The penalty is death.[1]

In the *Euthyphro*, Socrates actually states the indictment more accurately, namely that he is "a maker of gods," meaning that he brings in new gods, doesn't believe in the old ones, and thereby corrupts the youth. Socrates is trying to assimilate the new accusations to the old accusations of the *Clouds*: "For you yourselves used to see these things in the comedy of Aristophanes. A certain Socrates was carried around there claiming that he was treading on air and spouting much other drivel about which I have no expertise either much or little" (19c).

The phrase "much or little" recurs throughout the text, and I don't like the translation. The Greek is *mega* and *mikron*, and you could translate that as "great" and "small." The reason why I think "great" and "small" are better is that they bring to mind the *Clouds* where Socrates is shown investigating things great

---

[1] Diogenes Laertius, *Lives of the Eminent Philosophers*, II, 40, trans. Pamela Mensch, ed. James Miller (Oxford: Oxford University Press, 2018).

and small: gnats' anuses and fleas' feet and also the courses of the heavenly bodies and the contours of the whole earth.

But the Socrates of the *Clouds* doesn't investigate the middle-sized things, namely the realm of human things about which he's conspicuously ignorant and in which his behavior is conspicuously foolish. This "much or little" or "great or small" phrase recurs constantly here. Socrates has no expertise "great or small" about these things, which is not to deny that he has any medium-sized expertise.

"And I do not say this to dishonor this sort of knowledge" (19c). He's not attacking natural philosophy. He just says that he has no share of what they know, the great and the small, and then he says, "I offer the many of you as witnesses and maintain that you should teach and tell each other, those of you who have heard me conversing, and there are many such among you. Tell each other, then, if any of you ever heard me conversing about such things either great or small" (19d). He says, 'There's no evidence of this.'

There probably was some evidence, but he's simply asserting there isn't. Maybe he's depending on the fact that those who heard the Socrates of the *Clouds* more than 20 years before might not all be around anymore. Also, those who are accustomed to listening to him at close quarters might not be inclined to accuse him. But his defense is simply to say, 'Let somebody come forward and accuse me of this.' And no one does. It's a pretty weak defense: 'I didn't do it, and let someone accuse me of doing it.' But that's not what he's on trial for. Other accusers *have* come forward with other accusations, and he needs to deal with them, not Aristophanes.

When Socrates denies the charge of educating people, he is very careful about his formulations. He denies the charge "that I attempt to educate human beings and make money from it" (19d). Well, did he educate anybody for free? That would be the logical question.

Socrates denies that he ever educated anybody, but later he admits "the young follow me of their own accord. Those who have the most leisure, the sons of the wealthiest, enjoy hearing human beings examined" (23c). Of course they do, because it's comical to see people's pretensions punctured. "And they themselves often imitate me, and in turn they attempt to examine others" (23c). This is teaching by example, which is a form of education.

Socrates also denies having an "art" (*techne*) of teaching at a price (20b-c; cf. 31b-c), which is what the sophists did. "As for myself, I would be pluming and priding myself if I had knowledge of these things [namely what the sophists do]. But I do not have knowledge of it, men of Athens" (20c). Socrates denies that he has an educational art, and he denies that he educates for money. However, that's not equivalent to denying that he educates for free, and it's not equivalent to denying that he has a non-technical way of educating people.

Socrates also admits he exhorts people to take better care of their souls, to value virtue more than money or reputation (29d-e, 36b). I'd call that education.

When Socrates says he tests people who have a reputation for being wise, that's also educating them. He is teaching them a lesson. "Okay, Socrates, you didn't 'educate' anybody. Did you teach them any lessons?" Well, yes! He did. He certainly taught them lessons, lessons that they didn't often want to learn.

HUMAN VS. DIVINE WISDOM

Then Socrates says, "Perhaps then one of you might retort, 'Well, Socrates, what is *your* affair? Where have these slanders against you come from?'" If there's smoke, there's fire. What are these slanders based upon?

> Now, perhaps I will seem to some of you to be joking. Know well, however, that I will tell you the whole truth. For I, men of Athens, have gotten this name, this reputation, through nothing but a certain wisdom. Just what sort of wisdom is this? That which is perhaps human wisdom; for probably I really am wise in this. But those of whom I just spoke might perhaps be wise in some wisdom greater than human [namely the natural philosophers and the sophists] or else I cannot say what it is. For I, at least, do not have knowledge of it, but whoever asserts that I do lies

and speaks in order to slander me. (20d-e)

Socrates is admitting to a human wisdom, *anthropine sophia*. The wisdom that he denies is a more than human wisdom, an art of producing virtue and knowledge of things great and small. But he doesn't deny knowledge of the human soul and human character, and he doesn't deny knowledge of the human world or knowledge of middle-sized things. Not great, not small, but medium-sized things where we live. He actually is claiming that he's got a certain human wisdom about that.

SOCRATES VS. THE ORACLE

Then Socrates offers a witness, namely the god Apollo at Delphi. He tells a story about his friend Chaerephon, who is dead now and can't be called to testify. That's convenient, but Socrates does say that Chaerephon's brother is there to back him up. Chaerephon, of course, is Socrates' companion in the *Clouds*. Chaerephon went to the oracle of the god Apollo at Delphi and asked, "Is there anyone wiser than Socrates?" And the oracle said, "No." Socrates was shocked:

> When I heard these things, I pondered them like this. "Whatever is the god saying, and what riddle is he posing? For I am conscious that I am not at all wise either much or little." [I would translate that as "I am not wise in anything great or small." That would clearly bring in the sense of denial of natural philosophy.] So whatever is he saying when he claims I am the wisest? Surely, he is not saying something false, at least; for that is not sanctioned for him. (21b)

There he goes again. Socrates is getting into trouble by saying that the gods can't lie. The Greek gods could lie. He's claiming that Apollo can't lie, and that itself is a deeply impious claim, because it's equivalent to saying that the cherished view that the gods are tricky and clever is false and that the gods are subject to some higher power that commands them not to lie.

Socrates continues:

> ... for a long time, I was at a loss about whatever he [the god] was saying, but then very reluctantly I turned to something like the following investigation of it. I went to those reputed to be wise, on the ground that there, if anywhere, I would refute the divination ... (21b–c)

Then Socrates describes how he sought to refute the oracle. He went to men who were reputed to be wise and questioned them about their wisdom, hoping to discover that they were wiser than him and the oracle was wrong. But how is it pious to disbelieve the god's oracle and try to refute it? Socrates likens this process to the heroic labors of Heracles (22a).

As we observed in the *Euthyphro*, Socrates' method is to ask people to articulate what they know. When they fail to articulate their knowledge, Socrates concludes that they have none. This method hinges on the "Socratic fallacy," the very dubious assumption that you don't know what you can't say.

Socrates spoke first to an unnamed politician:

> ... it seemed to me that this man seemed to be wise, both to many other human beings and most of all to himself, but that he was not. And then I tried to show that that he supposed he was wise, but was not. So from this I became hateful both to him and to many of those present. (21c)

Socrates continues: "After the politicians, I went to the poets, those of the tragedies and dithyrambs, and the others" (22a–b). They too proved to be unwise. Socrates asked the poets to give a rational account of their work and found them incapable of it. Thus he concluded that they based their poetry on inspiration rather than knowledge. It is interesting that Socrates doesn't mention comedy in particular. It is surely included among "the others," but he leaves open the possibility that some comic poets, such as Aristophanes, could be wise.

Socrates specifically likens poets to diviners and oracles, who also speak based on inspiration rather than knowledge and thus cannot offer a rational account of their supposed superior knowledge. Euthyphro, of course, was a diviner who could not define piety, which he claimed to know better than anybody else.

It is significant that Socrates mentions that oracles also speak from inspiration rather than knowledge, which implies that Socrates can't take them seriously either. This contradicts Socrates' backstory, which is premised on taking the oracle of Apollo seriously.

Then Socrates questioned the craftsmen. He discovered that they have genuine knowledge, namely of their arts. But they wrongly thought that their expertise in one area made them wise about all things.

Socrates claims his three accusers represent the three groups whose pretensions of wisdom he punctured: Meletus on behalf of the poets, Anytus on behalf of the craftsmen, and Lycon on behalf of the politicians.

Socrates ends the tale of how he became unpopular by saying, "This is the truth for you, men of Athens. I'm hiding nothing from you either great or small in my speech nor am I holding anything back" (24a). Of course, by saying he's hiding nothing great or small, that leaves open the possibility that he's omitting something that falls between the great and small.

SOCRATES VS. MELETUS

Then Socrates begins his attack on the new accusers. As we shall see, his arguments are sophistical and his manner when cross-examining Meletus is arrogant, sarcastic, and badgering.

Socrates first asks Meletus about his accusation that Socrates corrupts the youth. Socrates asks 'Who benefits the youth?' Meletus' answer is the laws. But that seems to imply that everybody in Athens benefits the youth, except for Socrates. Socrates simply laughs off the idea that everybody benefits the youth but him. But he hasn't refuted the claim that he corrupts the youth.

Socrates asks Meletus if he believes that Socrates corrupts the youth voluntarily or involuntarily. Meletus says voluntarily. To which Socrates replies that he would never corrupt the youth voluntarily, because "if I ever do something wretched to my associates, I will risk getting back something bad from him . . ." (25e). Socrates scoffs at the idea that he'd be so naïve as to corrupt the sons of his neighbors and not expect anything bad to happen to him. But there are people that naïve. One of them is Socrates in the *Clouds*.

Then Socrates addresses the charge that he brings in new gods and disbelieves in the old gods. First, he gets Meletus to formulate his charge of "disbelief in *the gods of the city*" as "disbelief in *any gods at all*." Then, as soon as Meletus does that, Socrates says, in effect, 'Well, Meletus, you also assert that I believe in a *daimonion*, right?' 'Yes.' 'Well, aren't *daimonia* the offspring of gods? You can't have a *daimonion* without gods. It would be like believing in mules without believing in horses and asses, because mules are the offspring of horses and asses just as *daimonia* are the offspring of gods. If I believe in *daimonia*, I must believe in gods.'

Notice that this doesn't refute the real charge, namely that Socrates disbelieves in the gods *of Athens*. But by getting Meletus to change the charge to 'He doesn't believe in any kind of gods,' Socrates can then show that Meletus contradicts himself when he says that Socrates brings in new gods, because how can you believe in new gods when you don't believe in any?

Of course, the natural philosophers did precisely that: They introduced new gods, namely divinized natural phenomena, to conceal the fact that they believed in no gods at all. Moreover, Socrates hasn't actually refuted the claim that he disbelieves in *the gods of the city*, because he could believe that his *daimonion* is the offspring of a foreign god. Socrates actually refers to foreign gods from time to time. For instance, in the *Apology* itself, he swears an oath "by the dog" (21e), which is an Egyptian god (probably the jackal god Anubis).

Socrates' defense from the charge of corrupting the youth is similarly weak. He simply states, in effect, 'If I have corrupted any of the youth, let them come forward to accuse me, or let someone come forward on their behalf' (cf. 33d). This is absurd for two reasons. First, even if Socrates had corrupted some of the people present, who wants to raise his hand and claim to have been corrupted? So the lack of accusers does not imply the lack of a crime. Second, haven't Meletus, Anytus, and Lycon already come forward to accuse Socrates on behalf of the people he corrupted? If so, doesn't Socrates need to respond to their charges, instead of pretending that they don't exist?

Yet again, Socrates gives the impression of refuting the charges against him, but he hasn't actually accomplished that. It's such a systematic pattern throughout the *Apology* that maybe it is there for a reason. Plato is trying to show us the political predicament of philosophy if hauled before the bar and forced to justify itself publicly. It can't truthfully justify itself, so it's forced to be systematically deceptive.

WHAT IS SOCRATES DEFENDING?

Another way of approaching this issue is with a question: What is Socrates defending in the *Apology of Socrates*? Is it Socrates' apology *for Socrates*, or is it Socrates' apology for *something else*, or both? If Socrates is defending himself, he's doing a pretty lousy job. He makes a show of answering the charges, but his arguments fail, often spectacularly.

Beyond that, Socrates defends himself in a manner guaranteed to anger the jury and prejudice them against him. For instance, before Socrates is convicted, he talks about why he avoided politics. He tells the jurors that they do injustice, and if Socrates were to oppose them, they would destroy him. In short, Socrates is accusing the jurors of being bad men. That's not designed to ingratiate himself. He says this near the end of the speech, right before they're going to vote, so it will be fresh in their minds. Then after the jury votes to convict him, Socrates proposes the counter-penalty to death of free meals at public expense, which could only anger the jury still more (36d).

Socrates' behavior here indicates that whatever he's defending, he's not defending himself, because if he is defending himself, then he's not a very clever speaker. But we know that he's a very clever speaker.

So, what is Socrates defending? He's defending *philosophy*. But he's defending philosophy in a way that shows the *difficulties* of defending philosophy in a public context.

Near the end of his initial speech, Socrates says, in effect, 'I'm not going to flatter you. I'm not going to beg. I'm not going to bring my family out here, and I'm not going to tell you the things you want to hear. Why? Because the person who tells you what you want to hear rather than what's *good* for you to hear is a flatterer not a friend, and flatterers are corrupters.'

In the *Gorgias*, Socrates tells the fate of a wise man who tells people the harsh and unflattering truths they need to hear for the care of their souls. If such a man were put on trial in a democracy like Athens, he would be in the same situation as a doctor prosecuted before a jury of children by a pastry chef. The pastry chef corrupts their health with sugary treats, whereas the doctor improves their health with bitter medicines. But children are too foolish to understand that. Thus, the doctor would be unable to acquit himself.

Socrates would suffer the same fate. As a moral philosopher, Socrates is a doctor of the soul. He's been accused of dispensing bitter medicine to the people of Athens by those who manufacture mind-candy that flatters the egos but corrupts the souls of the people. Socrates, however, will not further corrupt them by pandering to their already corrupted tastes, even to save his life.

SOCRATES ON THE FEAR OF DEATH

Having "refuted" the new accusers in the slippery fashion we've seen, Socrates then deals with the question "Aren't you afraid of death?"

> Perhaps then someone might say, "Then are you not ashamed, Socrates, of having followed the sort of pursuit from which you now run the risk of dying?"
>
> I would respond to him with a just speech: "What you say is ignoble, fellow, if you suppose that a man who is of even a little benefit should take into account the danger of living or dying, but not rather consider this alone whenever he acts: whether his actions are just or unjust, and the deeds of a good man or bad? For, according to your speech, those of the demigods who met their end at Troy would be paltry, especially the son of Thetis [namely Achilles, who constantly risked death over honor]." (28b–c)

A man who is willing to risk his own physical survival for what he considers to be right is heroic. This is Socrates' ethic too:

> This is the way it is, men of Athens, in truth. Whenever someone stations himself, holding that it is best, or whenever he is stationed by a ruler, there he must stay and run the risk, as it seems to me, and not take into account death or anything else compared to what is shameful. (28d)

Then he talks about how when he was sent off to battle for Athens, he did his duty properly:

> I stayed . . . where they stationed me and ran the risk of dying like anyone else, but once the gods stationed me, as I supposed and assumed, ordering me to live philosophizing and examining myself and others, I have not then left my station because I fear death or any matter whatever. (28e)

Then Socrates makes some very interesting knowledge claims. He says, first of all, that people who fear death are really pretending to be wiser than they are, because they claim to know that death is a bad thing. Now, that's really not true. People who fear death can simply fear the fact that they *don't know* what death holds. They don't necessarily fear death because they *know* that they're going to be roasted slowly on a spit for all eternity. People fear death because it's an unknown.

But Socrates apparently doesn't fear the unknown. This is an aspect of the philosophical temperament. He's constantly *searching* for what's unknown, what's unfamiliar. For natural philosophy, that means what lies outside the human realm: nature, both great and small. This is how Socrates began to philosophize, as depicted in the *Clouds*.

But the philosophical quest is not necessarily for the new, but for the true. Sometimes the true isn't all that new. Sometimes one discovers truth in the old and familiar. Thus Socrates turned from the non-human to the human realm, from the great and small to the middle, from the unfamiliar to the familiar, which in the light of nature had begun to seem strange and questionable as well.

But then Socrates goes on:

> But I, men, am perhaps distinguished from the many human beings also here in this, and if I were to say that I am wiser than anyone in anything, it would be in this: that since I don't know sufficiently about the things in Hades, so also I suppose that I do not know. (29b).

Socrates is saying, 'I'm just like you. I don't know anything about the afterlife. But unlike you, I know that I don't know.' Saying that one knows nothing about the afterlife is like saying one knows nothing about the gods. For there are gods in the underworld too. It implies disbelief in the gods of the underworld. It implies that what the jurors believe about the afterlife is false or groundless, hence it is not knowledge.

"But I do know," Socrates says (and here's a knowledge claim from Socrates who's supposed to know nothing):

> that it is bad and shameful to do injustice and to disobey one's better, whether god or human being. So compared to the bad things which I know are bad, I will never fear or flee the things about which I do not know whether they even happen to be good. (29b)

In sum: 'I know that being evil is bad, but I don't know that being dead is bad. Therefore, given the choice, I'd prefer to die than be evil.' Death might be a profit. But Socrates is certain that evil is never a profit, which is a strong knowledge claim.

WHY SOCRATES CHOSE DEATH OVER EVIL

Then Socrates deals with the suggestion that he might cease and desist from philosophy in exchange for his life: "Socrates, for now we will not obey Anytus; we will let you go, but on this condition: that you no longer spend time on this investigation or philosophize; and if you are caught still doing this, you will die" (29c). Socrates refuses that deal:

> If you would let me go, then, as I said, on these conditions,

> I would say to you, "I, men of Athens, salute and love you, but I will obey the god rather than you; and as long as I breathe and am able to, I will certainly not stop philosophizing, and I will exhort you and exclaim this to whomever of you I happen to meet, and I will speak just the sorts of things I am accustomed to: "Best of men! You are an Athenian, from the city that is greatest and best reputed for wisdom and strength; are you not ashamed that you care for having as much money as possible, and reputation, and honor, but that you neither care for nor give thought to prudence and truth, and how your soul will be the best possible?" (29d–e)

This is Socrates' refrain. You're putting money and reputation ahead of the quality of your own soul, which is not to say that money and reputation are bad but simply that they're not the highest things to pursue and certainly not things to pursue at the expense of your own moral corruption.

> If one of you disputes it and asserts that he does not care, I will not immediately let him go, nor will I go away, but I will speak to him and examine and test him. And if he does not seem to me to possess virtue, but only says he does, then I will reproach him saying that he regards the things worth the most as the least important, and the paltrier things as the more important. I will do this to whoever, younger or older, I happen to meet, both foreigner and townsman, but more so to the townsman inasmuch as you are closer to me in kin. (29e–30a)

Even as a philosopher, Socrates admits to a partiality for Athenians because they are kin. He continues:

> Know well, then, that the god orders this. And *I* suppose that until now no greater good has arisen for you in the city than my service to the god. [In other words, 'I'm God's gift to Athens.'] For I go around and do nothing but persuade you, both younger and older, not to care for bod-

ies and money before, nor as vehemently, as how your soul will be the best possible. I say "Not from money does virtue come, but from virtue comes money and all good things for human beings both privately and publicly." (30a–b)

What about people who prosper from vice? What about the multi-billion-dollar porn industry? What about the multi-billion-dollar gambling industry? What about the multi-billion-dollar alcohol and drug and tobacco trades?

Socrates' answer is that one might get very rich from vice, exploiting the vices of others being a vice in itself. But without virtue, life is not worth living. Without virtue, all the things that money can buy cannot be used rightly, to make one genuinely happy. Indeed, rich fools have it worse than poor ones, because wealth gives them more opportunities for self-ruin. So as long as they are foolish, they'd be better off poor and homeless.

Rich fools can buy lots of thrills. They might *feel* good a lot, but happiness for the Greeks does not mean *well-feeling* but *well-being*. It means a state of harmony and health in the soul. It's possible to suffer physical pain while still having harmony and health in your soul, and it's possible to enjoy physical pleasure and still be in a state of spiritual disharmony and disease.

The question is: Which is the most important? If you could, you'd have both: physical pleasure and spiritual well-being. But if you have to choose, you choose what is the most important: the healthy soul.

Of course, the Athenians don't like to hear that, so there is an uproar in the court. Socrates says, in effect, 'If you kill me, this will hurt you more than it hurts me. Why? Because I'll be dead, but you'll be villains. You won't have harmed me spiritually. You'll merely have killed me. But I'm 70 years old. I'll be dead soon enough anyway. I'll die well, whereas you'll become bad men.'

SOCRATES THE GADFLY

Then Socrates raises the issue of what his defense speech is defending. He admits that he's not doing a very good job of defending himself, which at this point should be obvious to anyone. Then he makes matters worse by saying that he's actually speaking in defense of the jurors. His mission is to make the Athenians better men:

> So I, men of Athens, am now far from making a defense speech on my own behalf, as someone might suppose. I do it rather on your behalf, so that you do not do something wrong concerning the gift of the god to you by voting to condemn me. (30d)

Socrates then famously likens himself to a stinging pest, the gadfly:

> For, if you kill me, you will not easily discover another of my sort, who—even if it is rather ridiculous to say—has simply been set upon the city by the god as though upon a great and well-born horse who is rather sluggish because of his great size and needs to be awakened by some gadfly. Just so, in fact, the god seems to me to have set me upon the city as someone of this sort: I awaken and persuade and reproach each one of you, and I do not stop settling down everywhere upon you the whole day. Someone else of this sort will certainly not easily arise for you, men. Well, if you obey me, you will spare me. But perhaps you will be vexed, like the drowsy when they are awakened, and if you obey Anytus and slap me, you would easily kill me. Then you would spend the rest of your lives asleep, unless the god sends you someone else in his concern for you. (30e–31a)

What Socrates says is intellectually defensible. But, again, he goes out of his way to annoy his audience. Ordinary life really can be likened to sleep, insofar as reality is hidden by falsehoods and half-truths and we are distracted from pursuing genuine well-being by its counterfeits, like pleasure, wealth, and fame. Just as physical health sometimes requires the tough love of the druggist's purgatives and the surgeon's knife, spiritual health sometimes requires the tough love of being roused from our slumbers by Socratic questioning, even though it might be humiliating.

But it seems rather perverse and self-defeating for Socrates to liken this process to being stung by a gadfly, which is a disgusting blood-sucking insect.

Maybe there is something to Xenophon's claim in his *Apology* that Socrates spoke this way to inflame the jury and guarantee a conviction. Is there a philosophical point to this behavior? Or is Socrates just letting his anger and pride carry him away? Is this reason speaking—or *thumos*?

One might wonder: Is there really a fundamental incompatibility between philosophy *as such* and the public at large? Or is there just an incompatibility between Socrates' prickly personality and the public at large? Could philosophy and the city be harmonized with a suaver and—dare I say it?—more sophisticated rhetoric? Maybe Socrates was just not up to the job. Maybe the problem is not opinion as such, but simply the fact that Socrates had a bad reputation, and not just because of the *Clouds* but because he was also a bit of an asshole.

I think the Platonic answer to this is that philosophy *as such* is doomed to a bad reputation because it dissolves conventions that are the cement of society. So the problems faced by Socrates are faced by all philosophers, even the most affable and easy-going ones.

WHY SOCRATES AVOIDED POLITICS

At this point in the argument, it is natural to wonder: If Socrates is such a great boon to the city, then why did he not try to lead it? Hence Socrates deals with that question: "It might seem to be strange that I do go around counseling and being a busybody in private, but that in public I do not dare to go up before your multitude to counsel the city" (31c). Then he says that the *daimonion* began for him in childhood and always counseled him against this. Again, I don't think it began in childhood. I think that it began after the *Clouds*. But in any case, prudence dictates that Socrates not get involved in politics because it is too dangerous. Even though he would help his fellow countrymen, they would be ungrateful and repay help with harm:

> Now do not be vexed with me when I speak the truth. For there is no human being who will preserve his life if he genuinely opposes either you or any other multitude and prevents many unjust and unlawful things from happening in the city. Rather, if someone who really fights for the just is going to preserve himself even for a short time, it is necessary for him to lead a private rather than a public life. (31e–32a)

As soon as we are born, we fall into illusions and distractions, i.e., false beliefs and trivial pursuits that interfere with what we all really want, namely pursuing well-being. Isn't it obvious, then, that we should try to wake everyone up?

Plato's answer is: No, because not everyone is suited for enlightenment. Euthyphro is an example of a man who has been made worse rather than better by popular enlightenment. He would have been a better man if he had clung to the conventional concept of piety that philosophers are quick to dismiss as an illusion.

If not everyone is suited for enlightenment, then it is not responsible to broadcast philosophy to the public at large. One will make people worse off rather than better. And this will provoke the guardians of public order to swat philosophers like flies. Therefore, if you're going to lead a life pursuing wisdom and perfecting one's soul, you must do it privately.

To find kindred souls, philosophers must sift and sort humanity one-to-one, face-to-face, privately rather than publicly.

Does this mean that most men are doomed to unhappiness? Not necessarily. Although most people are not benefitted from being deprived of illusions and distractions altogether, they can be benefitted by purging away unhealthy illusions and distractions and replacing them with healthier ones.

True philosophy must always fight a two-front war: against the unhealthy conventions that enslave men and against the unhealthy intellectuals who would liberate us from convention altogether.

How Socrates Served Athens

After Socrates has been condemned, he mentions philosophy's second front against misguided intellectuals:

> I affirm, you men who have condemned me to death, that vengeance will come upon you right after my death, and much harsher, by Zeus, than the sort you give to me by killing me. For you have now done this deed supposing that you will be relieved from giving an account of your life, but it will turn out much the opposite for you as *I* affirm. There will be more who will refute you, whom I have now been holding back: you did not perceive them. And they will be harsher, inasmuch as they are younger, and you will be more indignant. (39c–d).

Who has Socrates been holding back? People like Euthyphro. People like the Socrates of the *Clouds*: vain, alienated, intellectuals; father beaters and corrupters of the youth. Socrates has been reining such people in. The jurors don't understand that, because constructive and destructive philosophy all look pretty much the same to unpracticed eyes. But without Socrates' moderating influence, bad ideas will be running amok. The Athenians think they are getting rid of a gadfly, but actually he's been holding back far more insidious forms of philosophizing.

Socrates was a hard friend. But he rendered unique and indispensable benefits to his city. The Athenians may never understand why, but they will be worse off once he is gone.

Plato's *Crito*

Plato's *Crito* is a very short dialogue. On the surface it's about Socrates' refusal to escape from prison and go into exile. But below the surface, the *Crito* is a very subtle meditation on the nature of political order. Underlying it is a distinction between three levels of human association, which I shall call pre-political, political, and trans-political association.

Pre-Political Association

Pre-political association is found in the smallest organic communities and has three dimensions. First, there is kinship, which is primarily a biological relationship but also involves erotic love of one's mate and "love of one's own," which is based in the spirited part of the soul. Second, there are personal attachments to friends and neighbors, which involve spirited love of one's own. Third, there are economic relationships based on self-interest, whether mutual (trade) or exploitative (slavery), all of them rooted in the desiring part of the soul.

Generally, within the pre-political realm, the relationships that exist between families, friends, and neighbors are governed by affection, whereas the relationships between strangers are governed by self-interest. The ethics of pre-political association boils down to: 'A good man is one who helps his friends and harms his enemies.' Plato discusses this view of justice in the first book of the *Republic*.

The Greek city-state was imposed upon these pre-political forms of association—including families, clans, and tribes—and existed in uneasy tension with them throughout its entire existence. These pre-political forms of justice are present in *Euthyphro* in the distinction between civil and criminal laws. If someone was murdered, it was treated as a civil case, meaning it was for the victim's own kin, his pre-political associates, to handle. The state took no interest in the matter. The state had an interest in it only in the sense that it gave a legal form to private vendettas, which is basically what civil law does today. If you were murdered and no one was left to bring a case on your behalf, the state wouldn't do it. That wasn't their job.

Strepsiades in the *Clouds* can be described as a pre-political individual. He is entirely concerned with his family and himself. He has a very tenuous sense of what it is to be a good citizen. So he's willing to cheat his fellow citizens. He's willing to twist and break the law, except, of course, when the laws are in his own interest. Then he appeals to them loudly. Strepsiades has no unconditional attachment to the law, no civic spirit. His only relationship to the law is self-interested. He's for the law when it's in his interest, and he's against it when it's not. He's not so much a citizen as just a legal consumer or shirker, depending on his interests.

POLITICAL ASSOCIATION

Political association is different. Political association, first of all, requires a certain scale. You're never going to have political order in a group of people small enough for them to all know one another and interact face-to-face. You don't need it. You can pretty much ensure social order simply based on personal relationships and affections. Hunter-gatherer bands, for instance, are pre-political associations. They're extended families, or groups of extended families, who all know one another personally.

But once communities get too large for everyone to know everyone else, then you must pass from pre-political to political association. When members of your community are strangers, your relations need to be mediated by something more than just self-interest or sentiments of attachment. We need impersonal rules to secure justice and harmony.

Once you start having laws, you can increase the scale of society dramatically. You could conceivably have a political society of hundreds of trillions of individuals, as long as all the laws function, because through these laws you can relate to trillions of other human beings with whom you could never form a personal relationship.

TRANS-POLITICAL ASSOCIATION

Trans-political association is above the laws made by human beings. Instead, it's regulated by an appeal to the laws of nature.

In the light of a notion of an unchanging and common nature, and an unchanging common natural right or justice, humanity appears to be one. In a radical sense, it's different than saying people would be one if they were all citizens of the same global state, because the laws are natural rather than conventional.

Politics is always conventional, and, although you can conceive of a global *polis*, there are many distinct political societies. This is why the concept of a global society is an odd thing. You can only get to it by eliminating all the fundamental distinctions that exist between the political societies in the world today. But that would lead to a world unrecognizable as our own. Political association involves a plurality of different political orders distinguished by different sets of conventional rules or norms for integrating and harmonizing people's actions.

Trans-political association requires the development of rationality to a high degree, because one comes to know nature only through reason. You don't need highly developed rational faculties, or any rational faculties at all, to be a good citizen. You just need the sentiments that attach you to your own group, to your fatherland, to your fellow citizens. But one of the conditions of trans-political association is the cultivation of rationality to a high degree.

The cultivation of reason leads to the notion of a life of the mind that transcends conventional distinctions. People with opposed political loyalties can associate harmoniously on the trans-political plane. My favorite example is Alexandre Kojève, the Stalinist, and Leo Strauss, the ultra-conservative, who were fast philosophical friends. How? Because their form of association was trans-political, based on the life of the mind. Within the life of the mind, a lot of the distinctions of the Cold War era melted away. Neither one of them saw that big a difference between Western capitalism and communism, when they viewed them from a suitably distant perspective. But, of course, they were always able to slip back to their political selves and take up opposite sides in the Cold War. But that wasn't their main form of association, and they just agreed to disagree on the Cold War.

If Strepsiades belongs down on the pre-political level, Socrates truly belongs up on a trans-political level. He orients himself by what's right by nature. Euthyphro is somewhere above the political, but not far enough above it to orient himself by what is right by nature. Euthyphro wants to get beyond a political level of life, and Socrates tries to get Euthyphro to turn around and resubmit himself to more conventional forms of association. He wants him to be a better citizen and a better son, to be more pious in terms of the conventional forms of Athenian piety.

WHO IS CRITO?

The Crito for whom this dialogue is named is very much like Strepsiades, a totally pre-political individual. But in this dialogue, Socrates tries to lead Crito up from pre-political association to political association, and that requires teaching him to respect conventional laws. Even though Socrates himself can look to natural law for guidance, he's trying to teach Crito to be concerned with conventional law and guide himself by that, rather than by the dual ethic of pre-political life which is helping your friends and harming your enemies.

Crito was an old friend of Socrates, and, appropriately enough, their form of friendship is entirely pre-political. They grew up near one another. They were members of the same *deme*, which was a pre-political division that existed in Athens, or, more precisely, a political division that took into account pre-political tribal distinctions that existed long before Athens became a city-state, in the manner of the different US states, which used to be considered sovereign entities but today have no real sovereignty whatsoever. But the same borders still exist for many of them, and they have their capitals and governments and flags and seals. In that sense, we still recognize a status that they once had but no longer enjoy. The *deme* had the same status for the ancient Athenian.

Crito is quite conventional, and his friendship with Socrates is not based on the life of the mind. They were born near one another; they grew up together; they've known one another all their lives; they have a certain fondness for one another. But it's a pre-political kind of fondness. Crito is no philosopher.

Crito did write some Socratic dialogues. I really wish they had survived, because they probably were fairly unimaginative reports of actual discussions that they'd had, since Crito wasn't the kind of guy who would depart too much from what had actually happened, and if he did, it would probably be easy to detect.

THE SETTING OF THE *CRITO*

Socrates has been condemned, and he's being held in prison. However, he's been held in prison for some time because there was a custom that a ship would be sent from Athens to Delos every year to pay respects to the god Apollo. The ship departed the day before Socrates' trial, and there could be no executions in the city while the ship was away. Because of adverse winds, the trip took 31 days. So, Socrates had a 30-day stay of execution. But the ship is returning, and Socrates will soon die.

Crito comes to him before daybreak. Socrates wakes up, and Crito tells him that he has made preparations for Socrates to escape so he can go into exile. Socrates says he's not going to do this, and they have the discussion that transpires here. Crito is convinced not to oppose Socrates, so Socrates simply stays for his execution.

DARKNESS & DREAMS

The dialogue begins before dawn. It's dark. There is no indication that the sun ever breaks over the horizon in the whole course of the conversation. In fact, there's no indication that Socrates even gets out of bed.

Socrates begins by relating a dream that he's had, and near the end of the text he relates a speech that the laws of Athens would give to him. Socrates says, "What if the laws and the community of the city should come and stand before us who are about to run away?" (50a). The Greeks frequently said dreams "stand before" the person dreaming. In this case, they would stand before both Socrates and Crito in a shared dream. Thus the Crito has a somnolent and dreamlike quality from beginning to end.

Later Socrates says, "Know well, my dear comrade Crito, that these things [namely, what the laws say] are what *I* seem to hear, just as the Corybantes seem to hear the flutes, and this echo of these speeches is booming within me and makes me unable to hear the others" (54d). The Corybantes took part in ecstatic dances in honor of the mother goddess Cybele. This suggests that the laws have a power of enchantment, possession, beguilement, and enthrallment. The authority of conventional laws is not, like the laws of nature, based simply on reason. The laws appeal to our non-rational nature.

The symbolism of darkness and dreams—especially shared or collective dreams—brings to mind the Allegory of the Cave in the *Republic*. The cave refers to the social world, which is bound together by shared illusions. In this case, the cave is pre-political opinion. It's the world of Crito.

Crito is not an enlightened fellow, and this shows in his preferences.

> SOCRATES: Have you just come, or have you been here long?
> CRITO: Fairly long.
> SOCRATES: Then why didn't you wake me up right away, instead of sitting beside me in silence?
> CRITO: . . . I kept from waking you on purpose, so that you would pass the time as pleasantly as possible. (43a–b)

Socrates' preference is to be awake, but Crito can't think of anything more pleasant than being asleep. This is an indication of their characters. Crito is a person who likes sleeping and dreaming. That's a wonderful symbol of a relatively unenlightened state of consciousness. Whereas Socrates wishes to be awake all the time, and that's an indication that his philosophic nature always seeks and prefers enlightenment.

Although Socrates wishes that Crito had awakened him rather than let him sleep, it is remarkable that Socrates is sleeping at all, for he is in prison and will soon die. When Crito asks Socrates how he can sleep so well at a time line this, Socrates replies, "That's because it would be discordant, Crito, for someone of my age to be vexed if he now must meet his end" (43b). What's the opposite of discord? Harmony. Socrates' capacity to sleep at a time like this is a result of his deep, composed harmony of soul. This, of course, is true of any person whose mind is made up. They don't dither.

CRITO PROPOSES A JAILBREAK

After Socrates relates his dream, Crito informs him that he has bribed the guard to allow Socrates to escape. Once he escapes, his friends will spirit him into exile. The first act we hear about is Crito breaking the law and corrupting its servant. Why is he breaking the law? Why is he corrupting the guard? He's doing it for a friend. Crito's preference is to always take care of his friends, and the laws really don't matter that much for him.

Crito appeals to Socrates to escape based on his duty to himself, his sons, and his friends. He never says anything about Socrates' duty to his fatherland, to the laws. Those sorts of duties don't exist in Crito's mind, or they're very tenuous. Again, the only time that Crito would probably appeal to the law is if it would be on his side, just like Strepsiades.

MINDING PUBLIC OPINION

Crito is not just worried about losing his friend Socrates, he's worried about losing face:

> But, *daimonic* Socrates, even now obey me and save yourself, since if you die, for me it is not just one calamity: apart from being deprived of such a companion as I will never discover again, I will also seem to many, those who don't know you and me plainly, to have been able to save you had I been willing to spend money, but not to have cared. And yet what reputation would be more shameful than to seem to regard money as more important than friends? For the many will not be persuaded that you yourself were not willing to go away from here although we were eager for it. (44b–c)

Crito is concerned about the opinions of strangers, and not so much their opinions of what *really* went on, but their opinions of what *seems* to have gone on. He thinks it would be awful if strangers thought that he didn't care enough for his friend to spend his money to help him escape. Helping his friends, harming his enemies: that's Crito's ethic. But he is also concerned with the good opinion of strangers.

Socrates says, "But why do we care in this way, blessed Crito, about the opinions of the many? For the most decent men, whom it is more worthy to give thought to, will hold these things to be done in just the way they were done" (44c).

Socrates immediately makes a distinction between types of opinion. There's the opinion of the many, and there's the opinion of decent men. We should only care about the opinions of decent men, the people who will know that things have been done properly. Crito has nothing to fear from them.

Crito responds: "But surely you see that it is necessary, Socrates, to care also about the opinion of the many" (44d). Why? Crito says, "The present situation makes it clear that the many can produce not the smallest of evils, but almost the greatest if someone is slandered among them" (44d). They can kill you, in other words.

THE GREATEST GOOD & THE GREATEST EVIL

Socrates' response is extremely rich and interesting. Socrates says, "Would that the many could produce the greatest evils, Crito, so that they could also produce the greatest good" (44d). This reply depends on the Greek premise that if you have an art, it gives you power over opposites. The art of the doctor gives one the capacity to cure or to kill. The same with the art of the pharmacist. The pharmacist can be the wiliest of poisoners or dispense the curative dose. Socrates is saying that there's an art that the many don't have. It's an art of creating the greatest of goods and also the greatest of evils.

What are the greatest of goods and the greatest of evils? Socrates says, "[The many] aren't capable of making someone prudent or imprudent" (44d). The Greek word for prudence is "*phronesis*," and another translation for that would be "wisdom" in the practical sense. There are two Greek words for wisdom: "*sophia*" and "*phronesis*." *Sophia* is generally used to refer to either wisdom in a generic sense or theoretical wisdom, the kind of wisdom that Socrates in the *Clouds* possesses. "*Phronesis*" refers specifically to practical wisdom, the kind of wisdom that

Socrates doesn't have in the *Clouds*. In fact, Strepsiades has more of it than Socrates.

The greatest good, apparently, is to be prudent, and the greatest evil is to be imprudent. The greatest good is to be wise, and the greatest evil is to be foolish. Does this mean that Socrates no longer cares about *sophia*, or wisdom in the theoretical sense? Not necessarily, because we could explain the absence of a reference to *sophia* by the fact that he's addressing Crito, who is a deeply practical man, so the only face wisdom would show to Crito would be practical wisdom.

The *Phadeo* shows that Socrates was still interested in theoretical issues to the day he died, for before his death, he discusses arguments for the immortality of the soul. But at a certain point, he recognized that not only is practical wisdom important, but in a sense practical wisdom is more important than theoretical wisdom, because theoretical wisdom without practical wisdom really isn't wisdom at all. It's just the kind of extravagant folly displayed by the Socrates of the *Clouds*.

Put it this way: theoretical knowledge without the ability to make right use of it really isn't wisdom at all. It's just a kind of comprehensive knowledge, and knowledge by its nature is neither good nor evil. It needs to be given that direction by practical wisdom. But the best thing is to have both kinds of wisdom.

The greatest good is to be wise, and the greatest evil is to be foolish, and the many can't produce either one of them.

Crito then says, in effect, 'Look, Socrates, if you're worried that we'll get arrested, that the informers will turn us in, that it will produce a great source of trouble for us, don't worry about it. We're wise in the ways of the world. We can take care of these things.' And Socrates says, "I am worrying over the prospect of these things, Crito, and of many others" (45a).

Crito sees Socrates' primary concerns as being practical and assures him that such contingencies have been taken care of. This is an indication of the kind of man Crito is. Socrates isn't disdainful of practical concerns, by any means, but at the same time he thinks that there are more important concerns, and those concerns come out fairly quickly. Socrates has *moral* concerns about the proper care of the soul.

Crito Puts Socrates on Trial Again

Then, in effect, Crito puts Socrates on trial again. He charges Socrates with betraying himself by allowing his enemies to get the better of him. He charges him with betraying his sons, not sticking around to educate and nurture them. Socrates is also betraying his friends, both by denying them his company and also by making them look bad. Then Crito tells Socrates that if he can't defend himself, then he has to leave prison with Crito.

Now, the second charge really isn't that much of an issue, because if Socrates fled, he probably couldn't have taken the children with him anyway. And even if the trial had never happened, given that he was a 70-year-old man in a time before modern medicine, chances are he wouldn't be around much longer to oversee their upbringing.

Crito continues:

> Instead, one should choose what a good and manly man would choose [the Greek word for courage, *andreia*, also means manliness], particularly if one has claimed to care for virtue through his whole life. For my part, I am ashamed for you and for us, your companions, that the whole affair concerning you will seem to have been conducted with a certain lack of manliness on our part. The way the lawsuit was introduced into the law court, even though it was possible for it not to be introduced [this is very interesting if Socrates could have avoided the trial entirely]; the way the judicial contest itself took place; and now this, the ridiculous conclusion of the affair, will seem to have escaped us completely because of a certain badness and lack of manliness on our part, since we didn't save you, nor did you save yourself, although it was possible and feasible if we had been of even a slight benefit. (45e–46a)

Socrates replies:

> Dear Crito, your eagerness is worth much if some correctness be with it. If not, the greater it is, the harder it is to

deal with. So we should consider whether these things are to be done or not, since I, not only now but always, am such as to obey nothing else of what is mine than that argument which appears best to me upon reasoning. (46b).

In this light, Socrates' last words in the dialogue are interesting: "Then let it go, Crito, and let us act this way since in this way the god is leading" (54e). If the god is leading and reason is leading, then, in a sense, you can say that for Socrates what is divine is reason, or the right thing to do according to reason, which is what's right by nature. The moral truth discoverable by reason is the truly divine. This fits perfectly with our reading of the *Euthyphro*.

If Socrates listens only to reason, this also implies the *daimonion* that he obeys is really reason, not a divine being. As we have learned from the *Theages*, the *daimonion* is just a personification of his knowledge of the human soul.

THE OPINIONS THAT REALLY MATTER

In responding to Crito, Socrates first argues against Crito's excessive concern with public opinion. He asks, "Was it said nobly on each occasion or not, that one should pay mind to some opinions and not others?" (46c–d). The way that Socrates conducts this argument is interesting. Socrates is constantly saying, 'Crito, do you and I agree or not that this is the case?' He's trying to build upon past agreements. Now, what is another word for agreements between human beings? Conventions. Socrates is, in a sense, trying to lead Crito by getting him to submit himself to conventions that have been established between him and Socrates. That foreshadows what happens later in the text when Socrates tries to lead Crito to a reverence for law, which consists of conventions that have been established by an entire society and consecrated by use and tradition. He's trying to lead Crito towards a submission to the conventional laws of political association.

Socrates raises the question of what sort of opinions should be heeded:

SOCRATES: . . . the upright opinions but not the villainous?
CRITO: Yes.
SOCRATES: Aren't the upright ones those of the prudent, and the villainous ones those of the imprudent?
CRITO: Of course. (47a)

So, the only opinions you're supposed to pay any mind to are the opinions of the wise. These are the only opinions that really matter.

Then Socrates uses us an analogy from craft. What if a person is an athlete? Whose opinion should he listen to? The spectators on the sideline, or the trainer, or the doctor? (47b). There's a lot of ghoulishness among spectators. I love hockey. It's the only spectator sport that is fast enough for me. People in the stands are screaming "Kill! Kill!" So, if an athlete listens to the opinions of the spectators, he might be ruined. They don't necessarily have his best interests in mind. So, you should listen to the opinion of your trainer, the person who knows your limits. Trainers and doctors are the wise in the case of things athletic.

What does the athlete destroy when he listens to the cheers of the many rather than to the expert opinion of the one? He destroys his body, of course. Is life worth living with a corrupted body? Not really. So, if you listen to the many rather than the one, you're going to lead a life that's not worth living because your body will be ruined.

THE CARE OF THE SOUL

Socrates then likens the care of the body to the care of the soul:

> . . . in particular, concerning the just and the unjust and shameful and noble, and good and bad things of which we are now taking counsel, must we follow the opinion of the many and fear it rather than that of the one—if there is such an expert—whom we must be ashamed before and fear more than all the others? And if we don't follow him, we will corrupt and maim that thing which, as we used to say, becomes better by the just and is destroyed by the un-

just. Or isn't there anything to this? (47c–d)

Now, the question is: What becomes better by the just and is destroyed by the unjust? It's the soul! It's very interesting though that Socrates circumlocutes around the word "soul."

Socrates then asks, "But is life worth living for us with that thing corrupted which the unjust maims and the just profits?" (47e). It's a very obvious and wordy way of not saying 'the soul.' Is life worth living for us with a corrupted soul? The answer would be clearly no.

Compare this to the *Theages*, in which the soul is also not mentioned directly. I believe that in both dialogues, this indicates that Socrates is speaking to non-philosophers. Socrates is speaking of philosophical matters to a non-philosopher in a non-philosophical manner. If he were speaking to a philosopher, or someone with philosophical potential, he would speak of the soul explicitly, as he does in the *Republic* and *Phaedo*.[1]

Another indication that Socrates is speaking to a non-philosopher here is that when Crito informs Socrates that the ship will soon return from Delos, after which he will die, Socrates replies, ". . . if such is dear to the gods, such let it be" (43d). As we know from the *Euthyphro*, Socrates rejects the idea that piety is what is dear to the gods, but as we have seen from the *Apology*, Socrates appeals to this idea when speaking to the general public.

Now let's look more closely at this passage:

> And in particular concerning the just and unjust, and shameful and noble, and good and bad things about which we are now taking counsel, must we follow the opinion of the many and fear it rather than that of the one — if there is such an expert — whom we must be ashamed

---

[1] Crito is present in the *Phaedo*, but Socrates' discussion of the soul is primarily with two Pythagorean philosophers, Simmias and Cebes. Socrates, moreover, does not talk about the whole soul. He discusses reason and desire but omits *thumos*, the middle part of the soul, and barely mentions honor which is associated with *thumos*.

before and fear more than all the others? (47c–d)

He's saying *if* there is an expert on what's shameful and not, what's good and bad. Of course, there are such experts. We call them philosophers. But, like the soul, the expert on the soul is not named here. Instead, he is occluded in an odd way. He is put into question. He is under a shadow, in the same way that the soul is hidden in the shadows. And, of course, everything in this dialogue is in the shadows because it's before dawn.

The point is that the soul doesn't appear in the darkness of a political or pre-political life. It only appears once you've moved to the trans-political level, because the key to natural law is understanding the soul. We understand the whole of the cosmos and nature through understanding the soul. This is the position of the mature Socrates, and this is entirely different from the Socrates of the *Clouds*.

The many cannot deliver the best or the worst, namely wisdom and folly. But they can still kill us. Surely that's reason enough to worry about their opinion. And surely it is reason enough for Socrates to escape from jail. Socrates' response is that there is something more important than merely living, which is living well, which means living nobly and justly. If Socrates stays, he will be killed. But if he goes, he will have to pay for his escape in the form of spiritual corruption. But that's a bad bargain. That's trading gold for lead. Dying is not that important to Socrates. Living well is more important.

THE SECOND-BEST WAY TO VIRTUE

The best way to attain virtue is to lead the philosophical life of care for the soul. But philosophy is not for the many. It is for the few. The reason Socrates does not speak explicitly to Crito about the soul or the philosopher, who is the expert in caring for the soul, is that Crito is not a philosophical type. Crito cannot know what the soul is and what it requires. He cannot have the kind of expertise that can produce the greatest good and the greatest evil, namely wisdom. He will have to settle for something less.

The second-best route for learning virtue is the laws of the city, the conventional laws. This is why the whole argument moves forward, step by step, by means of establishing conventions between Socrates and Crito. This is why the dialogue ends with the dream-like and beguiling speech of the laws. Socrates is really trying to beguile poor Crito. But it's for Crito's own good, because Crito will become a better man if he can rise above this ethic of helping friends and harming enemies and attain, even at this late stage in his life, a certain reverence for law as such, even when it may not necessarily be in his interest.

Socrates says something very interesting at 48d–e:

> Let us consider in common, my good man [again, he's always bringing the two together in common discussion, establishing a common viewpoint], and if there is some way you can contradict my argument, contradict it, and I will obey you. But if not, blessed man, then stop telling me the same argument again and again, that I ought to go away from here although the Athenians are unwilling. For I regard it important to act after persuading you, not while you are unwilling. (48d–e)

Why is it important for Socrates to persuade Crito? Socrates is already in prison. He doesn't have to persuade Crito in order to stay. I think that Socrates is trying to persuade Crito because he thinks it will benefit Crito himself by making him a better citizen.

Aristophanes is not under any illusion that Strepsiades could know what's right by nature and act on it. Nor is Socrates under any illusion that Crito could do the same. Both men will be the best they can be if they can learn reverence for the law. And what does reverence for the law do? It takes you outside of your private and personal interests and allows you to contribute to civilization, to make a higher order of life possible. So, a good citizen is a very good thing indeed.

THE GOOD CITIZEN

Political life requires the creation of a conception of the common good that people will promote at the risk of their short-term private interests. Once people are willing to take that risk, they find that there are larger goods available to them. Political life is the basis of any higher form of civilization. This is why Aristotle was for the *polis*, because you can't find high culture in tribal societies.

We give the most moral credit to the man who does something because it is *right*, even if it isn't in his self-interest, especially when it entails loss. You don't give a person moral credit for doing what's right when it's convenient or easy. You give a person moral credit for doing what is right precisely when it's the most difficult.

Although the right and the legal often diverge, we give people the same kind of credit when they follow the law precisely when it's not convenient, because it is clear that their primary loyalty is to the law rather than to their own convenience. We call people like that good citizens. The trouble with a world of people who only follow the laws when somebody's looking is that there are circumstances when someone isn't watching, then the law breaks down.

Consider the "prisoner's dilemma." The police arrest two men near the scene of a crime. The police are pretty sure they have the crooks. But they don't have any evidence. So what do they do? They put them in separate interrogation rooms and offer each of them a deal. If you rat on your friend, we'll give you lenient punishment.

Now, the best situation for both of them is to be able to trust the other guy not to rat on him, and not rat on the other guy as well. Then they both go free. But the only way to get the best outcome is if they trust one another. But that requires that both are willing to take the *risk* of putting their mutual good (both getting off) before their individual interests (ratting on their accomplice). If a person isn't willing to take that risk, the common good becomes unattainable.

The only thing that takes individuals or groups out of the competitive, cut-throat "state of nature" of pre-political association and brings them into political order is being willing to take the *risk* of laying down one's short-term individual interests and submitting oneself to a legal order that can produce a larger good that everybody can enjoy. If you can't take that risk, then political order will either collapse or never come into existence.

In societies where trust begins to break down, people stop following the laws. They say, 'I'm only going to follow the law when it's in my interest. I can't count on my fellow man being a decent human being who will reciprocate in kind if I take the risk of decency.' All one needs to unravel the trust that holds up society are a few well-established cases of good people being exploited because of their goodness.

One of my students told me that a street gang decided to induct new members by sending them out in a car at night with their headlights off, and they were supposed to shoot at the first good citizen who flashed their lights to indicate that they were driving with their lights off. All you need is one case of that, and suddenly people don't take the risk of good citizenship.

You can have political order only if you take individuals who are self-seeking (for themselves and their families) and induce them to submit to common impersonal rules, even though submitting to those rules entails the risk of being exploited if one's good citizenship is not reciprocated.

One needs another motivating factor that counter-balances one's calculations of self-interest. That factor is the idea of the noble. The noble person does his duty, follows the law, even when it is difficult and does not redound to his selfish interests. Without nobility, political society collapses into pre-political society.

THE GOOD MAN & THE GOOD CITIZEN

A good citizen follows the laws of his society and is willing to subordinate his private interests to ensure its survival and flourishing. But the good citizen is not the highest human possibility. The good citizen is relative to particular regimes and their laws. But above the laws of men stand the laws of nature. But the laws of nature—like the soul, and philosopher who cares for it—are only hinted at in the *Crito*, because they are largely invisible to Crito, and Socrates' purpose is to make him into a good citizen.

At 49c Socrates states ". . . surely there is no difference between human beings doing evil and doing injustice." Crito replies, "What you say is true." But is it true? Is there no difference between doing evil and doing injustice? If there is a difference, what is it? Injustice means breaking the laws of the city. Being a bad citizen. What does doing evil mean? Breaking the laws of nature. Being a bad man.

Doing evil and doing injustice would only be the same thing if the laws of the state were in complete harmony with the laws of nature, and that's not always the case. In fact, it's very seldom the case. Thus when Socrates equates doing evil and doing injustice, this is one of those questionable premises that he throws out hoping for someone to say, 'Wait a second here!' But Crito sees no problem, because Crito doesn't see anything above the conventional law, and even that is a bit hazy for him.

But Socrates does recognize a higher law. The clearest indication is in the *Apology*. Remember when Socrates says, 'What if you were to offer me the following deal: "We'll let you live. Just don't do philosophy"?' And what does he say? 'No way!' But the enactments of the courts were laws. He would not obey a law against philosophizing, because philosophy is right by nature, and no human law can contravene that, certainly no human law that Socrates will respect. So Socrates believes in civil disobedience. Socrates believes in breaking the laws, if the laws of the state contradict the laws of nature. This is especially important to keep in mind when you read the speech from the laws that follows.

However, Crito doesn't have access to that higher standard, so he doesn't see any difference between evil and law-breaking, between what's legal and what's moral. That's the limitation of the good citizen. The good citizen, by identifying what is legal with what is moral, can sometimes very piously and zealously do evil things because they are duly enacted by the state.

THE LAWS SPEAK

Let's turn to the speech of the laws. Again, it's cast in the language of a dream-like apparition. These are the kinds of flickering, beguiling shadows that one sees down in the cave. Socrates is using these to beguile Crito. Why? To make him a better man.

What if the laws and the community of the city should

come and stand before us who are about to run away (or whatever name we should give it) from here and ask: "Tell me, Socrates, what do you have in mind to do? By this deed you're attempting, what do you think you're doing if not destroying us laws and the whole city, as far as it lies in you? Or does it seem possible to you for a city to continue to exist, and not to be overturned, in which the judgments that are reached have no strength, but are rendered ineffective and are corrupted by private men?" (50a–b).

The private man is the pre-political man. This is a good question. How can political order exist if the judgments of the laws are turned over by private men? This is the anti-civil disobedience argument. If everybody just says, 'I'm going to opt out of obeying the law, because of my conscience,' we'll have chaos. There's truth to that, too. This is why it's a delicate issue. I would rather live in a dictatorship than in a state of anarchy, because bad laws are better than no laws at all. That's an important issue, and the laws are raising a valid question.

> SOCRATES: What shall we say, Crito, to these and other such things. For someone, especially an orator, would have many things to say on behalf of this law if it were destroyed, the law that orders that the judgments reached in trials be authoritative, or shall we tell them the city was doing us injustice and did not pass judgment correctly? Shall we say this or what?
> CRITO: Yes, this, by Zeus, Socrates!
> SOCRATES: Then what if the laws should say, "Socrates, has it been agreed to by us and you to do this or to abide by whatever judgments the city reaches in trial?'" (50b–c)

And so he's saying, 'Socrates, you've agreed to abide by our judgments. You've signed on the dotted line.' It's a sort of social contract view. But it's very important to ask the question: On what grounds does Crito so readily agree that we should tell the city that it's doing injustice? Is it an appeal to natural law over and above the enactments of convention, or is it an appeal to some other notion of right and wrong?

The city's doing injustice by harming my friend! That's why he's so ready to agree to this. Socrates wants to give up that attitude. Socrates says, 'But I've made a convention with the city, a compact to obey the laws.' He goes on to explain later that it's a sort of tacit agreement—that he had every right to leave the city once he was an adult, but he chose not to, and, therefore, by tacit consent he has agreed to obey all the judgments of the laws.

But before Socrates goes into that, he gives a completely different ground for the authority of the laws: The laws say, in effect, 'Didn't we bring you into existence? Your mother and father begat you, but you weren't a bastard. They weren't farm animals. They were man and wife, legally wed, and you were their legitimate offspring. By what? By us, the laws.'

Human beings, unlike farm animals, marry and breed under law, and, therefore, we have legal marriages and legal offspring. So, the laws say, 'We are the third begetter of you, Socrates. We are just as much your parent as your parents were. We brought you into this world, and we can take you out, too.' The laws ask, 'Didn't we nurture and educate you?'

They continue: "What about those that concern the nurture and education in which you, too, were educated of the one born? Or didn't those laws among us which have been ordered for this end order your father nobly when they passed along and commanded him to educate you in music and gymnastic?" (50d-e). Now, gymnastic educates the body, and music—which refers to all things connected with the muses, not just music proper—educates the tastes and sentiments and the spirited part of the soul. But there's no mention of the laws providing for the education of the higher part of the soul. Specifically, the laws don't provide for the cultivation of reason.

If, however, you look at the educational regime in the *Republic*, the *kallipolis*, the "city in speech," we find that beyond music and gymnastic education is another level of education that cultivates reason, which ultimately culminates in the production of philosopher-kings. The laws of Athens make no provision for that. Thus the laws are indicating that they make possible a certain kind of political excellence, but not the highest form of human excellence, which is, in a sense, trans-political—namely the cultivation of rationality. Because the laws don't make this possible, there are grounds for breaking the laws, not because you're *beneath* them, but because you're *above* them.

The Laws continue in a passage filled with echoes of the Just and the Unjust Speeches of the *Clouds*: "Well then, since you were born and nurtured and educated too, could you say first that you are not ours, both our offspring and slave, you yourself as well as your forbearers? And, if this is so, do you suppose that justice is equal for you and for us?" (50e).

Remember the Unjust Speech? Remember Pheidippides? Pheidippides, who listens to the Unjust Speech, thinks that justice is equal between fathers and sons. He doesn't see that there is an inequality between fathers and their children and between ancient laws and the modern *demos*, because he also says about the laws of the city: 'Men made those laws. I'm a man. So why can't I make new ones?' That's the teaching of the sophists, or the Unjust Speech, that justice is equal, that there are no unequal relationships. Here the laws offer a Just Speech that's far more powerful than the weak, flimsy Just Speech in the *Clouds*:

> . . . do you suppose that it is just to do in return whatever we attempt to do to you? Now, in regard to your father (or a master if you happen to have one), justice was not equal for you, so that you didn't also do in return whatever you suffered. You didn't contradict him when he spoke badly of you, nor did you beat him in return when you were beaten, or do any other such thing. So, is it then permitted to you to do with regard to the fatherland and the laws so that we, believing it to be just, attempt to destroy you then you too, to the extent that you can, will attempt to destroy us laws and the fatherland in return. (50e–51b)

In effect, they're saying: 'We can destroy you, but you have no right to destroy us. Justice is not equal between us.'

I'm sure you're thinking, "Eeek, the 'fatherland'! It sounds awful." But Socrates is trying to instill an entirely proper and salutary reverence for the laws. That reverence gives the laws the power to trump one's personal interests. One goes to them not on equal terms for a self-interested exchange. There are certain things a citizen owes that might not be in his interest. That's what nobility requires.

Philosophy & the Law

Now one might ask if political association is a necessary antecedent—a prerequisite—to the trans-political. Yes it is. The laws say, 'Socrates, you obviously loved Athens and us enough that you never wanted to leave.' Well, there are other explanations for why Socrates didn't leave Athens, other than because he loved the laws so much. In fact, the laws in Athens were in chaos, and he thought the laws in Sparta and Crete were better. But he didn't go to Crete or Sparta.

Why? Because Crete or Sparta, though they had excellent laws and produced excellent citizens, did not have the freedom or the flourishing culture that Athens had. That kind of freedom and high culture are two primary conditions for the creation of philosophy. It's precisely because Athens was so decadent, in some ways, and so badly governed, that there was an atmosphere conducive to philosophizing.

For a very long time, people have recognized that philosophy flourishes best in slightly seedy and decadent climates, because theory lags behind practice, so you can philosophically understand what's good about a particular society only when it is already in decline. Hence Hegel's metaphor: "The owl of Minerva takes flight only at dusk." Wisdom, represented by the owl of Minerva, only emerges in the twilight of a civilization, when it's a little too ripe. Of course, decadent societies can last for hundreds of years.

But let's listen to the laws, and try to imagine some Wagner playing in the background.

> And will you say that in doing this you are acting justly, you, who in truth care for virtue? Or are you so wise that you have been unaware that fatherland is something more

honorable than mother and father and all the other forbearers, and more venerable, and more holy, and more highly esteemed among gods and among human beings who are intelligent? And that you must revere and give way to and fawn upon a fatherland more than a father when it is angry with you and either persuade it to do whatever it bids and keep quiet and suffer if it orders you to suffer anything, whether to be beaten or to be bound? Or if that it leads you to war to be wounded or to be killed, this must be done? And that this is just and that you are not to give way or retreat or leave your station, but that in war and in court and everywhere, you must do whatever the city and the fatherland bid, or else persuade it what the just is by nature. (51a–c)

This notion of the "just by nature" is the clearest indication in the dialogue of the trans-political. The laws recognize that the only way to get above them is to appeal to what is just by nature. But, of course, Socrates is aware of how difficult this task is.

How could he persuade the people in the court that the life of philosophy is just by nature? We saw what he had to do. We saw the artful perjury he engaged in, particularly his tale of how philosophy is dear to the god Apollo. That's what he had to say. There's no way of communicating what's just by nature to the Strepsiadeses and the Critos of the world, and that's the rub.

This is why philosophers who recognize the nature of political life give up on any utopian dream that they can completely transform the world with philosophy. That doesn't mean that they give up entirely while the world goes to wrack and ruin. But they recognize that the political realm, especially a direct democracy, is not the sort of place where philosophy can have much of an impact.

If you want an image of how philosophy can play a positive role in society, you have to look at the whole drama of the *Republic*, because in the *Republic* Socrates is working to educate Glaucon, a young man from a well-connected family, namely Plato's family. Philosophy can have a very powerful effect on politics through education, specifically educating the people who lead or who will lead, but certainly not by going out and persuading the masses.

Socrates concludes by saying that he has no answer to the laws. He asks Crito if he has an answer. Crito has none. Then Socrates says, in effect, 'So, we have to abide by what the laws say. They brought me into this world, they nurtured me, they educated me, and I owe them a debt that I can't repay.'

There is a certain truth to that, when you think about your relationship to your parents and to your society, provided that your parents aren't monsters and your society isn't so bad that you would be better off being raised by wolves.

Even imperfect parents do things for you that you can't ever repay, like create you. So, the relationship between parent and child is never going to be on equal terms. There's always going to be an indebtedness that can't be repaid, although kindness and respect are good starts. Even when they're old fools, you have to respect them and treat them well.

It's the same with a society. A society does all kinds of things for you that are fundamental to your very identity. It too is a debt that can't be repaid, except with a bit of respect.

Socrates also gives another set of reasons for staying, a sort of social contract. He had every opportunity once he grew up to leave, and if he didn't take advantage of that, it's an indication that he agrees with the laws. It doesn't really follow, but he says he has no answer, and Crito can't think of any answer to that either. So Socrates says, 'Well, Crito, I'm persuaded by this, and so I'm going to stay.' We know, though, that Socrates does not have this view of law.

Why, then, *did* he stay? That's an important question. Socrates was an old man. Even if he did leave, he'd lead the life of an old man in exile in a hostile world. That wouldn't be a very enviable fate. It's certainly not a good fate for somebody who believes that life at any price is not really desirable. So I think that he regarded staying as the noblest thing to do, not because the conventional laws of the city, but because of a higher, transpolitical viewpoint.

Plato's *Phaedo*

Plato's *Phaedo* depicts the final conversations and death of Socrates. The *Phaedo* takes place the day after the *Crito*. While Crito was trying to convince Socrates to escape, other friends of Socrates were waiting outside the prison to spirit him away. Among them were two Pythagoreans from Thebes, Simmias and Cebes, who had brought the money to bribe the guard. When Socrates refused to escape, Simmias, Cebes, and the rest joined Socrates in his cell and spent the day talking about philosophy. The Athenians were quite generous and humane in allowing condemned citizens visits from their families and friends. When Socrates' friends left the prison at sundown, they were informed that the sacred ship had returned from Delos, thus on the next day, Socrates would die.

The next morning, more than 15 of Socrates' friends gathered before dawn to talk about philosophy and to say goodbye. The *Phaedo* is a long, densely argued, and densely narrated discussion of topics that were naturally foremost in the minds of a condemned man and his friends: the nature of the soul, whether it can survive the death of the body, and its post-mortem prospects. These topics deserve a whole book of their own. I will bring the present book to an end by looking at selections from the *Phaedo* that relate back to the *Clouds*, *Apology*, and *Crito*. Then we will read the final pages where Socrates dies.

The *Phaedo* takes its name from its narrator, Phaedo of Elis, a student of Socrates who was present at his death. Phaedo told the story to Echecrates and other Pythagoreans who had settled in Phlius, in the Peloponnese, after having been expelled from Southern Italy. Socrates' primary partners in the dialogue are two other Pythagoreans, Simmias and Cebes, who studied with the great Pythagorean Philolaus of Croton (although they don't seem to have learned that much). There is also a strong Pythagorean cast to Socrates's arguments about the nature and immortality of the soul.

The conversation began in the morning and ended at sunset,

when Socrates was executed by drinking hemlock (*Conium maculatum*), which causes paralysis starting in the feet. Eventually, one falls asleep and then stops breathing due to paralysis of the respiratory muscles. It is not a bad way to die.

PHILOSOPHY AS PREPARATION FOR DEATH

Death is a frightening thing. It is frightening if you believe it is simply annihilation. It is frightening if you believe it is the passage to another world, especially for the Greeks, who had a grim and amoral vision of the afterlife. It is even frightening if you simply don't know what it will bring. Thus most people try to stave off death as long as possible. But Socrates not only chose to stay and be executed, he was astonishingly cheerful the whole time he was in prison. Naturally, his friends wanted to know why. What was his secret?

The topic of death arises when Socrates tells Cebes to convey his farewell to Evenus, a sophist mentioned in the *Apology*. He also asks Cebes to tell Evenus, "if he is wise, to follow me [into death] as soon as possible" (61b).[1] Simmias interjects that, based on his knowledge of Evenus "he is not at all likely to follow [Socrates' advice] willingly" (61c). Evenus, it seems, puts a premium on self-preservation, as did the Socrates of the *Clouds*, who — after a long train of provocations — only expelled Strepsiades when he suggested suicide as an escape from his debts. What is the connection between sophists and self-preservation? And why does Socrates maintain that "every man who partakes worthily of philosophy" will be willing to die (61c)?

Socrates hastens to add, though, "Yet perhaps he will not take his own life, for that, they say, is not right" (61c).

Then Plato adds a significant detail: "As he said this, Socrates put his feet on the ground and remained in his position for the rest of the conversation" (61d). For us and the ancient Greeks, having one's feet on the ground connotes contact with concrete

---

[1] Plato, *Phaedo*, trans. G. M. A. Grube, in *Plato: Complete Works*, ed. John M. Cooper (Indianapolis: Hackett, 1997). Grube's translation is generally quite good, but I will make small amendments from time to time.

reality. As opposed to what? Floating in a basket, like the Socrates of the *Clouds*, for one. This is important, because the *Phaedo* is one of Plato's most metaphysical and otherworldly dialogues. Yet no matter how far out Socrates' arguments take him, he takes pains to remain anchored to concrete reality. Thus Socrates is very precise in distinguishing myth, hope, hearsay, likely stories, and hypothetical reasoning from firmly established truths.

When Cebes asks, "How do you mean, Socrates, that it is not right to do oneself violence, and yet that the philosopher will be willing to follow one who is dying?" (61d), Socrates replies that he will speak about this from "hearsay," but he is happy to share what he has heard, "for it is perhaps most appropriate for one who is about to depart yonder to tell and examine tales about what we believe the journey to be like" (61d–e). Here the word "tales" translates a form of the Greek "*mythoi*," from which we get the word myths.

Socrates offers an explanation "in the language of the mysteries," namely that "we men are in a kind of prison, and that one must not free oneself or run away," although Socrates cautions that this "impressive doctrine" is "not easy to understand fully" (62b). This, of course alludes quite directly to Socrates' situation. He is in prison, and when offered the chance to escape, he refused to, for reasons we explored in the *Crito* chapter.

Socrates is, however, more willing to stand by the statement that "the gods are our guardians and that men are one of their possessions" (62b). Killing oneself, on this account, is analogous to breaking out of jail or being a runaway slave. In both cases, we are asserting our own will in defiance of the will of the gods. Therefore, suicide is a bad thing.

Simmias and Cebes, however, turn this argument against Socrates. After all, by choosing to stay to be executed, isn't Socrates in effect committing suicide? If human beings are the property of the gods and are better off under their care, then shouldn't Socrates do anything he can to delay his death, including break out of jail? Although Simmias and Cebes do not point this out, Socrates' refusal to break out of jail could be considered impiety, which is what landed him in jail to begin with.

Socrates sees the force of this objection: "You are both justified in what you say, and I think you mean that I must make a defense against this, as if I were in court"(63b). In short, Socrates is back on trial again and must offer another defense speech. "Come then . . . let me try to make my defense to you more convincing than it was to the jury" (63b).

Cebes argues that if "a god is our protector and we are his possessions" then "it is not logical that the wisest of men should not resent leaving [by being executed] this service in which they are governed by the best of masters, the gods, for a wise man cannot believe that he will look after himself better when he is free" (62d). Based on our reading of the *Euthyphro*, Socrates would reject this claim, because he believes that it is possible for the wise to go over the heads of the gods themselves and learn what is right by nature. Therefore, we don't have to worry about what the gods think.

Cebes is assuming the standard polytheist idea that there are many gods, each of which has a finite jurisdiction. Socrates replies that:

> I should be wrong not to resent dying if I did not believe that I should go first to other wise and good gods. . . . if I insist on anything at all in these matters, it is that I shall come to gods who are very good masters. That is why I am not so resentful, because I have good hope that some future awaits men after death, as we have been told for years, a much better future for the good than for the wicked. (63b–c)

Note that Socrates describes this belief as "good hope" based on what we have been "told." This is far short of claiming to know.

Socrates seems to be assuming that Cebes objects to Socrates leaving the care of this world's good gods for the afterlife, which presumably is under the rule of bad gods, indifferent gods, or no gods at all. Thus Socrates emphasizes that he believes that the afterlife is ruled by good gods as well. This is completely consistent with the Socratic view that any and all genuine gods are necessarily good. But Cebes is not objecting to Socrates leaving our good gods for different kinds of gods. He is simply objecting to Socrates leaving this world's gods at all. If we are the property of the gods, it is not really our choice.

Socrates then states the thesis that he will defend in his new *Apology*:

> I want to make my argument before you, my judges, as to why I think that a man who has truly spent his life in philosophy is probably right to be of good cheer in the face of death and to be very hopeful that after death he will attain the greatest blessings yonder. . . . the one aim of those who practice philosophy in the proper manner is the practice for dying and death. (63e–64a)

Again, note the language of probability, cheer, and hope, all of which fall short of strong knowledge claims.

Even though he is in a somber mood, Simmias laughs at this description of philosophy because he says that in Thebes, people think that philosophers are nearly dead and the majority think they should be (64b). This brings to mind the Thinkery in the *Clouds*, whose students look sickly, starved, and at death's door.

At this point, Socrates offers a series of arguments on the nature of death, the nature of philosophy, and the nature and immortality of the soul. These arguments are the core of the *Phaedo*, but we will not discuss them here. I note, however, that at one point Socrates inserts a reference to the *Clouds*: "I do not think, said Socrates, that anyone who heard me now, not even a comic poet, could say that I am babbling and discussing things that do not concern me . . ." (71b–c). Indeed, for a dying man, the nature of the soul and the possibility of survival after death are of vital importance. They are not topics for idle speculation.

SOCRATES & NATURAL PHILOSOPHY

The *Phaedo*'s most sustained allusion to the *Clouds* is Socrates' intellectual autobiography, in which he admits that he was indeed a natural philosopher for a time:

> When I was a young man I was wonderfully keen on that wisdom which they call natural science [*peri physeos histo-*

rian, more literally "investigation of nature"], for I thought it splendid to know the causes of everything, why it comes to be, why it perishes, and why it exists. I was often changing my mind in the investigation, in the first instance, of questions such as these: Are living creatures nurtured when heat and cold produce a kind of putrefaction, as some say? Do we think with our blood, or air, or fire, or none of these, and does the brain provide our senses of hearing and sight and smell, from which come memory and opinion, and from memory and opinion which has become stable, comes knowledge?

This is a pretty recognizable depiction of pre-Socratic natural philosophy. One can imagine Socrates speaking this way in the *Clouds*.

So was Socrates guilty as charged by Aristophanes, the "first accuser"? Yes, at least for a time he was. But then he had a change of heart:

Then as I investigated how these things perish and what happens to things in the sky and on the earth, finally I became convinced that I have no natural aptitude at all for that kind of investigation, and of this I will give you sufficient proof. This investigation made me quite blind even to those things which I and others thought that I clearly knew before, so that I unlearned what I thought I knew before, about many other things and specifically about how men grew.

Not only did Socrates not learn the causes of all things from natural philosophy, he actually unlearned things that he knew before, specifically about "how men grew."

What do men "know" before the emergence of science? It is a mixture of myth, custom, shared and individual opinions, and practical experience. Let's call it common sense. This too fits with the *Clouds*, where Socrates is shown to lack common sense.

What is common sense about? It is about everything, but first and foremost it is about us, for even our view of the universe is very much marked by human nature and human conventions. Since it embraces both nature and convention, let's call the object of common sense the human condition.

In terms of the *Clouds* and the *Apology*, the human condition is the middle-sized realm, in contrast to the non-human realms of the great and the small. It is the realm of "human wisdom" that Socrates admits to in the *Apology*, as opposed to "divine wisdom."

What common sense did Socrates lose about "how men grew"? The only example he gives is a very common-sensical but also materialistic understanding of physical growth, namely that we grow by eating. This is true, but Socrates later makes clear that it is not the whole story.

I believe that human growth also refers to child-rearing and education. Recall in the *Theages* and the *Euthyphro* how the topic of education is broached in terms of metaphors from agriculture: planting, tending, weeding, and growth. What is the common-sense understanding of the purpose of child-rearing and education? Obviously, to make the young live well. What happens when we forget common sense about these topics? We end up corrupting the youth. Read this way, Socrates is admitting to another of the accusations in the *Clouds*, namely that the study of natural philosophy turned him into a corrupter of the youth.

Socrates then summarizes some accounts of causation—drawn both from common sense and natural philosophy—that he came to reject. We'll skip over this. Parts of this discussion are quite obscure, but later on it becomes clear that he rejected these accounts of causality because they do not make use of what Aristotle later called "final causation," also known as teleology, meaning the idea that changes happen to bring about future states: aims or goals which are understood as *goods*. Things become the way they are because it is *good*.

> ... I do not any longer persuade myself that I know why a unit or anything else comes to be, or perishes or exists by the old method of investigation [namely, natural philosophy], and I do not accept it, but I have a confused method of my own. (97b)

Socrates' own "confused method" of investigation will be made clear later.

SOCRATES & ANAXAGORAS

Before clarifying his own method, Socrates talks about his encounter with Anaxagoras, who claimed that Mind (*nous*) is the cause of everything. Socrates was excited, because he thought this would introduce the idea of final causes. In the passage that follows, I will emphasize the language of final causality, which explains things in terms of pursuing the good and avoiding the bad.

> One day I heard someone reading, as he said, from a book of Anaxagoras, and saying that it is Mind that directs and is the cause of everything. I was delighted with this cause, and it seemed to me good, in a way, that Mind should be the cause of all. I thought that if this were so, the directing Mind would direct everything and arrange each thing in the way that was *best*. If then one wished to know the cause of each thing, why it comes to be or perishes or exists, one had to find what was the *best* way for it to be, or to be acted upon, or to act. On these premises then it befitted a man to investigate only, about this and other things, what is *best*. The same man must inevitably also know what is *worse*, for that is part of the same knowledge. As I reflected on this subject, I was glad to think that I had found in Anaxagoras a teacher about the cause of things after my own heart, and that he would tell me, first, whether the earth is flat or round, and then would explain why it is so of necessity, saying which is *better*, and that it was *better* to be so. If he said it was in the middle of the universe, he would go on to show that it was *better* for it to be in the middle, and if he showed me those things, I should be prepared never to desire any other kind of cause. I was ready to find out in the same way about the sun and the moon and the other heavenly bodies, about their relative speed, their turnings, and whatever else happened to them, how it is *best* that each should act or be

acted upon. I never thought that Anaxagoras, who said that those things were directed by Mind, would bring in any other cause for them than that it was *best* for them to be as they are. Once he had given the *best* for each as the cause for each and the general cause of all, I thought he would go on to explain the common *good* for all, and I would not have exchanged my hopes for a fortune. I eagerly acquired his books and read them as quickly as I could in order to know the *best* and the *worst* as soon as possible. (97b–98b)

Unfortunately, Anaxagoras' concept of Mind had nothing to do with teleology. Instead, it seems to have been merely another kind of matter:

This wonderful hope was dashed as I went on reading and saw that the man made no use of Mind, nor gave it any responsibility for the management of things, but mentioned as causes air and ether and water and many other strange things. (98b–c)

Socrates then offers a vivid example that makes quite clear why he rejected purely material and mechanical causes in favor of final causes. Again, I will emphasize the language of final causation.

That seemed to me much like saying that Socrates' actions are all due to his Mind, and then in trying to tell the causes of everything I do, to say that the reason that I am sitting here is because my body consists of bones and sinews, because the bones are hard and are separated by joints, that the sinews are such as to contract and relax, that they surround the bones along with flesh and skin which hold them together, then as the bones are hanging in their sockets, the relaxation and contraction of the sinews enable me to bend my limbs, and that is the cause of my sitting here with my limbs bent. Again, he would mention other such causes for my talking to you: sounds and air and hearing, and a thousand other such things, but he would neglect to mention the true causes, that, after the Athenians decided it was *better* to condemn me, for this reason it seemed *best* to me to sit here, and more *right* to remain and to endure whatever penalty they ordered. For, by the dog [an oath to a foreign god, the Egyptian god Anubis], I think these sinews and bones could long ago have been in Megara or among the Boeotians, taken there by my belief as to the *best* course, if I had not thought it more *right* and *honorable* to endure whatever penalty the city ordered rather than escape and run away. (98c–99a)

If Socrates is not sitting in jail merely because the hip bone is connected to the thigh bone, and the thigh bone is connected to the knee bone, etc., what is the status of material things connected together mechanically? Socrates explains that these are mere *means*, subordinated to final causes, which are *ends*:

To call those things [bones, sinews, etc.] causes is too absurd. If someone said that without bones and sinews and all such things, I should not be able to do what I decided, he would be right, but surely to say that they are the cause of what I do, and not that I have chosen the *best* course, even though I act with my Mind, is to speak very lazily and carelessly. Imagine not being able to distinguish the real cause from that without which the cause would not be able to act as a cause. It is what the majority appear to do, like people groping in the dark; they call it a cause, thus giving it a name that does not belong to it. (99a–b)

How comprehensive does Socrates wish to make teleological explanation? Does he think that *everything* can be explained by teleology? Or does he think that teleology is confined to one area of nature, such as human beings or living things, whereas other areas of nature are ruled by purposeless mechanical necessity? Socrates makes it quite clear that he envisions a comprehensive teleology that governs the whole universe, including the earth itself and the heavens:

> That is why one man surrounds the earth with a vortex to make the heavens keep it in place, another makes the air support it like a wide lid. As for their capacity of being in the *best* place they could possibly be put, this they do not look for, nor do they believe it to have any divine force, but they believe that they will some time discover a stronger and more immortal Atlas to hold everything together more, and they do not believe that the truly *good* and "binding" binds and holds them together. (99b–c)

Socrates likens universal teleology to a "divine force" disposing all things toward the best. He contrasts this with the natural philosophers' quest to explain everything in terms of material and mechanical necessity, likening this to "a stronger and more immortal Atlas" holding the universe together by force. Atlas, of course, was one of the titans, who were the chthonic adversaries of the Olympian gods.

This brings us to another question. Does Socrates think that all teleology involves *Mind*, namely *conscious* intention and design? Or does he think that there can be *mindless* teleology? For instance, plants don't have minds, but they still have goals.

There is no evidence that Socrates believed in any sort of mindless teleology. Recall that the whole discussion of teleology was occasioned by Socrates hearing that Anaxagoras made *Mind* the cause of *all* things. Socrates was serious about that. He was attracted to the idea that the whole universe was ordered toward the good by conscious intention, and such a universal and benevolent Mind could only be described as a god. Indeed, in Xenophon's *Memorabilia*, book 4, chapter 3, Socrates defends the idea of a cosmos ordered by the divine for the good, which influenced the Stoic doctrine of divine Providence. This is a full-blown form of theistic metaphysical "optimism," the claim that the world is ruled by a benevolent deity for the maximum possible good of all. This is the best of all possible worlds.

But remember: as he is saying this, Socrates has both feet firmly on the ground. Thus, as attractive as this image of the cosmos was to Socrates, he was not willing to affirm that it is *true*, because he found no proof for it, neither from other thinkers or from his own investigations:

> I would gladly become the disciple of any man who taught the workings of that kind of cause. However, since I was deprived and could neither discover it myself nor learn it from another, do you wish me to give you an explanation of how, as a second best, I busied myself with the search for the cause, Cebes? (99c–d)

Why can't he know that universal teleology under the direction of benevolent gods is true? He certainly knows that the pursuit of the good makes sense of human action. Why can't he go further? The reason becomes clear when we look at Socrates' "second best" method of investigation. This is the "confused method" that he mentioned earlier.

SOCRATES'S FLIGHT TO THE *LOGOI*

Socrates literally calls his second-best method his "second sailing," which is an allusion to a comment made earlier by Simmias:

> I believe, as perhaps you do, that precise knowledge on that subject [the immortality of the soul] is impossible or extremely difficult in our present life, but that it surely shows a very poor spirit not to examine thoroughly what is said about it, and to desist before one is exhausted by an all-round investigation. One should achieve one of these things: learn the truth about these things or find it for oneself, or, if that is impossible, adopt the best and most irrefutable of men's theories [*anthropinon logon*, human *logoi*] and, borne upon this, sail through the dangers of life as upon a raft, unless someone should make that journey safer and less risky upon a firmer vessel of some divine doctrine [*logou theiou*, divine *logos*]. (85c–d)

For Simmias, the best thing is to know the truth. The truth is a safe and firm vessel, a divine *logos*. But some truths—for instance whether or not the soul is immortal—are hard to know because they fall outside the realm of experience.

Shouldn't one just dismiss questions about things that lie outside ones' experience? One can't, because some of these things are of vital importance to how we lead our lives in this world. For instance, the question of the nature and immortality of the soul. While we are alive, we can't know what lies on the other side of death. Yet what we think about that has enormous implications for how we lead our lives here. As Socrates says after offering his final argument for immortality:

> It is right to think then, gentlemen, that if the soul is immortal it requires our care not only for the time we call our life but for the sake of all time and that one is in terrible danger if one does not give it that care. If death were an escape for everything, it would be a great boon for the wicked to get rid of the body and their wickedness together with their soul, but now that the soul appears to be immortal there is no escape from evil or salvation for it except for becoming as good and wise as possible, for the soul goes to the underworld possessing nothing but its education and upbringing which are said to bring the greatest benefit or harm to the dead right at the beginning of the journey yonder. (107c-d)

If we think that the soul is mortal, then death is the end, and we should plan only for one life. If we think the soul is immortal, then we have to plan for the afterlife as well. Thus human immortality is not just an academic question. We need to answer it, and if we can't answer it with a divine *logos* (which presupposes experience we don't have in this world) we need a second-best answer, a human *logos*, based on the human condition. Simmias likens human *logos* to a risky, makeshift raft to help us "sail through the dangers of life."

What is this "second-best" method? Simmias says that it is to "adopt the best and most irrefutable of men's *logoi*," knowing that these fall short of divine knowledge. Socrates says something similar:

> ... when I had wearied of investigating things, I thought that I must be careful to avoid the experience of those who watch an eclipse of the sun, for some of them ruin their eyes unless they watch its reflection in water or some such material. A similar thought crossed my mind, and I feared that my soul would be altogether blinded if I looked at things with my eyes and tried to grasp them with each of my senses. So I thought I must take refuge in discussions [*logoi*] and investigate the truth of things by means of them. (99d–e)

This passage is known in the literature as Socrates' "flight to the *logoi*," the plural of "*logos*." *Logos* can be translated as very broadly as discussion or speech. It can also be more narrowly construed as argument, theory, or account.

When Socrates refers to "investigating things," he is talking about his phase as a natural philosopher. He identifies natural philosophy as trying to "look" at things with one's eyes and "grasp" them with each of the senses. This seems like a sound method. The trouble with natural philosophy, however, is not what it learns from the senses, but what it *unlearns* before learning from the senses.

The early Greek natural philosophers began by stepping outside of society into nature. They had a very specific idea of the truth they were seeking. They conceived the truth about nature as *objective*, thus they tried to shake off anything subjective, anything connected with the human point of view. For instance, myths project human categories onto the universe to understand it. The truth about nature would also be *one* principle that could explain many phenomena. Beyond that, the truth they sought was an *unchanging* principle that could explain the ceaseless change of nature. Finally, the truth about nature was *theoretical*. It did not need to justify itself by practical applications.

From this point of view, the human realm seemed contemptible: rife with subjectivism; rotted with plurality, contingency, and change; enthralled and stultified by the merely practical.

Ordinary people tread on the earth. The natural philosophers sought to "tread on the air," as Aristophanes put it, in order to "contemplate the sun." This is why Socrates is floating in a basket when he is first introduced in the *Clouds*.

This is the "blindness" of the "soul" that follows from relying exclusively on the eyes. Recall that earlier Socrates said that natural philosophy "made me quite blind even to those things which I and others thought that I clearly knew before, so that I unlearned what I thought I knew before, about many other things and specifically about how men grew."

Again, the problem with natural philosophy is not that it appeals to the evidence of the senses. The problem is that it discards all other forms of knowledge that came before it: myth, opinion, custom, convention, practical skills, in short: the common sense that reflects the human condition.

This is important to grasp, because it implies that the way to correct the shortcomings of natural philosophy is not to close one's eyes to the world of nature but instead to reopen one's eyes to the human condition.

It is also important to note that both Simmias and Socrates are willing to reject strong knowledge claims about the nature of the soul and universal teleology precisely because these claims go far beyond the evidence of the senses. If Simmias and Socrates were natural philosophers, who discard the resources of the human condition, they would have to stop there. But Simmias and Socrates have powerful practical reasons not to give up. Thus they avail themselves of a second-best method, which involves "*logoi*."

Let's see what this entails. Socrates continues:

> . . . I started in this manner: taking as my hypothesis in each case the theory [*logon*] that seemed to me the most compelling, I would consider as true, about cause and everything else, whatever agreed with this, and as untrue whatever did not so agree. . . . It is nothing new, but what I have never stopped talking about, both elsewhere and in the earlier part of our conversation. I am going to try to show you the kind of cause with which I have concerned myself. I turn back to those oft-mentioned things and proceed from them. I assume the existence of a Beautiful, itself

by itself, of a Good and a Great and all the rest. If you grant me these and agree that they exist, I hope to show you the cause as a result, and to find the soul to be immortal. (100b)

Socrates begins with different theories (*logoi*). A theory is true if it corresponds with reality. But we can't know if a theory corresponds with reality if we can't experience what the theory is about, for example life after death or universal teleology. Thus Socrates ranks the different theories not in terms of truth but in terms of how "compelling" they are. Then he treats the most compelling theory *as if* it is true, as well as whatever agrees with it. In this case, Socrates takes the forms as true, then uses them to argue for the immortality of the soul.

It is very tempting to see this as the first formulation of what has become known as the "hypothetico-deductive" method in the sciences. One observes puzzling phenomena whose causes are hidden. One uses one's imagination to hypothesize a hidden cause. One then deduces other phenomena that could be observed if the hypothetical cause actually exists. Finally, one looks for empirical verification.

In Socrates' case, however, he does not deduce testable phenomena. Instead, he argues for the immortality of the soul, which is no more empirically verifiable than the forms.

THE TURN TO MYTH

If we look at the *Phaedo* as a whole, Socrates' flight to the *logoi* is more than just a method of arguing from hypothetical first principles. *Logoi* can be anything and everything that is said, including received opinions and myths. Recall that at the beginning of the *Phaedo*, Socrates treats "hearsay" and "myths" about the soul and the afterlife with utmost seriousness.

At the end of the *Phaedo*, he returns to such myths, weaving both established myths and natural philosophy together into his own comprehensive myth about the afterlife. After summarizing these myths, Socrates says:

No sensible man would insist that these things are as I

have described them, but I think it is fitting for a man to venture it, for the venture is a noble one, that this or something like this is true about our souls and their dwelling places since the soul is evidently immortal, and a man should repeat this to himself as if it were an incantation, which is why I've been prolonging my tale [*mythos*]. That is the reason that a man should be of good cheer about his own soul if during life he has ignored the pleasures of the body and its ornamentation as of no concern to him and doing him more harm than good but has seriously concerned himself with the pleasures of learning and adorned his soul not with alien but with its own ornaments, namely moderation, righteousness, courage, freedom, and truth and in that state awaits his journey to the underworld. (114d–115a)

Myths are at best likely stories. Thus it would be foolish to insist on their literal truth. Believing in myths is a gamble, because you might be wrong. Socrates also speaks of the immortality of the soul as a magic spell that must be repeated again and again. It is a form of beguilement, quite possibly a form of self-deception. But these too are *logoi*.

Socrates says that venturing such beliefs is a worthy gamble, a salutary beguilement, because of the consequences. If you believe in an afterlife, particularly one in which you are rewarded for your virtues and punished for your vices, you will lead a better life in this world. And you will have lived well even if death turns out to be a full stop.

The *Phaedo* is the beginning of a philosophical tradition of using practical rather than theoretical reason to argue for metaphysical convictions. If one wishes to argue that the universe is divinely ordered for the good, that the soul is immortal, and that our deeds in this life will be rewarded or punished in the next world, one must first take stock of one's resources. If mystical intuition or theoretical reason cannot establish these truths, then maybe there is a second-best method.

This method takes its ideas about the afterlife from many sources, including myth and tradition. It argues that such beliefs have beneficial moral (and political) consequences, disbelief negative ones. On this basis, it argues that it is reasonable to embrace such beliefs even if they are not strictly justifiable.

Elements of this sort of argument can be found in Pascal's *Pensées*, but it is most fully worked out in Rousseau's *Emile*, Kant's *Critique of Practical Reason*, and William James' essay "The Will to Believe." But Socrates inaugurates this tradition in the *Phaedo*.

This concludes the theoretical portion of the *Phaedo*. The rest is devoted to action: the death of Socrates.

THE DEATH OF SOCRATES

Today, every death is described as a tragedy, no matter how trivial the person or farcical his end may be. Thus we find it quite unsettling that Plato presents the death of Socrates as more comic than tragic. Not every drama can be categorized as either comedy or tragedy. Even the ancient Greeks had a third category, the satyr play. Thus it should be no surprise that the *Phaedo* contains a mixture of tragic and comic elements: tears and laughter. But the amount of levity is surprising. Socrates' friends expected his death to be a bitter experience. But thanks to Socrates, it was bittersweet.

The bittersweet quality of Socrates' death is made clear by our narrator, Phaedo, near the dialogue's start:

> I certainly found being there a wondrous [*thaumasia*] experience. Although I was witnessing the death of one who was my friend, I had no feeling of pity, for the man appeared happy both in manner and words as he died nobly and fearlessly . . . so that it struck me that even in going down to the underworld, he was going with the gods' blessing and that he would fare well when he got there, if anyone ever does. That is why I had no feeling of pity, such as would seem natural in my sorrow, nor indeed of pleasure], as we engaged in philosophical discussion as we were accustomed to do—for our arguments were of that sort—but I had a strange feeling, an unaccustomed mixture of pleasure and pain at the same time as I reflect-

ed that he was just about to die. All of us present were affected in much the same way, sometimes laughing, then weeping ... (58d–59a)

Phaedo found the death of Socrates a "wondrous" (*thaumasia*) experience. According to Socrates philosophy begins with "wonder" (*thaumazein*) (*Theaetetus* 155d). Socrates' death is thus a spur to philosophical reflection.

Aristotle famously observed that tragedy causes spectators to feel both pity and fear. Phaedo's lack of pity signifies a lack of tragedy. So does Socrates' fearlessness.

Phaedo is sad, of course, but he is primarily sad for himself. He is losing Socrates. But Socrates does not feel fear or pain, so neither does Phaedo by empathy.

Phaedo usually felt unalloyed pleasure when talking about philosophy, but now his pleasure was mixed with pain. A bit later, Socrates remarks on the connection between pleasure and pain after he is released from his chains (60b).

Let's return to the end of the dialogue. After completing his discussion of the afterlife, Socrates says, ". . . my fated day calls me now, as a tragic character might say." This nod to tragedy, however, is immediately canceled by a sardonic and detached remark: ". . . it is about time for me to have my bath, for I think it better to have it before I drink the poison and save the women the trouble of washing the corpse" (115a).

Then Crito asks Socrates for his instructions to his children and friends. Here Socrates makes a rather striking distinction between theory and practice, asserting the primacy of practice over theory. Socrates says it does not matter whether his friends agree with what he has just said about the soul and the afterlife, as long as "you take care of your own selves in whatever you do." Then he adds that even if they agree with him intellectually, it will not matter if they do not practice care of the soul (115b-c).

When Crito asked Socrates how he wanted his body to be disposed of, Socrates "laughed quietly" and told Crito to "be of good cheer," because Socrates is not his corpse, so his friends can dispose of it however they please.

After his bath, Socrates bid farewell to his wife and children.

His mistress Myrto, with whom he had his last two children, was probably among the women present as well. It was close to sunset when he returned to his friends. After speaking kind words to his jailer, Socrates said, "Let someone bring the poison [*pharmakon*] if it is ready . . ." (116d). The Greek word *pharmakon* is more neutrally translated, "drug." Most drugs can cure or kill, for the poison is in the dose.

Crito, however, urges delay. The sun has not yet set, and other prisoners delay well after sundown with meals and farewells. Socrates, however, refuses:

> It is natural, Crito, for them to do so . . . for they think they derive some benefit from doing this. But it is not fitting for me. I do not expect any benefit from drinking the poison a little later, except to become ridiculous in my own eyes for clinging to life and being sparing of it when none is left. (116e–117a)

I think one reason modern people are so frustrated and perplexed by Socrates' choice to remain and suffer execution is that we tend to think that life is unconditionally good. If life is always good, there's never a good time to die. We cling to life as long as possible, whereas the ancient Greeks accepted the inevitability of death and thus were more concerned to have a good death, a noble death. Socrates, in particular, did not think that life is unconditionally good. Only a good life is good.

For Socrates, the good life hinges on wisdom. The unexamined life is not worth living. Well, you can't pursue wisdom if you are dead. So why did Socrates not draw out his life for the sake of philosophy? There is a sense in which philosophy is an "infinite task," to use the words of Edmund Husserl. But it cannot be an infinite task for each individual philosopher. There is a Latin epigram that ultimately derives from Hippocrates: "*ars longa, vita brevis*" ("Art takes time; life is short.") Philosophy is only an infinite task for the philosophical tradition, which passes the torch from generation to generation. Beyond that, wisdom is not endlessly deferred. One picks it up along the way. And human beings learned a long time ago that death is inevitable, thus our only choice is to die in a dignified or an undignified manner. Obviously, the wise man chooses to die with dignity.

Socrates was 70, which was a pretty good lifespan in his time. Chances are, he did not have much time ahead of him, no matter what happened. So just as he was not going to make himself look silly by grasping for a few extra minutes, he was not willing to abandon home, friends, and family for a few extra months or years.

Philosophy is a trans-political activity, hence Plato carefully names the number of foreigners who were present at Socrates' death. He could have prolonged the activity of philosophy in their company in many other cities in Greece. But Socrates as a whole was not a trans-political being. He had roots. He had thumotic connections with particular persons and places. These roots were very much connected to his body, which as long as he lived, was very much part of him.

I have no doubt, however, that if Socrates had been a much younger man facing the same charges, he first would have taken pains to prevent the case from coming to trial. Barring that, he would have spoken more persuasively in court, hoping for an acquittal. And barring that, he would have left Athens readily if condemned to die.

In short, I accept Xenophon's claim in his own *Apology of Socrates* that we cannot understand Socrates' behavior before, during, and after the trial without knowing that Socrates had decided it was time for him to die. Then why not just slink off and commit suicide? Obviously, Socrates relished the drama. He wanted to go out in style, in a way that could secure his place in history. In that, he succeeded wildly well.

And now we come to the end:

> ... Crito nodded to the slave who was standing near him. The slave went out and after a time came back with the man who was to administer the poison, carrying it made ready in a cup. When Socrates saw him, he said, "Well, my good man, you are an expert in this. What must one do?" "Just drink it and walk around until your legs feel heavy and then lie down, and it will act of itself." And he offered

the cup to Socrates, who took it quite cheerfully without a tremor or any change of feature or color but looked at the man from under his eyebrows as was his wont and asked, "What do you say about pouring a libation from this drink? Is it allowed?" (117a–b)

A libation is a sacrifice. One pours out a portion of one's drink as an offering to the gods. This is genuinely funny, because pouring out one's wine is a sacrifice for oneself and an honor to the gods, but pouring out poison is no sacrifice to Socrates and no honor to the gods. It looks like a pious gesture, but in substance it is just the opposite. Of course, impiety is why Socrates is there in the first place. We know this is meant jokingly, though, because Socrates has pointedly rejected prolonging the inevitable.

> "We only mix as much as we believe will suffice," said the man [who apparently didn't think there was anything funny there].
> "I understand," Socrates said, "but one is allowed, indeed one must, utter a prayer to the gods that the journey from here to yonder may be fortunate. This is my prayer and may it be so."
> And while he was saying this, he was holding the cup and then drained it calmly and easily. Most of us had been holding back our tears reasonably well up until then, but when we saw him drinking it and after he drank it, we could not hold them back any longer. My own tears came in floods against my will, so I covered my face. I was weeping for myself, not for him, for my misfortune in being deprived of such a comrade. Even before me, Crito was unable to restrain his tears and got up. Apollodorus had not ceased from weeping before, and at this moment his noisy tears and anger made everybody present break down except Socrates. (117b–d)

It is important to note that Phaedo says he is crying for himself, not for Socrates. He is crying for himself because he is losing Socrates. But he is not crying for Socrates, out of empathy, because Socrates is not in emotional distress.

> "What is this," [Socrates] said, "you wondrous fellows [*thaumasioi*]? It is mainly for this reason that I sent the women away to avoid such unseemliness, for I am told one should die in good-omened silence, so keep quiet and control yourselves!"
> His words made us ashamed, and we checked our tears. (117d–e)

There are two very important ideas in this passage.

First, when Socrates refers to his friends as "wondrous fellows," the word for wondrous is a version of the word for the wonder (*thaumazein*) that Socrates says is the beginning of philosophy. Socrates, at the very end, has not lost his capacity for wonder. Beyond that, although his philosophical career began with wonder at the cosmos, at the end, he is experiencing wonder at his fellow men.

Second, in accordance with his earlier definition of philosophy as preparation for death, Socrates is teaching his friends how to die: "in good-omened silence" not tears. First and foremost, he is teaching by example. But when they do not follow his example, he shames them into controlling themselves. And it works. "His words made us ashamed, and we checked our tears." This is said about Socrates in the *Symposium* too. Alcibiades said, 'The only person in the world who ever made me feel ashamed was Socrates.' The capacity to evoke feelings of shame is a very important dimension of moral education. If you can't feel shame for anything, then you're morally dead.

> [Socrates] walked around, and when he said his legs were heavy, he lay on his back as he was told to do, and the man who had given him the poison touched his body and after a while tested his feet and legs, pressing hard upon his foot and asked him if he felt this, and Socrates said, "No." Then he pressed his calves and he made his way up his body and showed us that it was cold and stiff. He felt it himself, and he said that when the cold reached his heart

he would be gone. As his belly was getting cold, Socrates then covered his head. He had covered it and said these were his last words, "Crito, we owe a cock to Asclepius. Make this offering to him and do not forget it." "It shall be done," said Crito. "Tell us if there is anything else." But there was no answer. Shortly afterwards, Socrates made a movement. The man uncovered him, and his eyes were fixed. Seeing this, Crito closed his mouth and his eyes.

Such was the end of our comrade Socrates, a man who we would say was of all those we had known the best and also the wisest and the most upright. (117e–118a)

To give a cock to Asclepius is to sacrifice a rooster to the god of healing in order to recover. Nietzsche says this is just an expression of Socrates' poisonous pessimism and hatred of life. Life is a disease, and now he's being cured of it, and so he wants to sacrifice a cock to Asclepius for the cure to life, which is death.

I think Nietzsche's interpretation is a lot of nonsense. Socrates is about to die, and he says what is equivalent to, "Quick, call an ambulance!" It's a little bit of lightheartedness, some gallows humor. His last words were a joke.

It reminds me of St. Lawrence, who was being grilled alive by the Romans, and at one point he called out, 'Turn me over! I'm done on this side!' Such bravado is quite impressive and bucks up the morale of those left behind.

SOCRATES' SECRET

How did Socrates face death with such aplomb? Death is fearsome. Courage helps us overcome fear and retain self-control, emotional detachment, and dignity in the face of death. Good humor is a sign that one's courage has held and that one has mastered the situation.

Was Socrates courageous because he believed in the immortality of the soul and the moral order of the universe? I think Socrates did indeed believe in these things, and they certainly didn't hurt him. But he also emphasizes that one can cultivate virtues like courage even if one disagrees with him about metaphysical matters. Beyond that, Socrates was renowned for courage in battle and self-control throughout his life, perhaps long before he developed the ideas in the *Phaedo*.

Ultimately, I think Socrates' secret is simply that he did not value life as such, but only a good life. Part of a good life is dignity in the face of the inevitable, like death.

But we don't really need to understand Socrates' *reasons* in order to follow his *example*. In the *Apology*, Socrates mentions the Homeric heroes who faced death bravely. Socrates may have learned courage simply by imitating examples of heroism, and he can teach by example as well.

This is the genius of the Platonic dialogues, which do not merely rehearse abstract arguments but also memorably depict individual characters and concrete deeds. Socrates does not teach us how to die simply with arguments. He also teaches by example.

We will all face death someday, and when we do, I doubt any of us will recall a single one of Socrates' arguments. But maybe his example will see us through.

INDEX

Numbers in bold refer to a whole chapter or section devoted to a particular topic.

A
accusers, 128–30, 138, 144–45; old, 146–47; new, 146, 152, 154, 158–59, 161
Achilles, 161
adultery, 39, 84, 133
Aesop, 95
agriculture, *see* farming
Alcibiades, 4
Alcibiades I, 111, 120n4
Allegory of the Cave, 175, 187
Ameipsias, 56
Anaxagoras, 3, 22, **40–42**, 43, 44, 46, 74, 144
Anaximander, **33–35**, 36, 65
Anaximenes, **35–37**, 45
anthropomorphism, 34, 38–39
anthroposophy, 12
Antiphon, 28, **49–52**
Anonymous Heidegger Scholar, vi
Anubis, 159, 203
Anytus, 6, 130, 144, 146–47, 158–59, 163, 166
Aphrodite, 115
Apollo, 8, 149–51, 156, 158, 174, 192
Apollonia, 35, 45, 46, 74
Apollodorus, 215
Apology of Socrates, iii, v, 2, 7–8, 12, 13, 16, 25, 40, 88, 97, 104, 121, 130, **143–69**, 182, 187

Archelaus, 3, 22, 107
architecture, 23
Aristippus, 6
aristocratic ethos, 21
Aristophanes, v, 2, 55, 59–60, 64, 69, 70–71, 78, 83, 84, 85, 88–91, 96, 112, 119–20, 121, 129, 157, 184; see also *Clouds*, impiety
Aristotle, 2, 10, 18, 19, 37, 65, 185, 212
Asclepius, 217
atheism, 5, 11, 37, 38, 67–71, 74, 87, 135, 136, 140, 144, 152–53, 159, 163
Athenians, 3, 5–6, 9, 11, 26, 40, 65, 86, 111, 123, 127, 128, 144, 147, 164–66, 169, 184
Atlas, 19, 204
Athens, 2, 4–5, 8, 11, 31, 40, 45, 56, 57, 59, 60, 65, 71, 80, 86, 98–99, 104, 110, 111, 121–23, 136, 144, 148, 155, 158, 159, 161, 164, 169, 173–74, 184, 190, 191
Austen, Jane, 10
Authority, conventional, 175; natural, 83–84; of poets, 31

B
Bauhaus, 23
Blavatsky, Helena Petrovna, 12

body (as prison), 15
bohemianism, 70–71
Buddhism, 54
buggery, 65, 83, 85
Burke, Edmund, 60

C
Canaanites, 92
care of the soul, 8, **181–83**; *see also* erotic things, human nature, love, moral education, psychology
causality: *see* fate, fortune, luck, materialism, necessity, teleology
cave (Allegory of the Cave), 175, 187
Cebes, 182n1, **194–97**, 205
Cepheus, 14
Chaerephon, 57, 62–63, 156
change, 34, 37, 47, 60, 66, 77, 79, 207
chaos, 75, 76, 90, 180
chivalry, 86
Christianity, 31, 92
Cicero, 2, 19, 22
civic-mindedness, 171, 185; *see also* community spirit; duty (civic)
Cleary, Collin, vi
Clinias, 17
Clouds (Aristophanes), iii, v, 2, 5, **56–95**, 98, 102, 112, 121, 125, 127, 129, 141, 142, 156, 190; vs. the *Euthyphro*, 121, 125, 127, 131, 136, 142; relation to philosophy, 6, 28, 35, 42, 48–49, 51, 54–55, **59–61**, 70–71, 77, 88–89, 119, 143; impact on Socrates, 88, 119–20, 121, 129, 142; portrayal of Socrates, 5, 13, 28, 45, 55, 66, 78, 96, 104, 105, 110, 112, 121, 129, 146, 151–54, 159, 162, 167, 169, 177–78, 183; vs. the *Theages*, 96, 100, 103, 104, 106, 110, **118–20**
comedy, 56, 59, 96, 111, 118, 153, 157, 211
community spirit, 171, 185; *see also* civic mindedness; duty (civic)
conservatism, 59–61, 112, 126, 172
convention, vs. nature, 47–51, 59–60, 63, 66, 71–72, 136–37, 172–73, 175
Cooper, John M., 97n1; 195n1
corrupting, men's souls, 151, 176; the youth, 5, **112–13**, 116, 117, 124, 159, 200
courage, 4, 17–18, 79, 210, **217–18**
counter-culture, 70–71
Corybantes, 175
Cramer, Daniel, 15
Cratylus, 121, 126
Credit (moral), 185
Crete, 191
crime, 122–23, 137, 159, 170, 185
Crito, 2, 24, **170–93**
Crito, iii, 2, 7, 16, 26, 121, **170–193**
Cronos, 31, 74, 93, 127, 132
Cupid, 115
Cybele, 175

D

daimonion, **16**, 115–19, 124, 126, 138, 159, 167, 180
Damon, 3
death, 15, 25, 56, 150, **161–63**, 195, 206
death of Socrates, iv, v, 3–6, 10, 16–19, 121, 126, 143, 144, 148, 153, 160, 169, 174, 178, **211–18**
Delos, 174, 182, 194
Delphi, 8, 12, 149, 156
Delphic oracle, 8, 12, 76, 148–49, 156–58; *see also* divination, enthusiasm, oracles
demagogues, 98, **110–12**, 117
democracy, 48, 110, 112, 192
Demodocus, 96–103, 108, 112–14, 117, 125
Derrida, Jacques, 145
desire, 27, 32, 48, 50, 57, 76, 94, **102–109**, 128, 170, 201
Devlin, F. Roger, vi
Dew, Buttercup, vi
dialogue (as literary form), 106, 120, 145, 211, 218
Dianetics, 54
Die Fragmente der Vorsokratiker, 28n1
Diels, Herman, 28n1
dike, 29; *see also* justice
dinos, 74; *see also* vortex
dio, 74
Diogenes of Apollonia, 35, **45–46**, 74
Diogenes Laertius, **2–4**, 43, 153
Dionysia, the, 5, 56
dissimulation, 10; *see also* esotericism, irony, lying
divination, 126–28; *see also* Delphic oracle, enthusiasm, oracles
dreams, 174–75, 184, 187
duty (civic), 3; *see also* civic-mindedness, community spirit

E

Echecrates, 194
education, 9, **31**, 87, 89–90, 93–95, 101, 103, 125, 137, 154–55, 189, 192–93
Empedocles, 42, **43–45**, 46, 74
enthusiasm, **126–28**; see also Delphic oracle; divination; oracles
envy, 100, 128, 149
Erebus, 64
Eros, 15–16, 115
eros, **13–16**, **114–16**, 125–26, 152; see also love
erotic things or erotics, **13–16**, 114–16, 125–26, 152; *see also* care of the soul, human nature, love, moral education, psychology
esotericism, 54
Eupolis, 56
Euripides, 3, 18, 86, 108
Euthydemus, 17
Euthyphro, **121–42**, 151, 157–58, 168–69, 173
Euthyphro, iii, 2, 39, 68n4, 95, 119, **121–42**, 147, 150, 151, 153, 157, 170, 180, 182
Evenus, 195
evolution of species, 35
example, teaching by, 155,

216, 218
examples, moral, 85

F
family, 84, 87, 90, 93, 122-23, 130, 139-40, 142, 170-71
farming, 32, 99, 108-109, 125
fate, 34, 161, 193, 212; *see also* causality, fortune, luck, materialism, necessity, teleology
father beating, 58-59, 121-23
Forms, theory of, 41, 65, **131-32**; *see also* Ideas
Four Texts on Socrates: Plato's Euthyphro, Apology, and Crito and Aristophanes' Clouds, v, 7n9, 56n2
Fortune, good, 17-18, 78; bad, 88; *see also* causality, fate, luck, materialism, necessity, teleology
Freemasonry, 54
Freud, Sigmund, 14, 93
From Plato to Postmodernism, iv

G
gadfly, **166-67**, 169
Gilbert & Sullivan, 75
geometry, 54, 64-66
Glaucon, 192
gods, 5, 7-9, 11, 14, 16, 25, 30-32, 34-35, 37-40, 43, 45, 46, 47, 56, 60, 62, 67-68, 71, 76-78, 83-87, 89-90, 92-93, 98, 102, 109, 115, 123-24, 126-28, 131, 133-36, 138-42, 147-48, 150-53, 156-57, 159, 163, 166, 182, 192; *see also* myth, religion
good, the, 15, **17-18**, 105, 197; 201, 204-205, 210; good citizen, 184-87; good life, **17-18**, 26, 213-14, 218; moral goodness, 87
Gorgias, 113
Gorgias, 124, 137, 161
Gnostics, 15
Greater Dionysia, 56
Greece, 3, 7, 9, 20, 31, 48, 122, 143, 214
Greeks, 5, 9-10, 14, 18-19, 21, 30-31, 32, 39, 81, 82, 83, 85, 122, 123, 124, 126, 135, 136, 142, 143, 147, 149, 165, 174
Grube, G. M. A., 97n1; **195n1**
Gullick, Mark, vi

H
hedonism, 51, 82, 91; *see also* pleasure
hemlock, 5, 195
Hegel, G. W. F., 191
Hera, 31, 84, 133
Heraclides of Pontus, 20
Heracles (Hercules), 82, 83-84
Heraclitus, 28, 37, 67
Hermes, 87-88, 90
heroism, 218
Hesiod, 31, 39
Hinduism, 91
Hippocrates, 213
Homer, 9, 19, 31, 39, 82
Homeric heroes, 218
hubris, 89, 127, 130, 151
human condition, 23, 28, 66, 200, 208
human nature, 60, 66, 71, 73, 78, 85, 88, 90, 92, 96, 119,

200; *see also* care of the soul, erotic things, love, moral education, psychology
human wisdom, 9, 12–13, 55–56, 200
humanism, **22–23**, 27, 88
humanistic philosophy, 22–23, 27, 88
Hume's Philosophy of Common Life, vi
Husserl, Edmund, 213
hypocrisy, 84–85
hypothetical reasoning, 196, 209; *see also* science

I
Ideas (*eide*), **131–33**; *see also* Forms
ignorance, 4, 105–106, 142; Socratic, 9, **12–13**, 154
impiety, 5, 40, 118, 127; Socrates accused of, **123–24**; *see also* piety
initiatic spiritual orders, 54, 69, 73; *see also* mysteries & mystery religions
immortality, 53
incest, 86
inequality (natural), 10, 83–84, 86, 127, 190
Invisible College, The, iii, vi
invulnerability, 24–26
irony, 3, 8–11, 103–104, 106, 131–32, 149–52; Socratic, **9–11, 151–52**; *see also* dissimulation, esotericism, irony
Islam, 91

J
James, William, 211
Jesus, 1
Job, 24
Judaism (Orthodox), 92
Just Speech, 25, 60, **78–82**, **82–86**, 89–90, 102–103, 112, 127, 161, 190; *see also* rhetoric, sophistry & sophists, Tongue, Unjust Speech
justice, 15, 18, 24, 27, 34, 47, 49, 52, 87, 137, 138, 170–72, 187, 188–90; see also *dike*

K
Kant, Immanuel, 211
katabasis, 76
knowledge, 4, 12–13, 104–107, 113, 125, 154–58, 162–63, 178; moral, 17–18, 26, 115–16; of the soul and human nature, 14, 16, 18, 27, 71, 73, 99, 114–16, 119, 125–26, 152, 156, 180
Kojève, Alexandre, 172
kottabos, 82
Kranz, Walther, 28n1

L
Lamprocles, 2, 17
laughter, 119–20, **128–30**
St. Lawrence, 217
laws, 47, 49–53, 153, 158, 170–71, 173–76, 180, 184–93; moral, 21, 30, 46, 135; of nature, see *under* nature
Leon of Phlius, 20
Livingston, Donald W., vi
logocentrism, 145

logoi, 145, **205-209**
logos, 205; divine, **205-206**;
  human, **205-206**
love, 13-15, 43-44, 83, 86, 114,
  134, 164; tough, 130, 166-
  67; *see also* care of the soul,
  eros, erotic things, human
  nature, moral education,
  psychology
love of one's own, 170; see
  also *thumos*
luck, 17-18, 34, 50, 112, 152;
  see also causality, fate,
  fortune, luck, materialism,
  necessity, teleology
luxury, 21
Lyceum, the, 123
Lycon, 6
Lycurgus, 19
lying, 144; *see also*
  dissimulation, esotericism,
  irony

M

Magee, Glenn, vi
Magna Graecia, 21
magnanimity, 10, 149
Malden, Karl, 72
Martini, Mary Ann, vi
materialism, 41; *see also*
    causality, fate, fortune,
    luck, necessity, teleology
Meletus, 6
Menexenus, 3
Meno, 111, 130
metaphysics, 19, 27, 132, 210
metaxy, 13
Minerva, 191
Mind (*nous*), 41-42, 201-204
mind, life of, 172-73

moral character, 8; *see also*
  soul, care of the soul
moral education, **31**, 95, 216;
  see also care of the soul;
  erotics; love; human
  nature; psychology
moral philosophy, 6-9, 16, 21,
  24, 26, 27, 46, 88, 161
morality, 7, 9, **16-17**, 22, 31,
  40, 46-47, 48, 57, 71, 77, 85,
  87, 89-93, 95, 102, 115-16,
  122, 137, 140, 164, 178-80,
  185, 187
Morgan, John, vi
Myrto, 3, 213
mysteries & mystery
  religions, 53, 62, 69, 192;
  see also initiatic spiritual
  orders
mysticism, 15, 210
myth, 19, **30-31**, 33-34, 39, 46-
  47, 74, 85, 95, 196, 207-208,
  210; *see also* gods, religion

N

natural philosophy, iii, 5-6,
  22, 37-38, 43, 46-49, 53, 61,
  64, 66, 68, 69-71, 73, 78, 86,
  87, 89, 99, 152, 154-56, 159,
  162; and the sophists, 48-
  49, 55, 59-60, 70-71, 77-78;
  Socrates' opposition to,
  198-208; *see also* nature,
  pre-Socratic philosophy
natural right, 60, 140, 147, 172
nature, 5-6, 19-23, 29-30, 32-
  33, 37-38, 46-52, 59-61, 69,
  74-75, 77, 82-84, 86-93, 96,
  99, 152, 162, 172, 183; vs.
  convention, 47-51, 59-60,

63, 66, 71–72, 136–37, 172–73, 175; human, 60, 66, 71, 73, 75, 78, 85, 88, 90, 92, 96, 114, 116, 119, 125; natural law, 34, 60, 66, 90–92, 116, 135–37, 140–42, 147, 172–73, 175, 180, 183, 184, 186–87, 189, 192; see also natural philosophy

necessity, mechanical, 203–204; natural, **34–35**, 41, 45–46, 49, 51, 74, 82, 201; *see also* causality, fate, fortune, luck, materialism, necessity, teleology

Nestor, 19, 82

New Age, 70–71

Nietzsche, Friedrich, 1, 217

nihilism, 89

nobility, 21, 186, 191

nomos, 29, 47

nous (Mind), 41–42, 201–204

O

objectivity, 63

Odysseus (Ulysses), 19

Oedipus the King, v

Oedipus Trilogy, 56

Olympiodorus the Younger, 120n4

optimism, 204

oracles, 76, **157–58**; see also Delphic oracle; divination; enthusiasm

order, **29–30**, 42, 47, 87, 93, 122, 149, 150, 168, 170, 184, 185, 188, 217

Oresteia, 56

Orphism, 53, 54

Ouranos, 74, 127, 132

owl of Minerva, 191

P

pain, 51–52, 165, **211–12**

Pangle, Thomas, v, 14n10, 98n2, 103, 109, 115, 117

parabasis, 69

Parmenides, 28–29

Pascal, Blaise, 211

pederasty, 82–83

Peloponnesian War, 3–5, 99

Pericles, 40, 98, 110, 111, 144

pessimism, 217

Phaedo of Elis, 194, 211–12, 215

Phaedo, iii–v, 2, 17, 45, 64–65, 121, 182, **194–218**

Phaedrus, 152

Phaenarete (Socrates' mother), 2, 62

Pheidippides, **56–95**, 96, 100, 105–106, 119, 131, 190

Phlius, 20, 194

Philolaus of Croton, 194

philosophy, v, 1, 7, 9, 21, 30–31, 96–97, 100, 116–17, 143–44, 148, 150–51, 160, 162, 167–69, 182–83, 187, 191–92; see also humanistic philosophy, moral philosophy, natural philosophy, pre-Socratic philosophy

phronesis, 177; see also wisdom, practical

physiognomy, 124

piety, 5, 11, 37, 38, 40, 43, 79, 93, 102, 118, 122–24, 127, 131–35, 138–42, 144, 147–51, 158, 168, 173, 182

pity, **211–12**
Plato, v, 4, 15, 16, 18, 20, 26, 27, 28–29, 41, 65, 78, 88, 98, 102–103, 105–107, 113, 114, 118, 120, 121, 127, 143, 145, 160, 167, 168, 192; *see also* dialogue (literary form); Forms, theory of; Socrates; *Alcibiades* I, 111; *Apology of Socrates*, iii, v, 2, 7–8, 12, 13, 16, 25, 40, 88, 97, 104, 121, 130, **143–69**, 182, 187; *Cratylus*, 121, 126; *Crito*, iii, 2, 7, 16, 26, 121, **170–193**; *Euthydemus*, 17; *Euthyphro*, iii, 2, 39, 68n4, 95, 119, **121–42**, 147, 150, 151, 153, 157, 170, 180, 182; *Gorgias*, 124, 137, 161; *Meno*, 111, 130; *Phaedo*, iii–v, 2, 17, 45, 64–65, 121, 182; *Phaedrus*, 152; *Protagoras*, 111; *Republic*, 76, 95, 97, 100, 115, 135, 138, 170, 175, 182, 189, 192; *Seventh Letter*, 106; *Statesman*, 121; *Symposium*, 4, 13–14, 115, 119, 129, 152; *Theages*, iii–v, 2, 13, 16, 88, **96–120**, 125–26, 142, 152, 180, 182; *Theaetetus*, 32, 121
pleasure, 82, 85; *see also* hedonism
poetry, 9, 31, 58, 59, 66, 70, 71, 76, 85, 86, 157, 158
Polignano, Michael, vi
polis, 172, 185
politics, 6–7, 16, 32, 48, 66, 97, 100, 110, 122, 143, 151, 160, 167, 170–73, 175, 180, 183, 184–86, 188, 190, 191–93; *see also* pre-political society, transpolitical society
Polus, 113
practical reason, 208, 210; *see also* reason, theoretical reason
pre-political society, 122; *see also* politics, transpolitical society
pre-Socratic philosophy, iii, 1–2, 6–7, 19, 21–23, **28–55**, 60, 66, 67, 88, 119; *see also* nature, natural philosophy, science
prisoner's dilemma, 185
Prodicus, 113
Prometheus, 19
Protagoras, 144
Protagoras, 111
Proteus, 141
providence, divine, 38, 40, 46, 75, 204
Prufer, Thomas, v, 56
psychology, 16; *see also* care of the soul, erotic things, human nature, love, moral education
punishment, 137–38
Pythagoras, 20, 21, **53–55**
Pythagoreans, 15, **53–55**, 69, 182n1

Q
Quintilian, 10

R
reason, 22, 93, 167, 172, 175, 180, 189; *see also* practical reason, theoretical reason

religion, 30, 31, 38, 48, 54, 69, 71, 77, 89–95, 123, 140, 142; *see also* gods, myth
Republic, 76, 95, 97, 100, 115, 135, 138, 170, 175, 182, 189, 192
Rousseau, Jean-Jacques, 211
rhetoric, 4, 48, 66, 83, 86, 87, 110, 113, 145; *see also* Just & Unjust Speech, sophistry, Tongue

S
satyr plays, 56, 120, 211
science, 5, 6, 19, 21, 22, 30–31, 54, 61, 66, 67, 73, 77, 88, 89; *see also* hypothetical reasoning, pre-Socratic philosophy
self-control, 4, 17, 217–18; *see also* temperance
self-interest, 140, 170–71, 185–86, 191
self-preservation, 78, 195
Seventh Letter, 106
Shakers, 140
Simmias, 182n1, **194–96**, 198, 205–206, 208
Simplicius, 34
Slaughter, Kevin, vi
Smith, Nicolas D., iv
Socrates: and Aristophanes' *Clouds*, see under *Clouds*; *daimonion* of, 16, 115–19, 124, 126, 138, 159, 167, 180; on death, 150, **161–63**; death of, iv, v, 3–6, 10, 16–19, 121, 126, 143, 144, 148, 153, 160, 169, 174, 178, **211–18**; on the good life, 8, 17–19, 24–26, 150, 165, 181–83; role in the history of philosophy, 1, 6, 22, 27, 88; human wisdom of, 9, 12–16, 88, 114–16, 125–26, 156; on laws, 173–75, 183–84, 187–89, 191–93; life of, 2–5, 21; and the pre-Socratics, 19, 22–23, 28, 40–41, 45, 49, 55; on religion, 135–36, 140, 147; trial of, 5, 104, 119, 126, 129, **143–69**
Socratic fallacy, 132, 157
sophia, 177; *see also* wisdom, theoretical
sophistry & sophists, 6–7, 9, **47–48**, 49–51, 59–60, 64, 66, 82, 86, 87, 89, 96, 100–101, 108, 110, 111, 113, 117, 155, 119; and natural philosophy, 48–49, 55, 59–60, 70–71, 77–78; see also Just and Unjust Speech, rhetoric. Tongue
Sophocles, v, 56
Sophroniscus (Socrates' father), 2
Sophroniscus (Socrates' son), 3
soul, 8, 9, 14–16, 24, 53–54, 76, 96, 101, 114–16, 125, 137, 150, 152, 161, 165, 170–71, 178, 181–83, 186, 189, 196, 198, 205–206, 208–10, 212, 217; *see also* care of the soul, moral education, immortality, transmigration
Sowell, Thomas, 93
Sparta, 65–66, 191

speculation, 27; *see also* theory
speculative philosophy, 21, 22
spiritedness (*thumos*), 170
Statesman, 121
Steiner, Rudolf, 12
Stoa of Zeus the Liberator, 98
stoics, 204
Strauss, Leo, v-vi, 172
Strepsiades, **56-95**, 96, 100-102, 104-106, 112, 125, 131, 145-46, 171-73, 176, 178, 184, 192
suicide, 78
Symposium, 4, 13-14, 115, 119, 129, 152

T
Tacitus, 161
Tartarus, 64
teleology (final cause), **200-205**, 208-209; *see also* causality, fate, fortune, luck, materialism, necessity
temperance (self-control), 18
Thales, **32-33**, 34, 35-36, 63, 65
Theaetetus, 32, 121
Theages, **96-120**
Theages, iii-v, 2, 13, 16, 88, **96-120**, 125-26, 142, 152, 180, 182
Thebes, 194, 198
Theophrastus, 10
theoretical reason, 210; *see also* reason
theory (*theorein*), 21, 32, 39, 54, 66, 77; *see also* speculation
Theosophical Society, The, iii
theosophy, 12
Thinkery, 54, 57-59, 61-2, 64, 66, 68-69, 72-73, 75-79, 86, 88-90, 98, 101, 105, 115, 118, 146, 198
Thucydides, 98
Timon, 3, 88
Tongue (dramatic personification), 75, 87
thumos, 167, 183n1, 214; *see also* love of one's own
tradition, 29, 30, 59-61, 71, 83, 86, 89, 90, 93, 122, 126, 140, 180
transmigration (of soul), 53
transpolitical society, 170, **171-73**, 183, 190-93; *see also* politics, pre-political society
tragedy, 31, 56, **211-12**
tyranny, 94, **107-10**

U
Ulysses (Odysseus), 19
"unexamined life," **8-9**, 26, 148, 150
Unjust Speech, 51, 60, 62, 77, **78-85**, 89, 93, 102, 190; *see also* Just Speech, rhetoric, sophistry & sophists, Tongue

V
values, objective, 134; subjective, 134
Veyne, Paul, 31
vice, 4, 31, 89, 149-50, 165,
virtue, 4, 23-26, 155, 164-65, 179, 183-84, 191
vortex, 41-42, 44, 46, 74-75, 87, 90-91, 204; see also *dinos*

W

Wagner, Richard, 191
way of things, **29–30**, 47
weakness of will (*akrasia*), 18–19
West, Grace, v
West, Thomas G., v
wisdom, v, 9, 12–14, 16–20, 26, 69, 73, 84, 86, 88–89, 96, 100, **103–106**, **107–10**, 120, 128, 130, 141, 149, 150, **155–56**, 157, 158, 168, 177–78, 183, 191; divine, 12, **155–56**; human, 155–56; practical, 17, 26, 150, **177–78**; theoretical, 19, 177–78; see also *phronesis*
wonder, 211–12, 215–16

X

Xanthippe, 2–3, 4, 17
Xenophanes, **38–40**, 43
Xenophon, 2, 5–6, 16, 28, 58, 124, 167, 214; *Apology of Socrates*, 214; *Memorabilia*, 58, 204

Z

Zeus, 31, **73–75**, 77, 83, 84, 87, 89–90, 92–93, 98, 105–106, 127, 130, 132, 133, 135, 136
Zsutty, David, vi

About the Author

Greg Johnson, Ph.D., is Editor-in-Chief of Counter-Currents Publishing Ltd. and the Counter-Currents.com webzine.

In addition to the present volume, he is the author of eighteen other books (all published by Counter-Currents, unless otherwise noted): *Confessions of a Reluctant Hater* (2010, 2016), *Trevor Lynch's White Nationalist Guide to the Movies* (2012), *New Right vs. Old Right* (2013), *Son of Trevor Lynch's White Nationalist Guide to the Movies* (2015), *Truth, Justice, & a Nice White Country* (2015), *In Defense of Prejudice* (2017), *You Asked for It: Selected Interviews*, vol. 1 (2017), *The White Nationalist Manifesto* (2018), *Toward a New Nationalism* (2019), *Return of the Son of Trevor Lynch's CENSORED Guide to the Movies* (2019), *From Plato to Postmodernism* (2019), *It's Okay to Be White: The Best of Greg Johnson* (Ministry of Truth, 2020), *Graduate School with Heidegger* (2020), *Here's the Thing: Selected Interviews*, vol. 2 (2020), *Trevor Lynch: Part Four of the Trilogy* (2020), *White Identity Politics* (2020), *The Year America Died* (2021), and *Trevor Lynch's Classics of Right-Wing Cinema* (2022).

He is editor of *North American New Right*, vol. 1 (2012); *North American New Right*, vol. 2 (2017); *The Alternative Right* (2018); Julius Evola, *East & West: Comparative Studies in Pursuit of Tradition* (with Collin Cleary, 2018); Collin Cleary, *Summoning the Gods: Essays on Paganism in a God-Forsaken World* (2011); Collin Cleary, *What Is a Rune? & Other Essays* (2015); Francis Parker Yockey, *The Enemy of Europe* (Centennial Edition Publishing, 2022), Charles Krafft, *An Artist of the Right* (The Mystic Sons of Charles Krafft, 2022), Alain de Benoist, *Ernst Jünger: Between the Gods & the Titans* (Middle Europe Books, 2022), and many other volumes.

His writings have been translated into Arabic, Czech, Danish, Dutch, Estonian, Finnish, French, German, Greek, Hungarian, Norwegian, Polish, Portuguese, Russian, Slovak, Spanish, Swedish, and Ukrainian.

www.ingramcontent.com/pod-product-compliance
Lightning Source LLC
Chambersburg PA
CBHW030106170426
43198CB00009B/514